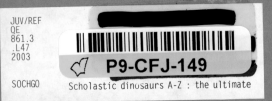

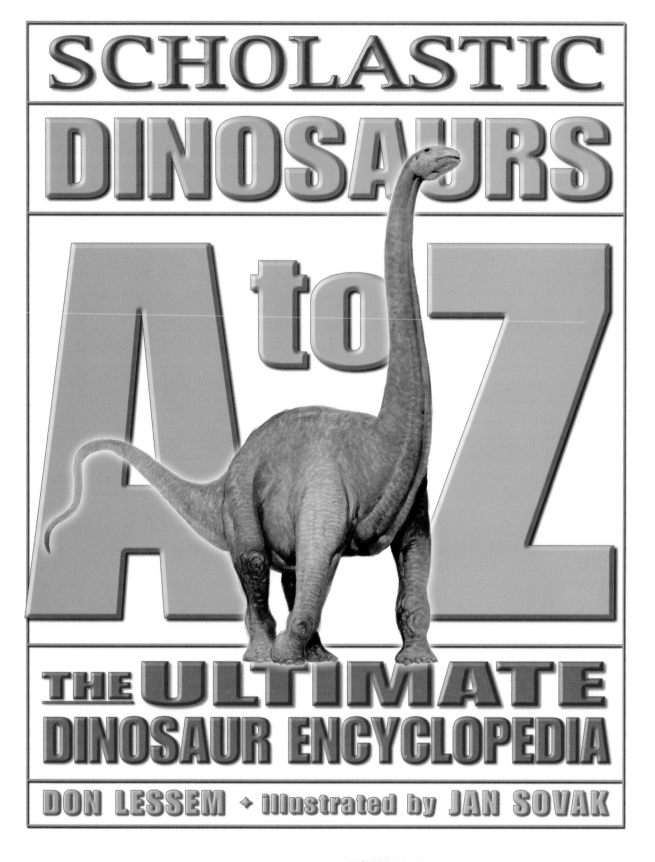

SCHOLASTIC

DINOSAURS

A to Z

THE ULTIMATE DINOSAUR ENCYCLOPEDIA

DON LESSEM • illustrated by JAN SOVAK

Gilmoreosaurus
see page 89

Photo Credits: © Don Lessem: pages 5, 6(t), 38, 55, 86, 142; © Jan Sovak: page 6(b); © Francois Gohier/PRI: pages 18, 196; © PRI: page 19; © North Wind Picture Archives, Alfred, ME: pages 27, 110; © Photofest, NY/New World Pictures: page 90; © Tom Rich: page 114; © PRI/Science Photo Library: page 124; © CORBIS: pages 158, 199; © Joyce Photographies/PRI: 192(t), 192(b);

Expert Readers: Dr. Philip Currie, Royal Tyrell Museum of Palaeontology; Sunny Hwang, and Diego Pol, the American Museum of Natural History, New York

Library of Congress Cataloging-in-Publication Data: Lessem, Don. • Scholastic Dinosaurs A to Z / Don Lessem. • p. cm. • 1. Dinosaurs—Dictionaries, Juvenile. [1. Dinosaurs—Dictionaries.] I. Title. • QE861.3 .L47 2001 • 567.9'03—dc21 • 00-041304

10 9 8 7 6 5 4 3 2 1   03 04 05 06 07

ISBN 0-439-16591-1

Printed in the U.S.A.   24
First printing, September 2003

Book Design and Art Direction: Nancy Sabato
Composition: Kevin Callahan

Haplocanthosaurus
see page 95

Contents

Nodosaurus
see page 136

Acknowledgments

*To Valerie Jones, a.k.a. Irene Adler, explorer
and friend – D.L.*

*To Dr. Phil Currie, a dear friend who taught me so
much, and to the memory of Charles R. Knight and
Z. Burian who showed us how artistic reconstruction
should look. Thanks also to Nancy Sabato. – J.S.*

Research Assistants: Daniel Lipkowitz and Kelly Milner Halls
Special Thanks: To Wendy Barish, editor emeritus
extraordinaire and her staff and successors, Sheila Keenan
and Elysa Jacobs, for their remarkable and well-tested
patience with an author working on a schedule that would
be speedy only by geological time standards. I deeply
appreciate their not adding my name to those of the
extinct animals in this book.

I am indebted to dinosaur genera detectives Ben
Creisler, Don Glut, and George Olshevsky, who have
searched publications far and wide to keep a current listing
of all dinosaur discoveries. There are too many scientists
and amateur fossil finders to thank
individually for the hard work they
put into each dinosaur find, preparation,
study, and publication. But their dedication
and insight makes this and all other
dinosaur popularizations possible.

Lesothosaurus
see page 115

4

When I was six years old, I discovered my first dinosaur: a little plastic one hidden inside a box of cereal. I've been interested in dinosaurs ever since. In fact, I spend my life hunting dinosaurs from Canada to Argentina to Mongolia. I am lucky to live and work for a fossil museum in Alberta, Canada. Alberta is in the middle of one of the richest dinosaur fossil areas in the world.

Dr. Phil Currie excavating a dinosaur fossil in the Gobi Desert of Inner Mongolia

Books from my childhood told us dinosaurs were dead and gone and that there was little we could or would learn about them. Since then, our knowledge of dinosaurs has exploded. A new kind of dinosaur is found nearly every two weeks. And there are thousands of kinds of dinosaurs still waiting to be uncovered.

We've also learned so much lately about how dinosaurs lived and behaved and about the world in which they lived. Best of all for a dinosaur-lover like me, we found out dinosaurs are probably not dead at all! Most of us paleontologists now think dinosaurs live on as birds.

In this book, my friends, author Don Lessem and artist Jan Sovak, have presented a huge amount of up-to-date information about their favorite animals and mine. *Scholastic Dinosaurs A to Z* is the most current and thorough children's book I know of on dinosaurs. It will help all of us understand the magnificent animals that ruled the earth for 165 million years. Most of all, I hope this wonderful book will help create a new generation of lifelong dinosaur hunters.

PHIL CURRIE
Curator of Dinosaurs,
Royal Tyrrell Museum of Palaeontology,
Drumheller, Alberta, Canada

5

I have loved dinosaurs since I was five years old, and first stood in awe of an enormous *T. rex* skeleton. That was 45 years ago. Since then, ideas about dinosaurs have changed even more than I have. There are more than twice as many dinosaurs known as there were when I was a boy. Far more has been discovered about how dinosaurs lived and died than I ever dreamed of as a child.

There are also many more dinosaur books. I've written two dozen myself. But none has provided me with the one resource I would have wanted most as a child: a book describing every known dinosaur. Since I couldn't find such a book, I figured I'd write it.

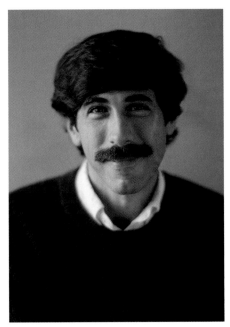

"Dino" Don Lessem, author

What's in This Book?

In *Scholastic Dinosaurs A to Z* you'll find just about every dinosaur named by science (and even those renamed!) What we can't tell you, at least for now, is what color these dinosaurs were, how tall they stood, or how much they weighed. It's difficult to estimate the height of two-legged dinosaurs

Jan Sovak, illustrator

because they didn't stand tall like us. They balanced like a teeter-totter, over their upright legs. And we can only guess at the weight of any dinosaur by studying its bones.

In this book, I've highlighted those dinosaurs we know well from their fossil remains and those with especially strange or significant features. To illustrate these dinosaurs, a talented artist, Jan Sovak, who worked on this book, must interpret how muscle, flesh, and skin would look over bones. Dents in the bones left by the insertion of muscles help artists gauge how muscular the animals were. Skin patterns are known from several dinosaur mummies.

But for many dinosaurs, there is not enough evidence to represent them accurately in lifelike drawings. The illustrations for these dinosaurs are based on fossils that have been uncovered so far; an important feature of the animal; or the only bone known to have come from it. The truth is that many dinosaurs are known from just a single tooth or bone. Dinosaur fossils are difficult to find. In nearly 200 years of searching, scientists have unearthed the remains of fewer than 1,000 different kinds of dinosaurs.

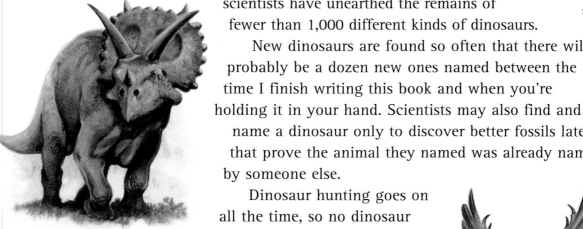

Drinker
see page 73

Arrhinoceratops
see page 38

New dinosaurs are found so often that there will probably be a dozen new ones named between the time I finish writing this book and when you're holding it in your hand. Scientists may also find and name a dinosaur only to discover better fossils later that prove the animal they named was already named by someone else.

Dinosaur hunting goes on all the time, so no dinosaur book can ever be entirely complete. But *Scholastic Dinosaurs A to Z* is as up-to-date as possible. You will find new information on dinosaurs you know and read about dinosaurs you've never heard of. In fact, some *scientists* do not know about a few of the animals in this book, because these dinosaur remains came from remote places or little-known digs.

You can keep up with the latest dinosaur discoveries, too. Let me know what you find out. And keep digging dinosaurs!

Rahonavis
see page 163

"DINO" DON LESSEM
Newton, Massachusetts

How Is This Book Organized?

After these introductory pages, you will find an alphabetical listing of dinosaur entries. Each entry includes information about a dinosaur's name, size, age, diet, and physical details and places where its remains were found. There is also an icon next to each dinosaur entry that shows the major scientific group or taxon to which it belongs. (You can read more about these groups in "How Are Dinosaurs Grouped?" on page 21.) The abbreviations in the captions stand for top (t.); bottom (b.); right (r.); left (l.); front (f.); and back (b.). At the back of the book, you'll find a "Recent Discoveries" page with the latest news about dinosaur finds; a glossary; and a list of resources for further study.

Here are some other notes about the information in each A-to-Z dinosaur entry:

NAME Not every dinosaur named is officially a dinosaur. (See "How Are Dinosaurs Named?" page 20.) A large number of the more than 900 dinosaurs known have been given names that are not yet valid or are no longer scientifically valid. Some of these names go with fossils that are still not fully identified. Other dinosaurs have been misidentified. Still more dinosaur names have been based on evidence from so few fossils that not much can be told about the dinosaur's true identity.

Scientists have different categories for many of these questionable names. In this book, scientifically valid dinosaur names are in italics in the main entries; those that are not are in quotation marks, followed by the phrase "Not a valid scientific name" and whatever brief information is available on the dinosaur.

SIZE Scientists rarely even estimate the weight of a dinosaur because its skeleton doesn't show the complete, fleshed-out dimensions of the living animal. And there aren't even full skeletons for most dinosaurs! Instead, they estimate the length of a dinosaur. Sometimes this is hard to do because there are only fossil fragments available or the only skeleton found belongs to a young dinosaur that was not fully grown.

Lambeosaurus
see page 113

TIME Dates when a dinosaur lived are estimates. (A single species appears to have existed for less than two million years on the average.) Figuring out the age of a fossil is an inexact science, unless the rock in which it was found is of volcanic origin. Volcanic rock can be precisely dated through chemical testing, but few fossils are preserved in volcanic rock.

Brachyceratops
see page 48

The dates and ages given for when a dinosaur lived are based on an estimate of the time of formation of sedimentary rocks in which its fossils were embedded. For other dinosaurs, the time period is estimated based on information about the age of the fossils of other, better-known animals found nearby.

There is a range of estimates given for the time that a single dinosaur might have lived, so we've chosen a single, representative date. But remember, this animal may have lived as much as 30 million years before that date.

PLACE We list where a dinosaur's fossils have been found, but the animal's actual range may have extended farther, across ancient landmasses.

Sometimes you'll find a question mark next to a dinosaur's group icon or within an entry. These question marks appear wherever there is information that's still in dispute or simply unknown by scientists. Fossil parts often don't indicate enough to easily measure or classify the dinosaur. The question marks in this book reflect the questions of scientists. For all the information that is known about dinosaurs, there is much more unknown.

Khaan
see page 110

What Is a Dinosaur?

Dinosaurs aren't mammals. They aren't reptiles. They aren't sea creatures or flying creatures. So what are they? I hear kids say that dinosaurs were giant meat-eating and plant-eating animals that lived a long time ago and became extinct. That's true — in part. For example, there were many small dinosaurs. And dinosaurs weren't the only giants who went extinct. There were other animals as large as dinosaurs that disappeared too. (Though one group of dinosaurs is *not* extinct — we call them birds.)

Dinosaurs were a group of animals that lived only on land, between 222 million and 65 million years ago. Like reptiles, their ancestors, dinosaurs laid eggs and had scaly skin. Birds also shared these features. Birds are the living relatives of meat-eating dinosaurs!

There are many features in the skeletons of birds and dinosaurs that show that they are different from reptiles. Among these differences are an S-shaped curve in the neck, and a hinge-like ankle that helped dinosaurs (and helps birds) walk with their limbs directly underneath their bodies. Reptiles walk with their limbs held out to the side (if they have any limbs at all!).

Some dinosaurs were enormous, as heavy as 20 elephants, as long as four school buses, or as tall as a

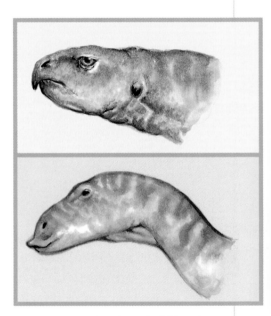

curved neck vs. straight neck

dinosaur posture vs. reptile posture

How some dinosaurs and a human measure up

six-story building. But some dinosaurs were no bigger than chickens. An average-size dinosaur was about as big as a mini-van.

Dinosaurs lived everywhere on Earth. Their bones have been found on every continent. Dinosaurs walked through forests and deserts and swam across rivers. Some saw snow. Most dinosaurs lived in warm lands with many plants but few flowers. All dinosaurs lived before the first blade of grass ever sprouted.

Dinosaurs, except for birds, disappeared 65 million years ago. No animals on land ever grew so big, ranged so far, or dominated their world for as long as the dinosaurs did.

When and Where Did Dinosaurs Live?

All the dinosaurs we know of, except for birds, lived during the three periods of the Mesozoic era: late in the Triassic Period (250 million to 200 million years ago), and throughout the Jurassic Period (200 million to 145 million years ago) and the Cretaceous Period (145 million to 65 million years ago). Our ancestors, the early mammals, also lived during the Mesozoic Era, but these ancient mammals never grew larger than house cats.

Remains of the same kinds of dinosaurs have been uncovered in one or more places, but how far dinosaurs actually ranged, and in what numbers, is a mystery. We only have a scattered sample of dinosaur fossils from different times and places, not a complete record of ancient life.

We do know that Earth changed enormously during the 163 million years that dinosaurs lived. We have fossil evidence not only of dinosaurs but of their changing environments.

The Triassic Period (250 million to 200 million years ago)

During the Triassic Period, all of the earth's land formed a single continent called Pangaea. Pangaea was close to the equator. The weather was hot; heavy rainstorms swept parts of the single continent, while other areas were dry. Giant ferns and other primitive trees without flowers towered over the land.

Reptiles were the dominant form of life in the Triassic period. Many reptiles were not even closely related to dinosaurs. But some had similar features. The

Late Triassic Period

228 million years ago
Eoraptor

220 million years ago
Massospondylus

Jurassic Period

200 million years ago
Dilophosaurus

rabbit-size *Lagosuchus*'s modified ankle bones helped it walk upright, the same way dinosaur ankles did. Some Triassic reptiles, such as *Saurosuchus,* grew to more than 20 feet (6.5 meters) long, longer than most Triassic dinosaurs.

The earliest dinosaurs we know of were dog-size meat eaters from the Late Triassic Period such as *Eoraptor* from Argentina. The largest of these early dinosaurs was *Herrerasaurus*, a meat-eater 15 feet (4.5 meters) long.

Two very different forms of dinosaurs, the **saurischian** and the **ornithischian**, developed during the Triassic Period. These forms survived through the rest of dinosaur time.

The **saurischian**, or "lizard-hipped," dinosaurs had a pubis bone that faced down and forward in its hips. Saurischians included both the meat-eating theropods and the giant four-legged plant-eating sauropods.

Ornithischians, or "bird-hipped," dinosaurs also appeared in the Late Triassic Period, around 200 million years ago. These dinosaurs had a pubis bone pointing down and backward. Ornithischians included many later kinds of plant-eaters, including stegosaurs and horned dinosaurs.

Around 230 million years ago, the first of the lizard-hipped plant-eaters, called **prosauropods**, appeared. They grew up to 20 feet (6.5 meters long). Prosauropods had small heads and walked either on two legs or on all fours. Bird-hipped plant-eaters, such as *Heterodontosaurus* appeared at the same time. These first ornithischians were no bigger than turkeys.

Earth: Triassic Period

13

170 million years ago
Omeisaurus

Brachiosaurus

125 million years ago
Iguanodon

145 million years ago

Allosaurus

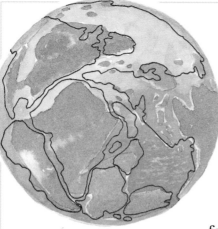

Earth: Jurassic Period

The Jurassic Period (200 million to 145 million years ago)

During the Jurassic Period the Earth continued to divide into northern and southern supercontinents. The land became drier in many areas and climates became more varied. Places that are land now were underwater then. (Seashells found from this time in what is now the Jura Mountains of France gave this period its name.)

The northeastern part of North America was underwater for much of the Jurassic Period and the Cretaceous Period that followed. But in other regions, like the American West, forests spread and shallow lakes formed. Evergreen plants, including conifer trees, grew in deep forests.

Dinosaurs grew to many new shapes and sizes during this period, while many other giant reptiles disappeared from the land. Dinosaurs became the dominant land animals in the Jurassic Period. The new bird-hipped groups included armored and plated dinosaurs, as large as the truck-size *Stegosaurus*. Giant, four-legged, plant-eating sauropods evolved from the prosauropods, including the six-story-high sauropod *Brachiosaurus*. Many other giant plant-eaters also appeared at this time. The longest of all dinosaurs were the whip-tailed diplodocids, including *Seismosaurus*, the 150-foot-long (45 m) "earth-shaker."

Meanwhile, meat-eaters grew as large as the 35-foot-long (11 m) *Allosaurus*, and as small as the beagle-size *Compsognathus*. The biggest meat-eaters were powerful hunters with strong jaws and arms. The small hunters were the fastest dinosaurs of the Late Jurassic. Small meat-eating dinosaurs much resembled the first birds, which appeared at this time. Giant sea reptiles and huge flying reptiles evolved in the Jurassic, too.

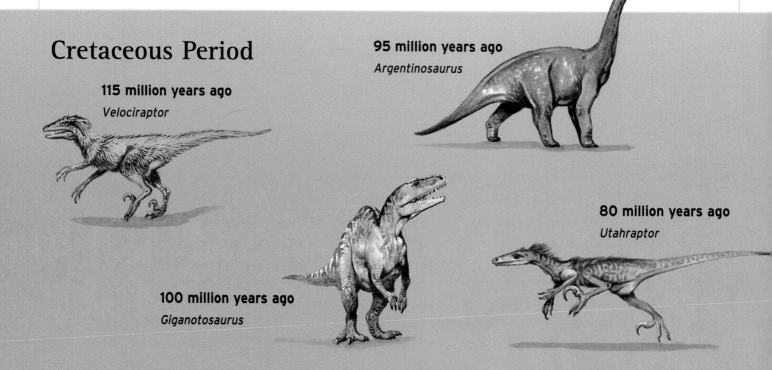

Cretaceous Period

95 million years ago
Argentinosaurus

115 million years ago
Velociraptor

80 million years ago
Utahraptor

100 million years ago
Giganotosaurus

The Cretaceous Period (145 million to 65 million years ago)

In this last dinosaur period, the landscape changed most of all. Flowering plants became common. The modern continents began to form as older landmasses broke up. Sometimes these new continents became huge islands or were partly flooded by the ocean. Sometimes they collided with other continents. North America was divided for part of the Cretaceous by a huge shallow sea with the western lands connected to Asia. South America and India became isolated island continents. Europe turned into a chain of large islands.

The world was warmer than it is today and there was no ice at the poles. Some areas became dry and desertlike; others became warmer and wetter. Early types of flowering plants and trees began spreading over the lands, replacing some of the conifers and ferns.

Dinosaurs lived in all these changing lands and different climates. Some saw snow during the dark winters in Alaska and Australia. Others lived nearer the equator in places as dry as the Gobi Desert today or in wetlands in North Africa where the modern Sahara Desert is.

Earth: Cretaceous Period

Sauropods took on many new and giant forms, including *Argentinosaurus,* the largest dinosaur known. Vicious, long-clawed "raptor" dinosaurs roamed the Northern Hemisphere.

Some meat-eaters grew feathers; others developed beaks instead of teeth. Bird-hipped plant-eaters evolved into armored, duck-billed, dome-headed, and horned dinosaurs the size of tanks. Some had highly specialized mouths packed with hundreds of grinding teeth.

15

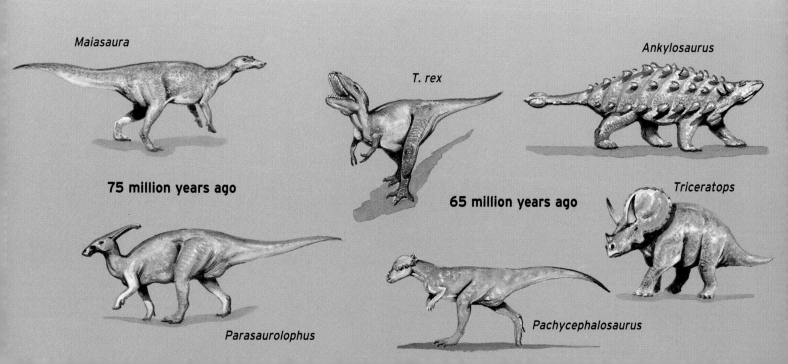

Maiasaura

Ankylosaurus

T. rex

75 million years ago

65 million years ago

Triceratops

Parasaurolophus

Pachycephalosaurus

What Happened to the Dinosaurs?

Dinosaurs were going extinct the whole time they roamed the earth. But as one kind of dinosaur disappeared, others filled its place. (Dinosaurs' closest relatives, birds, didn't die out.) What stopped this evolutionary parade of dinosaurs? Space rocks!

At least, many scientists now think so. Twenty years ago, scientists began

finding evidence that asteroids, rocks from space, crashed into Earth 65 million years ago. One huge crater, from just such an impact, has been found on the ocean floor in the Gulf of Mexico. That crater is 50 to 60 miles (80 to 110 kilometers) wide in the impact center. It could be 168 miles (270 kilometers) wide at its outer rim!

When asteroids hit Earth, they sent huge clouds of dust up into the air. The dust from a giant asteroid would have blocked the sunlight and changed Earth's temperature. The heat of the asteroid as it burned through Earth's

atmosphere would have set fires blazing. Smoke, heat, and clouds of ash would have spread across the planet.

Around the time that the asteroids hit, roughly 65 million years ago, many kinds of animals died out. Dinosaurs, as well as the giant reptiles of the sea and air, were among the life-forms wiped out in this great extinction. Birds, descended from meat-eating dinosaurs, lived on. Mammals, reptiles such as crocodiles, insects such as cockroaches, and many other kinds of life on sea and land also mysteriously survived.

Asteroids and weather changes might not have been the only causes of dinosaur extinction. At the end of the Cretaceous Period, seas were drying out. Changes in the sea levels may have created more extreme winter and summer weather in all lands. Other weather changes, caused by volcanoes or shifting sea currents, may have also affected the earth and its inhabitants.

Continents long separated were coming together again, too. Maybe mammals or other animals carried deadly diseases with them as they crossed newly linked landmasses. Animals that had been separated for so long would not be immune to each other's diseases. Any of these slow changes may have been as much the cause of the dinosaurs' extinction as the asteroid impact.

We don't know exactly what killed the dinosaurs. Maybe we will never have definite proof. But we do know enough about these amazing animals to picture them in our minds and appreciate how extraordinary dinosaurs were. We humans didn't come along until 64 million years after the last dinosaurs had died — yet they live on in our books, our movies, and our dreams.

We've learned most of what we know about dinosaurs from fossils, the preserved remains of dinosaurs and other ancient animals and plants. Studies of the age of rocks, the changes in Earth's magnetic fields, and the shifts in the seafloor also tell us about the age of the earth when dinosaurs lived.

Dinosaur fossils include teeth, claws, and footprints. There are also dinosaur skin impressions and even feathers preserved. Scientists have even found *T. rex* poop! They call dinosaur dung a coprolite.

Fossils form when plant or animal parts or traces are covered with sand or mud and protected while minerals enter into them to harden them. Over millions of years, this sand or mud hardens into stone and the fossil within it is protected, sometimes deep within the earth. If they didn't fossilize, skeletons would turn to dust in years or mere months from wind and rain erosion.

Dinosaur excavation requires teamwork.

Over millions of years, even rocks move. Forces within the earth can push rock from dinosaur time closer to the earth's surface. Erosion then exposes just a bit of a dinosaur fossil, most of which lies protected beneath the ground. Wind blows away the dust and exposes more layers of fossil-rich rock. The badlands, cliff faces, and modern deserts of the North American West, China, Mongolia, and Patagonia are particularly rich in dinosaur fossils. The bare desert ground, swept by wind, allows scientists and amateur prospectors the best chance to see the remains of dinosaurs.

Knowing where to look for dinosaur fossils requires knowledge of the ancient landscape. Sandstone layers produced from ancient streambeds are often the best for preserving dinosaurs. Still, luck plays a big part in fossil discoveries. Most new dinosaur discoveries are made by amateurs, not by professional researchers. Sometimes children are the ones to discover dinosaur remains.

In recent years, scientists have experimented with many methods, from radar to sound waves, to locate dinosaur bones beneath the surface of the ground. But to date, the best way to find a dinosaur is still the way it has always been done: walk the land and look down until you find a promising bit of fossil bone sticking up!

Once a dinosaur fossil is located, it is best if it is excavated by professionals. Paleontologists are scientists who specialize in fossils. Their tools are not complicated and most of their digging methods are a century old. Researchers chip away with pickaxes, hammers, and chisels to remove the rock on top of the fossils. Sometimes they even dynamite! When close to the fossil layer, scientists work with smaller tools such as awls and scrapers. The fossilized bone is removed from the ground with much of the surrounding rock still attached. At the dig,

A scientist measures the teeth in a *Mosasaurus* skull.

each bone or group of bones is wrapped in burlap or other fabric that is soaked in plaster. A thin separator material (such as toilet paper!) is used to keep the plaster from sticking to the bone. The plaster hardens to form a jacket that can weigh several tons. The plaster cast protects discoveries, while scientists dig for more fossils.

The good weather for digging is short, but the time needed to clean fossils is long. Scientists and their assistants spend winter months in their laboratories, cleaning fossils with tiny drills. Then they begin to piece together and examine fossil fragments.

Bone studies show whether the dinosaurs suffered from injuries or disease. These studies also reveal information about how fast the dinosaur grew. Looking at dinosaur poop under the microscope, or at the pattern of wear on a dinosaur's teeth, can tell us what it ate.

By patiently assembing individual bones and, if lucky, nearly entire skeletons, scientists can tell us more about the identity of a dinosaur. Measurements are taken of the length and shape of the bones and compared to those of other dinosaurs that are already known. If the bones are truly different from all other known samples, then the fossil may represent a new kind of dinosaur. In a carefully detailed report approved by other scientists, a researcher then names the new dinosaur.

How Are Dinosaurs Named?

Lessemsaurus
see page 115

Dinosaurs didn't call each other by name. Scientists invented names for the different dinosaur groups. The names are usually Latin or Greek translations of terms describing the dinosaur's appearance or place of origin. The very word *dinosaur* was invented in 1841 by a British scientist, Sir Richard Owen. Owen created his word from the Greek words *deinos* ("terrible") and *sauros* ("lizards"). He was describing a group of animals then known from just a few fossils.

Dinosaur names come from a variety of sources. Sometimes a dinosaur is named for the place where it was found, like *Utahraptor*. Most often a dinosaur is named for a key feature of its skeleton, although scientists use the Greek or Latin word for that feature. For example, *Corythosaurus* is a duckbill dinosaur named for its *corytho*, or helmetlike, crest. *Stegosaurus* is named for the *stego* plates on its back.

Sometimes a dinosaur is named after a person. I'm particularly fond of *Lessemsaurus,* a new plant-eating dinosaur from Argentina that scientist Jose Bonaparte kindly named for a dinosaur writer I know well – me! Like me, *Lessemsaurus* had a small head and large belly.

To be officially named, a newly discovered dinosaur must first be described in a scientific journal. The information is published only after review by other scientists. A key fossil, the holotype, of this new species must show features unlike those of any other dinosaur.

Often, however, a dinosaur is named before it is scientifically described and officially recognized. Or the dinosaur is given its name based on incomplete fossils or an incorrect interpretation of a fossil. It may take scientists many years and more dinosaur fossil finds to realize that a dinosaur already named is not a separate kind of dinosaur after all. In this book we include many dinosaurs mistakenly given separate names, but point them out as "Not a valid scientific name."

The most famous case of a mistaken dinosaur name is "Brontosaurus." This giant plant-eater was named in the late 1800s by the same researcher who had created the name *Apatosaurus* for a giant plant-eater he had found. By 1903, another scientist had proven *Apatosaurus*'s bones were from the same kind of animal as "Brontosaurus." So "Brontosaurus" was no longer a valid scientific name – but it was a familiar one, so people still use it informally today.

How Are Dinosaurs Grouped?

At the highest level of organizing animals, dinosaurs are traditionally grouped into one of two major branches of the dinosaur family tree: the bird-hipped ornithischians or the lizard-hipped saurischians. (One of the most confusing aspects of dinosaur anatomy and classification is that the meat-eaters, which don't belong to the bird-hipped group, are widely regarded as birds' closest relatives.)

Within the bird-hipped or lizard-hipped categories, dinosaurs are separated into groups once called orders, then into units called families. Each family is composed of different *genera* (the plural of genus) that have key features in common. For example, all the plate-backed dinosaurs, or *stegosaurs,* form a family.

We usually refer to dinosaurs by their genus name. Each genus, or kind, of dinosaur is significantly different from any other in the shape, and sometimes size, of many of its bones. For instance, *Albertosaurus* is a genus in the tyrannosaur family. All of the dinosaurs in this family are meat-eaters. They have common features, such as short front limbs with just two fingers.

The dinosaurs in this book are listed alphabetically by their genus names. Scientists also give dinosaurs species names, a still narrower classification. A species is a group of animals that cannot produce breeding young with any other kind of animal. Determining species among dinosaurs is difficult. *Tyrannosaurus rex* is one of the few dinosaurs everyone knows from its first (genus) and second (species) names.

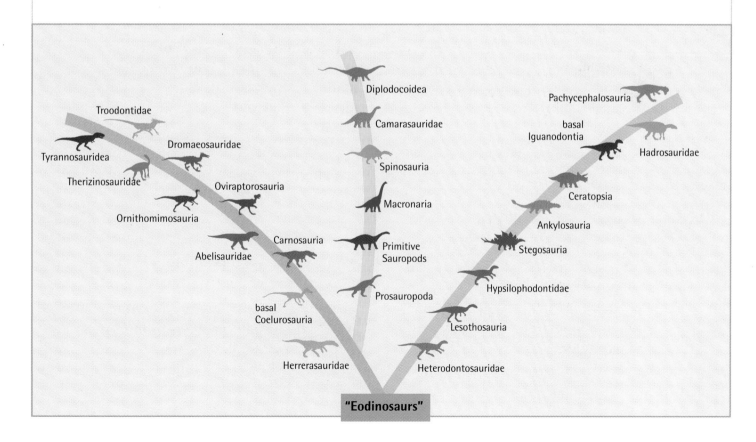

All of the dinosaurs in this book are grouped into the system listed below. It is one of the most recent and widely accepted of many scientific concepts for how to organize dinosaurs.

According to this system, all dinosaurs belong to:

DINOSAURIA: descendants of reptiles that walk tall. Their forelimbs and hind limbs do not sprawl but are held close to and beneath the body, more or less vertically. The Dinosauria are divided into:

SAURISCHIA AND THE ORNITHISCHIA. These are taxa, or groups, which are then divided into many other levels of taxa, or groups. Saurischia include two different major taxa (once called orders) at the highest level of organization:

- **Sauropodomorpha:** large plant-eating sauropods and their prosauropod ancestors, which grew to 20 feet (6.5 m) long.

- **Theropoda:** all the meat-eating dinosaurs and their descendants, birds.

These huge groupings, Sauropodomorpha and Theropoda, break down into smaller groups, once called families. These 26 smaller groups are described below. An icon represents each group. You'll find these icons next to the genus name in each dinosaur entry.

The icons below are grouped within the two major orders of dinosaurs; the lizard-hipped saurischians come first and are followed by the bird-hipped ornithischians. Additionally, the saurischian category is further divided into the plant-eating sauropods and prosauropods and the meat-eating theropods. Within each group, the taxa are organized from the most primitive to the most advanced members.

SAURISCHIANS

Sauropods and Prosauropods

Primitive sauropods: early members of the sauropodomorph group of large plant-eaters with five digits on their hind feet, and leaf-shape or spoon-shape teeth.

Macronaria: These sauropods had large nostrils on the sides of their skulls instead of on the front like other sauropods. Titanosaurs and brachiosaurs, the largest of all dinosaurs, are members of Macronaria. They were among the most widespread and long lasting of all dinosaur forms.

Camarasauridae and relatives: a group of sauropods that feature divided spines on a few of their backbones.

Diplodocoidea: sauropods with peglike teeth in the front of their mouths and nostrils atop their skulls. Most of their neck and back vertebrae had divided spines.

Prosauropoda: The fifth digit of the hind feet on these primitive plant-eaters is small or completely absent.

Theropods

Herrerasauridae: These early meat-eaters, or theropods, had four-digit hind feet and five-digit hands, though the fifth digit of the hand was very small.

Ceratosauria: theropods with three functioning toes, and another toe so small it did not make contact with the ground. They also had a grasping hand with four digits, including opposable "thumbs."

Abelisauridae: mid-sized theropods

from the southern continents in the Cretaceous Period. These animals featured shortened arms and slender hind limbs. *Abelisaurus* and *Carnotaurus* are among the Abelisauridae.

Spinosauria: These large theropods had cone-shaped front teeth in a cluster at the front of their snouts.

Carnosauria were large theropods with nongrasping three-digit hands.

Ornithomimosauria were ostrichlike dinosaurs – light, fast, and long-legged.

Basal Coelurosauria were small theropods, all of which may have had a form of nonflight feathers. They include *Compsognathus* and *Coelurus*.

Tyrannosauridae were theropods with two-digit hands. *Tyrannosaurs* are some of the last and largest carnivorous dinosaurs.

Therizinosauridae were theropods with wide hips and very large claws on their hands and feet.

Oviraptorosauria were theropods with toothless beaks.

Dromaeosauridae were theropods with a large claw on the second digit of each of their limbs, including the "raptor" claw of the dromaeosaurs.

Troodontidae were small birdlike theropods.

ORNITHISCHIANS

Lesothosauria were small primitive ornithischians with cheeks or tooth rows that curved inward where the cheeks would have been.

Ankylosauria had well-developed armor scutes over their bodies and include armored dinosaurs with and without tail clubs.

Stegosauria were ornithischians with plates and spikes along the neck, back, and tail.

Heterodontosauridae were small ornithischians with fanglike teeth at the front of their snouts.

Pachycephalosauria were thick-headed and usually small plant-eaters.

Ceratopsia were "horned dinosaurs" with a special beak bone (rostrum) at front of their snouts. They included *Triceratops* and many other familiar dinosaurs, with large horns, and some without.

Hypsilophodontidae were primitive ornithischian dinosaurs with a special notch on one of the bones in their pelvis (ischium).

Basal Iguanodontia were advanced ornithopods with three functional toes on their hind feet. Some had a spike on their thumbs. They also had specialized jaws for chewing plants, but their teeth were not as numerous and specialized as those of duck-billed hadrosaurs.

Hadrosauridae were large, advanced ornithopods with complex sets of teeth and wide beaks. Some had flattened skulls, while others had complex crests on their heads.

23

Abelisaurus

| Abelisauridae | Ankylosauria | basal Coelurosauria | basal Iguanodontia | Camarasauridae | Carnosauria | Ceratopsia | Ceratosauria | Dromaeosauridae | Diplodocoidea | Hadrosauridae | Herrerasauridae | Heterodontosauridae |

Abelisaurus

ah-**bell**-ih-**sor**-uhss

NAMED AFTER: Roberto Abel, Argentine museum director

CLASSIFICATION: Saurischia, Theropoda, Ceratosauria, Abelisauridae

LENGTH: 20 ft (6 m)

TIME: Late Cretaceous, 70 million years ago

PLACE: Argentina

DIET: meat

DETAILS: *Abelisaurus* chased its prey on long, slender hind limbs. Its arms were unusually short. It had a long, narrow head with no horns or ornamentation over its deep-set eyes. Its body style may have been similar to *Carnotaurus,* a closely related Argentinian meat-eater made famous in Disney's movie *Dinosaurs.* Only one incomplete skull of *Abelisaurus* has been discovered.

Abrictosaurus

a-**brick**-toe-**sor**-uhss

NAME MEANS: "awake lizard"

CLASSIFICATION: Ornithischia, Heterodontosauridae

LENGTH: 4 ft (1.2 m)

TIME: Early Jurassic, 195 million years ago

PLACE: South Africa

DIET: plants

DETAILS: When predators came near, this little browser escaped with quick bursts of speed on two powerful legs. *Abrictosaurus* was lightly built and very small for a dinosaur. Like all early bird-hipped dinosaurs, it had leaf-shape teeth for chewing plants.

Abrictosaurus

Abrosaurus

ab-roh-**sor**-uhss

NAME MEANS: "delicate lizard," because of the light construction of its skull

CLASSIFICATION: Saurischia, Sauropoda, Camarasauridae

LENGTH: 60 ft (18.3 m)

TIME: Middle Jurassic, 165 million years ago

PLACE: China

DIET: plants

DETAILS: A long-necked, four-legged sauropod, *Abrosaurus* had a small head with nostrils apparently set above its eyes. Very little is known about this mysterious plant-eating giant. It was named from just a few fossils found in 1986.

"Acanthopholis" (a-can-**thoff**-oh-liss) Not a valid scientific name. Too few fossil remains have been found to properly identify this animal as anything more specific than a nodosaur, or clubless, armored dinosaur.

Achelousaurus

ack-eh-**loh**-uh-**sor**-uhss

NAMED AFTER: Achelous, the shape-changing Greek and Roman river god

CLASSIFICATION: Ornithischia, Ceratopsia

LENGTH: 20 ft (6.1 m)

TIME: Late Cretaceous, 80 million years ago

PLACE: Montana, U.S.

DIET: plants

DETAILS: *Achelousaurus* carried its stocky body on four sturdy legs. It had a knob of bone on its snout and two long spikes at the back of its bony neck frill. It lacked the large horns of other horned dinosaurs. Only a single, partial skeleton of this dinosaur has been found.

*Achelousaurus (t.)
with a young ornithomimid (b.)*

Achillobator

uh-**kil**-oh-**bah**-tor

NAMED AFTER: Achilles, the legendary Greek warrior, and the Mongolian word for hero (*bator*)

CLASSIFICATION: Saurischia, Theropoda, Deinonychosauria, Dromaeosauridae

LENGTH: 20 ft (6.1 m)

TIME: Late Cretaceous, 75 million years ago

PLACE: Mongolia

DIET: meat

DETAILS: *Achillobator* was a large member of the deadly clawed "raptor" dinosaurs. It would have had a very thick Achilles tendon on its heel to support the slashing action of its claw. The proportions of its big skull were similar to those of larger meat-eaters, not the more narrow heads of other dromaeosaur "raptors." Some researchers think that the fossils identified as belonging to this animal may belong to two different types of dinosaurs.

Achillobator

Acrocanthosaurus

ack-row-**can**-thoh-**sor**-uhss

NAME MEANS: "high-spined lizard"

CLASSIFICATION: Saurischia, Theropoda, Carnosauria

LENGTH: 40 ft (12 m)

TIME: Early Cretaceous, 121 million years ago

PLACE: Oklahoma, Texas [U.S.]

DIET: meat

DETAILS: *Acrocanthosaurus* had spines as high as two feet (0.6 m) tall on its neck, back, and tail. The spines on its back were probably set in a ridge of flesh. These spines were not raised in a bony sail as in some later meat-eaters, such as *Spinosaurus* from North Africa.

Acrocanthosaurus (t.) and a small hypilophodont (b.)

Acrocanthosaurus had qualities in common with the earlier giant allosaurs of the Jurassic Period in North America. It also resembles giant meat-eaters that lived in South America nearly 50 million years later, such as *Giganotosaurus* and *Carcharodontosaurus*. Since *Acrocanthosaurus* lived in lands between the habitats of allosaurs and later giant carnivores, it may be a link between big meat-eaters before and after its time. It is the largest meat-eater known from the southern United States.

A nearly complete skeleton of *Acrocanthosaurus*, was recently purchased by the North Carolina Museum of Natural Sciences in Raleigh.

Adasaurus

odd-uh-**sor**-uhss

NAMED AFTER: Ada, an evil spirit from Mongolian mythology

CLASSIFICATION: Saurischia, Theropoda, Deinonychosauria, Dromaeosauridae

LENGTH: 6 ft (1.8 m)

TIME: Late Cretaceous, 70 million years ago

PLACE: Mongolia

DIET: meat

DETAILS: Like other fearsome meat-eating "raptor" dromaeosaurids, *Adasaurus* had a slashing claw on the second digit of each hind foot. But its "killer claw" was smaller than similar slashing weapons on *Deinonychus* and *Velociraptor*.

Aegyptosaurus

ee-**jip**-toe-**sor**-uhss

NAME MEANS: "Egyptian lizard"

CLASSIFICATION: Saurischia, Sauropoda, Macronaria

LENGTH: 47 ft (14.3 m)

TIME: Late Cretaceous, 99 million years ago

PLACE: Egypt

DIET: plants

Aegyptosaurus left femur

DETAILS: The fossils of this mysterious dinosaur were found in Egypt and brought to a German museum nearly a century ago. These fossils were all destroyed when the museum was bombed during World War II. Though *Aegyptosaurus* fossils were incomplete, leg bones and vertebra fragments suggest it was a large, four-legged plant-eater. Perhaps this is the same animal as the newly named *Paralititan*, found at a pre–World War II German dig site in Egypt.

Abelisauridae   Ankylosauria   basal Coelurosauria   basal Iguanodontia   Camarasauridae   Carnosauria   Ceratopsia   Ceratosauria   Dromaeosauridae   Diplodocoidea   Hadrosauridae   Herrerasauridae   Heterodontosauridae

Aeolosaurus

ee-oh-loh-**sor**-uhss

NAMED AFTER: Aeolus, the Greek god of the winds

CLASSIFICATION: Saurischia, Sauropoda, Macronaria

LENGTH: 47 ft (14.3 m)

TIME: Late Cretaceous, 70 million years ago

PLACE: Argentina

DIET: plants

DETAILS: One of the last of the large four-legged plant-eaters, *Aeolosaurus* had a long, flexible neck. Some scientists think this sauropod had dermal plates, or armor, on at least some portions of its body. This fossil discovery, like most dinosaur discoveries, was far from complete. *Aeolosaurus* was about the same size as *Aegyptosaurus*.

Aeolosaurus dermal plate

"Aepisaurus" (ee-pih-**sor**-uhss) Not a valid scientific name. Too few fossils have been found to fully identify this large four-legged plant-eater, discovered in France in 1853.

"Aetonyx" (ay-eat-**on**-icks) Not a valid scientific name. See *Massospondylus*.

Afrovenator

aff-row-vee-**nay**-tor

NAME MEANS: "African hunter"

CLASSIFICATION: Saurischia, Theropoda, Carnosauria

LENGTH: 20 ft (6 m)

TIME: Early Cretaceous, 132 million years ago

PLACE: Niger

DIET: meat

DETAILS: This three-fingered carnivore was discovered in the

Afrovenator

Sahara Desert. *Afrovenator* was a relative of large and primitive meat-eaters such as the huge *Torvosaurus* of western North America in the Late Jurassic Period and the spinosaurs from Cretaceous North Africa.

"Agathaumas" (ag-uh-**thaw**-muss) Not a valid scientific name. Probably *Triceratops* or *Torosaurus*.

Agilisaurus

ad-jih-loh-**sor**-uhss

NAME MEANS: "agile lizard"

CLASSIFICATION: Ornithischia, Hypsilophodontidae

LENGTH: 4 ft (1.2 m)

TIME: Late Jurassic, 165 million years ago

PLACE: China

DIET: plants

DETAILS: This little dinosaur was one of a worldwide family of small, bird-hipped plant-eaters. It had several sharp front teeth designed for slicing leaves. Because *Agilisaurus* had a small body with strong hind limbs, it was probably a fast runner. A nearly complete skeleton was named in 1990.

Agilisaurus

Heads or Tails?

Edward Drinker Cope (1840–1887) was a rich Philadelphia scientist. He spent his fortune collecting dinosaur bones. Cope paid teams of diggers to unearth fossils of the great beasts in the American West. He also engaged in a bitter battle with Othniel Charles Marsh (see page 110). Both men in the 19th-century "bone wars" used treachery and wealth to see who could find and name the most dinosaurs. Marsh once publicly embarrassed Cope by pointing out that the Philadelphia scientist had placed the skull of a marine reptile on the wrong end of its body. Marsh's workers invaded Cope's dig sites. Cope's men raided lands Marsh thought he had reserved for fossil hunting.

Cope named many of the backboned animals known in his time, an amazing accomplishment. Among them were many kinds of dinosaurs, including the first Triassic meat-eaters from Arizona and "Agathaumas," the first horned dinosaur named from North America.

Edward Drinker Cope

"**Agrosaurus**" (**ag**-row-**sor**-uhss) Not a valid scientific name. The bones of this dinosaur were mislabeled and were once thought to have come from Australia. They actually were found in England.

Agustinia

ah-guh-**stee**-nee-uh

NAMED AFTER: Agustin Martinelli, a young Argentine fossil-finder

CLASSIFICATION: Saurischia, Sauropoda, Macronaria

LENGTH: 25 ft (7.6 m)

TIME: Early Cretaceous, 121 million years ago

PLACE: Argentina

DIET: plants

DETAILS: *Agustinia* was the size of an ice-cream truck and featured spiky armor, not commonly known on the sauropod dinosaurs. *Augustinia* was recently named by Argentine paleontologist José Bonaparte.

Alamosaurus

al-a-mo-**sor**-uhss

NAMED AFTER: Ojo Alamo, New Mexico

CLASSIFICATION: Saurischia, Sauropoda, Macronaria

LENGTH: 67 ft (20.4 m)

TIME: Late Cretaceous, 66 million years ago

PLACE: New Mexico, Texas, Utah, U.S.

DIET: plants

DETAILS: This large sauropod was perhaps the last giant four-legged plant-eater to live in the North American West. It weighed roughly 30 tons—as much as six elephants. *Alamosaurus* was descended from the South American dinosaurs that moved northward once the landmasses of the Americas were reunited near the end of the dinosaurs (about 65 million years ago). It came the farthest north of any dinosaur native to South America known at this time. Some of its relatives had armor, but it is not known if *Alamosaurus* shared that trait.

Albertosaurus

al-**bert**-oh-**sor**-uhss

NAMED AFTER: Alberta, Canada

CLASSIFICATION: Saurischia, Theropoda, Tyrannosauridae

LENGTH: 25 ft (7.6 m)

TIME: Late Cretaceous, 70 million years ago

PLACE: Alberta, Canada

Albertosaurus (b.), and *Lambeosaurus* (t.).

DIET: meat

DETAILS: *Albertosaurus* prowled western North America five million years before its giant cousin, *Tyrannosaurus rex*. With a huge skull and sharp, serrated teeth, this ferocious carnivore sawed through flesh with ease. Its two-fingered hands were small, as were its arms. But strong back legs gave *Albertosaurus* strength and bursts of speed. Its brain was comparatively large. This meat-eater probably had a keen sense of vision and smell compared with most dinosaurs, making it a highly efficient carnivore. Big as it was, it was not much more than two thirds the size of *T. rex*.

Alectrosaurus

a-**lek**-tro-**sor**-uhss

NAME MEANS: "mateless lizard"

CLASSIFICATION: Saurischia, Theropoda, Tyrannosauridae

LENGTH: 20 ft (6.1 m)

TIME: Late Cretaceous, 88 million years ago

PLACE: China, Mongolia

DIET: meat

DETAILS: A huge meat-eater from the Late Cretaceous, *Alectrosaurus* was a puzzle to paleontologists for many years. Only its arm bones and leg bones were found in the Gobi Desert in the 1920s—100 feet (30 m) apart. In the early 1970s, more specimens were discovered, including a skull, complete with a smooth snout and long, razor-sharp teeth. Its strange name was chosen because the animal did not appear to be closely related to other types of tyrannosaurs. Later it was learned that the big arms and clawed hands found with the skeleton belonged to a completely different kind of dinosaur, a therizinosaur.

"**Algoasaurus**" (al-**go**-uh-**sor**-uhss) Not a valid scientific name. Probably a young sauropod plant-eater named for Algoa Bay in South Africa, near where it was found.

Agustinia

Hypsilophodontidae Lesothosauria Macronaria Ornithomimosauria Oviraptorosauria Pachycephalosauria Primitive sauropods Prosauropoda Spinosauria Stegosauria Therizinosauridae Troodontidae Tyrannosauridae

Alioramus

al-ee-oh-**ray**-muss

NAME MEANS: "different branch"

CLASSIFICATION: Saurischia, Theropoda, Tyrannosauridae

LENGTH: 20 ft (6.1 m)

TIME: Late Cretaceous, 65 million years ago

PLACE: Mongolia

DIET: meat

DETAILS: *Alioramus* was considerably smaller than other tyrannosaurs. It had a greater number of smaller teeth in a longer, more slender skull. The single skeleton discovered so far indicates that it had a long snout with six small horns.

Alioramus

Aliwalia

al-ih-**wall**-ee-uh

NAMED AFTER: Aliwal, the South African location of the first fossil find

CLASSIFICATION: Saurischia, Theropoda, Herrerasauridae

LENGTH: 25 ft (7.6 m)

TIME: Late Triassic, 215 million years ago

PLACE: South Africa

DIET: meat

DETAILS: *Aliwalia* is one of the first large meat-eating dinosaurs, the biggest yet known from the Triassic Period. It was as heavy as a car and almost twice as long. The dinosaur is known from a large upper jaw and parts of a leg. Other members of the herrerasaur group are known from Europe, the American Southwest, and South America. These finds indicate that herrerasaurs probably hunted all over the world when it was a single landmass more than 200 million years ago. The first bones of this dinosaur were found by a prospector along a creek near his home in South Africa. He shipped bones to an English geologist in London, who passed them on to a famous paleontologist, Thomas Henry Huxley. Huxley identified both *Aliwalia* and a plant-eater from the bones. A second shipment of *Aliwalia* was lost and apparently surfaced in a Vienna museum. A third batch was sent to a Paris museum. Not until 1985 did a paleontologist identify several of the bones in Vienna as belonging to *Aliwalia,* not the plant-eater.

Allosaurus (t.) and a sauropod (b.)

Allosaurus

al-oh-**sor**-uhss

NAME MEANS: "strange reptile"

CLASSIFICATION: Saurischia, Theropoda, Carnosauria

LENGTH: 37 ft (11.3 m)

TIME: Late Jurassic, 145 million years ago

PLACE: Colorado, Utah, Wyoming, Montana [U.S.]

DIET: meat

DETAILS: During the Late Jurassic Period, the mighty *Allosaurus* ruled western North America. More than 70 three-inch-long (8 cm) teeth lined its powerful jaws. Huge, muscular back legs enabled *Allosaurus* to sprint at relatively high speeds for a dinosaur. Its forearms featured three razor-sharp claws as long as 10 inches (25 cm) in adults. *Allosaurus* also had short, pointed horns, one above each eye. Thousands of allosaur bones were discovered in one Utah quarry. The bones may have been concentrated in quicksand, which trapped many predators over time.

"Alocodon" (a-**lock**-oh-don) Not a valid scientific name. A small plant-eater, named for the vertical grooves in its teeth. The teeth are the only fossils known of this animal.

Altirhinus

al-tee-**rye**-nuss

NAME MEANS: "high nose"

CLASSIFICATION: Ornthishichia, basal Iguanodontia

LENGTH: 25 ft (7.6 m)

TIME: Early Cretaceous, 140 million years ago

PLACE: Mongolia

DIET: plants

DETAILS: *Altirhinus* was one of many closely related

Altirhinus

members of the iguanodon family, which lived around the world. Iguanodontids, including *Altirhinus,* appeared early in the Cretaceous Period, when flowering plants were starting to spread. Perhaps iguanodontids were better suited to eating these new forms of vegetation than earlier plant-eaters. Certainly iguanodontids had strong grinding teeth and jaws as well as large thumb spikes. Their spikes may have been used in feeding or defense. This plant-eater was identified in 1998.

"Altispinax" (al-tih-**spy**-naks) Not a valid scientific name. This large European meat-eater was first named for vertebrae with high spines, but was mistakenly used again to name a dinosaur from a tooth. See *Becklespinax.*

Alvarezsaurus

all-vah-ress-**sor**-uhss
NAMED AFTER: Argentine fossil-finder Don Gregorio Alvarez
CLASSIFICATION: Saurischia, Theropoda, Alvarezsauridae
LENGTH: 7 ft (2.1 m)
TIME: Late Cretaceous, 90 million years ago
PLACE: Argentina
DIET: meat
DETAILS: *Alvarezsaurus* is the first known example of what may be a family of lightly built meat-eaters from the South America, North America, and Asia. It was probably a fast runner.

This small, birdlike dinosaur was found on a riverbank near the University of Comahue's Museum of Natural Sciences in western Patagonia.

Alwalkeria

al-waw-**keer**-ee-uh
NAMED AFTER: Alick Walker, British paleontologist
CLASSIFICATION: Saurischia, Theropoda, Herrerasauridae
LENGTH: 5 ft (1.5 m)
TIME: Late Triassic, 225 million years ago
PLACE: India
DIET: meat
DETAILS: This little predator is one of the oldest known dinosaurs. A long and narrow snout containing teeth

Alwalkeria

without grooves and the lack of a ridge of bone beneath the skull opening near the eye indicate that it was a very primitive meat-eater. The oldest known Asian dinosaur, *Alwalkeria* may also have been discovered in Texas.

Alxasaurus

all-shah-**sor**-uhss
NAMED AFTER: Alxa Desert in Inner Mongolia
CLASSIFICATION: Saurischia, Theropoda, Therizinosauridae
LENGTH: 13 ft (4 m)
TIME: Early Cretaceous, 112 million years ago
PLACE: China, Mongolia
DIET: unknown, perhaps plants and insects
DETAILS: *Alxasaurus* is considered one of the most primitive of the strange and mysterious

Alxasaurus

Amargasaurus

Abelisauridae   Ankylosauria   basal Coelurosauria   basal Iguanodontia   Camarasauridae   Carnosauria   Ceratopsia   Ceratosauria   Dromaeosauridae   Diplodocoidea   Hadrosauridae   Herrerasauridae   Heterodontosauridae

therizinosaurs. It was descended from meat-eaters but did not have sharp meat-slicing teeth. This long-legged and long-clawed animal may have had a beak. It may have eaten bugs, which it dug with its claws. Some animals related to *Alxasaurus* have been found with feathery body coverings.

Amargasaurus

ah-**mar**-gah-**sor**-uhss

NAMED AFTER: La Amarga, a canyon in Argentina

CLASSIFICATION: Saurischia, Sauropoda, Diplodocoidea

LENGTH: 28 ft (8.5 m)

TIME: Early Cretaceous, 132 million years ago

PLACE: Argentina

DIET: plants

DETAILS: One of the most unusual-looking of the sauropod plant-eaters, *Amargasaurus* had a double row of spines running from its neck to its tail vertebrae. According to one theory, the spines were a defense against predators trying to bite *Amargasaurus*'s neck. Other researchers have suggested the tall spines may have acted as a cooling system, drawing heat away from the animal's body. *Amargasaurus* was small compared to giant plant-eaters of its group.

Ammosaurus

am-oh-**sor**-uhss

NAME MEANS: "sand lizard" or "sandstone lizard"

CLASSIFICATION: Saurischia, Prosauropoda

LENGTH: 13 ft (4 m)

TIME: Early Jurassic, 195 million years ago

PLACE: Connecticut, Arizona, U.S.; Nova Scotia, Canada

DIET: plants

DETAILS: This primitive plant-eater could walk on its hind legs or on all fours, like all prosauropods. More remains of this animal would be known if they hadn't been chopped up by stone workers in a Connecticut sandstone quarry in the 1800s. Many *Ammosaurus* bones were left in the sandstone blocks that were used to build bridges in that state. Only the rear half of the dinosaur was retrieved by scientists. More *Ammosaurus* fossils were retrieved from a bridge when it was demolished in 1969. What is now known includes three vertebrae, some hipbones, and hind limbs. *Ammosaurus* had a bulky body, small feet, big hands with thumb claws, and a long tail.

Ampelosaurus

am-**pell**-oh-**sor**-uhss

NAME MEANS: "vineyard lizard"

CLASSIFICATION: Saurischia, Sauropoda, Macronaria

LENGTH: 47 ft (14.3 m)

TIME: Late Cretaceous, 71 million years ago

PLACE: France

DIET: plants

DETAILS: Based on an incomplete skeleton named in 1995, this large, long-necked plant-eater had a bulky body with some armor and a long, stocky tail. *Ampelosaurus* belongs to the titanosaur group of large plant-eaters, with four legs nearly equal in size. Titanosaurs were the most common of all sauropods worldwide in the Cretaceous Period. But titanosaurs are not well known in Europe, and the only ones from North America named so far are *Alamosaurus* and *Venenosaurus*.

Ampelosaurus armor plate

Amphicoelias

am-**fih**-**seal**-ee-uhss

NAME MEANS: "hollow at both ends" (vertebra)

CLASSIFICATION: Saurischia, Sauropoda, Diplodocoidea

LENGTH: 70 ft (21.3 m)

TIME: Late Jurassic, 155 million years ago

PLACE: Colorado, U.S.

DIET: plants

DETAILS: *Amphicoelias* has been a poorly known giant dinosaur since it was described in 1877. It was originally known only from two vertebrae and leg bones, but new finds may fill in major details. A giant bone found in 1878 was the largest dinosaur vertebra ever discovered. The famous 19th-century dinosaur paleontologist Edward Drinker Cope decided the bone belonged to *Amphicoelias*. Cope kept this nearly eight-foot-long (2.4 m) backbone in his Philadelphia home, but the enormous vertebra has disappeared — it may have come from a dinosaur up to 160 feet (49 m) long!

"Amphisaurus" (**am**-fih-**sor**-uhss) Not a valid scientific name. Now known as *Anchisaurus*.

"Amtosaurus" (**ahm**-toe-**sor**-uhss) Not a valid scientific name. Known from bits of a skull found in Mongolia. Named in 1982, "Amtosaurus" was thought to be an armored dinosaur, but the bones may belong to a duck-billed dinosaur.

"Amurosaurus" (ah-**moo**-roh-**sor**-uhss) Not a valid scientific name. This crested duck-billed dinosaur from the Russian side of the Amur River, which borders China, has not yet been described in detail.

"Amygdalodon" (am-ig-**dal**-oh-don) Not a valid scientific name. A large South American plant-eater named from just a single tooth.

Anasazisaurus

ah-nah-**saw**-zee-**sor**-uhss
NAMED AFTER: the Anasazi people of the American Southwest.
CLASSIFICATION: Ornithischia, Hadrosauridae
LENGTH: 31 ft (9.4 m)
TIME: Late Cretaceous, 84 million years ago
PLACE: New Mexico, U.S.
DIET: plants
DETAILS: This large, crestless hadrosaur, which may be the same animal as *Kritosaurus,* was named in 1993 from a skull found in the desert.

"Anatosaurus" (a-**nate**-oh-**sor**-uhss) Not a valid scientific name. A mistaken name for a duckbill, a large plant-eater named *Edmontosaurus.*

Anatotitan

a-nate-oh-**tie**-ton
NAME MEANS: "giant duck"
CLASSIFICATION: Ornithischia, Hadrosauridae
LENGTH: 40 ft (12.2 m)
TIME: Late Cretaceous, 65 million years ago
PLACE: Montana, South Dakota, U.S.
DIET: plants
DETAILS: This large duck-billed dinosaur weighed more than four tons. It had strong, grinding teeth, though the front half of its flattened muzzle was toothless. *Anatotitan* had narrower, longer limbs and a flatter head than its close relative, *Edmontosaurus.*

Anatotitan

Anchiceratops

Anchiceratops

ang-kee-**sayr**-a-tops
NAME MEANS: "near (a link to) horned face"
CLASSIFICATION: Ornithischia, Ceratopsia
LENGTH: 20 ft (6.1 m)
TIME: Late Cretaceous, 70 million years ago
PLACE: Alberta, Canada
DIET: plants
DETAILS: *Anchiceratops* was a medium-size horned dinosaur with a large head and a long, wavy frill near its neck. It had two long, pointed horns at the brow and a shorter, almost stubby, horn at the snout. Some *Anchiceratops* had an extra knob sticking up from the back of their frills — perhaps these were the males. This dinosaur was first found by the man who discovered *T. rex,* "Mr. Dinosaur" Barnum Brown. He named the first *Anchiceratops* specimen in 1914. Since then five more skulls have been found, all in Alberta, Canada.

Anchisaurus

ang-kee-**sore**-uhss
NAME MEANS: "near lizard"
CLASSIFICATION: Saurischia, Sauropoda, Prosauropoda
LENGTH: 7 ft (2.1 m)
TIME: Early Jurassic, 195 million years ago
PLACE: Connecticut, Massachusetts, U.S.; Nova Scotia, Canada

DIET: plants

DETAILS: Much like *Ammosaurus,* another dinosaur of the same time and place. It had finely serrated, leaf-shape teeth for snipping leaves from their stems or vines. *Anchisaurus* had relatively large eyes for its small head. Its neck was long and it had strong forelimbs with large, five-digit hands. Nearly complete specimens have been unearthed in Connecticut and Massachusetts. *Anchisaurus* was named by famed Yale University dinosaur scientist Othniel C. Marsh in 1885.

Andesaurus

an-dee-**sor**-uhss

NAMED AFTER: the Andes, the South American mountain range

CLASSIFICATION: Saurischia, Sauropoda, Macronaria

LENGTH: 85 ft (25.9 m)

TIME: Early Cretaceous, 112 million years ago

PLACE: Argentina

DIET: plants

DETAILS: This gigantic sauropod carried itself on four sturdy legs. Its exact length is not known. The bones found suggest that it was one of the largest of all dinosaurs. Each of its tail vertebrae was more than two feet (61 cm) long. Unlike other titanosaurs, these tailbones were flat on the ends. *Andesaurus* was named in 1991.

Andesaurus

"Angaturama" (**on**-gah-too-**rah**-muh) Not a valid scientific name. Named in 1996 from parts of a single skull found in Brazil, it may be the same animal as the meat-eater recently named *Irritator.*

Animantarx

an-ih-**man**-tarks

NAME MEANS: "living fortress"

CLASSIFICATION: Ornithischia, Ankylosauria

LENGTH: 10 ft (3 m)

TIME: Late Cretaceous, 99 million years ago

PLACE: Utah, U.S.

DIET: plants

DETAILS: This squat dinosaur belonged to the nodosaurs, armored browsers without tail clubs. *Animantarx* is named for its elaborate armor, which covered all of its body, even its eyelids. *Animantarx* was smaller than the later armored dinosaurs of the North American West, which were three times longer.

Ankylosaurus

ang-kill-oh-**sor**-uhss

NAME MEANS: "fused lizard"

CLASSIFICATION: Ornithischia, Ankylosauria

LENGTH: 30–35 ft (9.1–10.7 m)

TIME: Late Cretaceous, 65 million years ago

PLACE: Montana, Wyoming, U.S.; Alberta, Canada

DIET: plants

DETAILS: Perhaps the last and largest of the armored dinosaurs called ankylosaurs, *Ankylosaurus* is often described as a "walking tank." The low-slung and heavy animal showed an intricate arrangement of thick, bony plates across its back, head, and other vulnerable areas. The bones of the last third of its tail were held rigidly together by overlapping connections; the tail itself ended in a large, bulbous club. The stiffened tail and club could have delivered a blow to an attacking predator.

"Anodontosaurus" (an-oh-**don**-toe-**sor**-uhss) Not a valid scientific name.

"Anoplosaurus" (**an**-o-ploh-**sor**-uhss) Not a valid scientific name. Identified as an armored dinosaur in 1879 in England from a few bones. The bones may belong to a duck-billed dinosaur or even be from two kinds of dinosaurs.

Anserimimus

an-sayr-ih-**my**-muss

NAME MEANS: "goose mimic"

CLASSIFICATION: Saurischia, Theropoda, Ornithomimosauria

LENGTH: 10 ft (3 m)

TIME: Late Cretaceous, 80 million years ago

PLACE: Mongolia

DIET: small animals

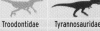

DETAILS: *Anserimimus* was a member of the ostrichlike dinosaur group, all of which had long legs and were lightly built for speed and agility. This dinosaur is based on a single specimen without a skull. It is presumed to be toothless or nearly so, like other ornithomimids. Without teeth, this small meat-eater may have used its strong arms and shovel-like claws to dig for insects or scoop out dinosaur eggs from nests. It also may have hunted small mammals and lizards.

Antarctosaurus

an-**tark**-toe-**sor**-uhss
NAME MEANS: "southern lizard," after South America
CLASSIFICATION: Saurischia, Sauropoda, Macronaria
LENGTH: 100 ft (30.5 m)
TIME: Late Cretaceous, 99 million years ago
PLACE: Argentina
DIET: plants
DETAILS: This giant, long-necked sauropod was among the biggest dinosaurs ever to walk the Southern Hemisphere. It weighed as much as 50 tons. Like other titanosaurs, it probably had a tiny head with weak jaws, and teeth only in the front of its mouth. It was discovered in Argentina in 1916. Other possible specimens were later found in Uruguay and Chile.

Antarctosaurus

"**Antrodemus**" (an-**trod**-eh-muss) Not a valid scientific name. See *Allosaurus*.

"**Apatodon**" (a-**pat**-o-don) Not a valid scientific name. Based on a piece of backbone of a meat-eater that may have been *Allosaurus*. The fossil was first thought to be part of a lower jaw. It was later lost.

Apatosaurus

a-**pat**-oh-**sor**-uhss
NAME MEANS: "deceptive lizard"
CLASSIFICATION: Saurischia, Sauropoda, Diplodocoidea
LENGTH: 90 ft (27.4 m)

Apatosaurus

TIME: Late Jurassic, 145 million years ago
PLACE: Oklahoma, Utah, Wyoming, Colorado, U.S.
DIET: plants
DETAILS: This animal was widely known as "Brontosaurus" until 1911, when it was discovered that the fossils given that name actually belonged to the previously named *Apatosaurus*. Adding to the confusion, this long-necked sauropod was for many years reconstructed with the wrong head. That head turned out to be from another dinosaur found in the same quarry. Although originally given a boxy, *Camarasaurus*-like skull, *Apatosaurus* is now recognized as one of the

Fossil Puzzles

Finding fossils is fun. Figuring out which fossil belongs to which dinosaur is hard work. Fossilized dinosaur parts are often just fragments no longer linked in a skeleton. If you have studied dinosaur skeletons, however, you can often determine where that fossil piece might fit into a dinosaur's body. It's like solving a huge jigsaw puzzle. When new fossils are discovered, scientists compare them with known fossils. This is very tricky work. A new fossil could indicate a new species of dinosaur. Or it could be a body part of an animal already named. Sometimes even trained scientists don't recognize what they've found.

"Nanotyrannus," the "pygmy *T. rex*," was named several years ago from a skull that had sat in a museum drawer for 50 years. The skull had been mislabeled as a young *Gorgosaurus* and given plaster horns. Some researchers think that "Nanotyrannus" was a young *Tyrannosaurus rex*; others think it was a separate kind of dinosaur.

Mapping a fossil quarry

Abelisauridae   Ankylosauria   basal Coelurosauria   basal Iguanodontia   Camarasauridae   Carnosauria   Ceratopsia   Ceratosauria   Dromaeosauridae   Diplodocoidea   Hadrosauridae   Herrerasauridae   Heterodontosauridae

whip-tail diplodocid dinosaurs. It had a long, low snout tipped with peglike teeth. *Apatosaurus* was three times the length of a school bus and more solidly built than most other diplodocid plant-eaters.

Aragosaurus

air-uh-go-**sor**-uhss
NAMED AFTER: Aragón, an area in Spain
CLASSIFICATION: Saurischia, Sauropoda,Camarasauridae
LENGTH: 60 ft (18.3 m)
TIME: Early Cretaceous, 130 million years ago
PLACE: Spain
DIET: plants
DETAILS: Much like North America's *Camarasaurus,* this bulky, four-legged plant-eater had a powerful, muscular tail and a heavy body. Only a single partial skeleton was found.

Aralosaurus

air-uh-loh-**sor**-uhss
NAMED AFTER: the Aral Sea
CLASSIFICATION:
Ornithischia,
Iguanodontia, Hadrosauridae

Aralosaurus

LENGTH: 28 ft (8.5 m)
TIME: Late Cretaceous, 94 million years ago
PLACE: Kazakhstan
DIET: plants
DETAILS: This Cretaceous duckbill, similar to Canada's hook-nosed hadrosaur, *Gryposaurus,* had a toothless beak at the front of its jaws and a stiff tail. Its fossils were found in a group, suggesting that this dinosaur lived in herds like other duckbills.

"Araucanoraptor" (are-ow-**kah**-no-**rap**-tor) Not a valid scientific name. Based on remains of what may have been a relative of the child-size meat-eater *Troodon,* it has never been formally described.

Archaeoceratops

ahr-kee-o-**sayr**-a-tops
NAME MEANS: "ancient horned face"
CLASSIFICATION: Ornithischia, Ceratopsia
LENGTH: 3 ft (0.9 m)
TIME: Early Cretaceous, 130 million years ago
PLACE: China
DIET: plants
DETAILS: One of the first and smallest of all the ancestors of the true horned dinosaurs, this poodle-

Archaeoceratops

size dinosaur had no horns. A partial skeleton of this animal was located in Chinese Inner Mongolia and named by Chinese and Japanese scientists in 1996.

"Archaeoraptor" (**ark**-ee-oh-**rap**-tor) Not a valid scientific name. Parts of the specimen were altered by unethical fossil hunters. It was first identified as a feathered raptor dinosaur, but it is now known to be made from the parts of two different and perhaps individually important animals, one a fossil bird, now called *Archaeovolans,* the other a raptorlike dinosaur, *Microraptor.* Some recently described early fossil birds from China, such as *Jeholornis,* actually have long, bony tails similar to those of raptor dinosaurs.

Archaeornithoides

are-kee-or-nih-**thoy**-deez
NAME MEANS: "ancient bird form"
CLASSIFICATION: Saurischia, Theropoda, basal Coelurosauria?
LENGTH: 3 ft (0.9 m)
TIME: Late Cretaceous, 84 million years ago
PLACE: Mongolia
DIET: meat, insects
DETAILS: Only the partial skeleton of a young *Archaeornithoides* has been found. In some ways its teeth and jaws look similar to those of *Archaeopteryx,* the first bird. Scientists are still not sure exactly how to classify this small, meat-eating dinosaur.

Archaeornithomimus

ar-kee-or-**nith**-o-**my**-muss
NAME MEANS: "ancient bird mimic"
CLASSIFICATION: Saurischia, Theropoda, Ornithomimosauria
LENGTH: 7 feet (2.1 m) long
TIME: Late Cretaceous, 85 million to 75 million years ago

Archaeornithomimus
partial foot

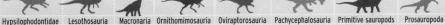

Like Father, Like Daughter

In the Patagonian desert of far western Argentina, Professor Rodolfo Coria works hard at uncovering fossils of truly gigantic dinosaurs. Sometimes he gets a little help. His daughter Ludmila has been helping him dig since she was just four years old.

Professor Coria, born in 1956, lives with his family in Plaza Huincul, a small city just a few hours from some rich dinosaur grounds. There Coria has unearthed bones of *Argentinosaurus*, the world's largest plant-eater, and *Giganotosaurus*, the largest known meat-eater. He has also uncovered many other new kinds of dinosaurs as well as vast nesting grounds full of dinosaur eggs and embryos.

Rodolfo Coria with his wife, Claudia, and daughter Ludmila

38

PLACE: Inner Mongolia
DIET: meat; insects; fruit; plants; nuts
DETAILS: *Archaeornithomimus* is the earliest known ornithomimid dinosaur. This primitive ostrichlike dinosaur is known only from an incomplete fossil that lacks a skull, so it's not known whether *Archaeornithomimus* was toothless like most other ornithomimids. (Some primitive members of this group did have teeth, though.) *Archaeornithomimus's* hand and ankle bones are less lightly built than those of the faster, and probably later, ostrich-mimic dinosaurs of North America and Asia.

Argentinosaurus

are-jenn-**teen**-oh-**sor**-uhss
NAMED AFTER: Argentina
CLASSIFICATION: Saurischia, Sauropoda, Macronaria
LENGTH: 123 ft (37.5 m)
TIME: Early Cretaceous, 99 million years ago
PLACE: Argentina
DIET: plants
DETAILS: *Argentinosaurus* was the largest animal ever to roam the earth. The first of its known remains were brought to scientists by a rancher in western Patagonia in 1989. The rancher initially mistook its five-foot-long (1.5-m) shinbone for a piece of

fossilized wood. Several of the dinosaur's vertebrae have been uncovered, as well as parts of its hips. Its largest backbones found are more than 4.5 feet (1.5 m) wide and five feet (1.7 m) tall. They are the most massive dinosaur backbones ever discovered. These fossils filled with minerals over time. Now, each backbone weighs more than two tons.

Argyrosaurus

are-jih-roh-**sor**-uhss
NAME MEANS: "silver lizard"
CLASSIFICATION: Saurischia, Sauropoda, Macronaria
LENGTH: 65 ft (19.8 m)
TIME: Late Cretaceous, 73 million years ago
PLACE: Argentina
DIET: plants

Argyrosaurus upper arm bone

DETAILS: The first large plant-eater unearthed in South America in the late 1800s, *Argyrosaurus* was probably larger than *Apatosaurus,* and one of the biggest dinosaurs. Only an oversize forelimb and scattered foot bones have been confirmed as fossilized *Argyrosaurus* bones. This sauropod's name refers to Argentina's reputation as the "land of silver." Its remains may also have been found in Uruguay.

"Aristosaurus" (a-**riss**-toe-**sor**-uhss) Not a valid scientific name. See *Massospondylus.*

"Aristosuchus" (are-**riss**-toe-**sue**-cuss) Not a valid scientific name. This small meat-eating dinosaur was originally thought to be similar to a crocodile.

"Arkansaurus" (**ar**-kan-**sor**-uhss) Not a valid scientific name. Its fragmentary fossils may belong to a primitive ostrichlike dinosaur found in Arkansas.

Arrhinoceratops

a-**rye**-no-**sayr**-a-tops
NAME MEANS: "without nose-horn face"
CLASSIFICATION: Ornithischia, Ceratopsia
LENGTH: 25 ft (7.6 m)
TIME: Late Cretaceous, 70 million years ago

Arrhinoceratops

Argentinosaurus

Hypsilophodontidae   Lesothosauria   Macronaria   Ornithomimosauria   Oviraptorosauria   Pachycephalosauria   Primitive sauropods   Prosauropoda   Spinosauria   Stegosauria   Therizinosauridae   Troodontidae   Tyrannosauridae

PLACE: Alberta, Canada

DIET: plants

DETAILS: Despite its "noseless" name, this horned dinosaur had a short, thick nose horn and a pair of medium-size horns above its eyes. However, *Arrhinoceratops'* nose and face was shorter than those of horned dinosaurs previously discovered. Only two skulls of these plant-eaters have been discovered.

"Arstanosaurus" (**are**-stah-no-**sor**-uhss) Not a valid scientific name. Fossil bits found in Kazakhstan indicate what may have been either a horned dinosaur or a duck-billed dinosaur.

Asiaceratops

ay-zhuh-**sayr**-ah-tops

NAME MEANS: "Asian horned face"

CLASSIFICATION: Ornithischia, Ceratopsia

LENGTH: 6 ft (1.8 m)

TIME: Early Cretaceous, 112 million years ago

PLACE: Uzbekistan; Kazakhstan

DIET: plants

DETAILS: Much like its North American counterpart, *Montanoceratops*, this dinosaur was a small protoceratopsian, a relative of the large North American horned dinosaurs but without horns. It was named in 1989.

Asiaceratops

"Asiamericana" (**ay**-zhuh-mare-ih-**con**-uh) Not a valid scientific name. Based on three teeth found in the central Kyzylkum Desert of Uzbekistan, Central Asia, this animal was classified as a meat-eating dinosaur from the spinosaur family, but its fossils may actually have been teeth of a carnivorous fish.

"Asiatosaurus" (**ay**-zhee-at-oh-**sor**-uhss) Not a valid scientific name. A description for a giant plant-eater from Mongolia based on teeth-shaped fossils like those of *Camarasaurus*.

"Astrodon" (**as**-stroh-don) Not a valid scientific name. See *Pleurocoelus*. Maryland's state dinosaur was named "star tooth" for the pattern inside its plant-eating tooth. (This pattern is visible when looked at in cross section under a microscope.) Its species name, *johnstoni*, honors a dentist. This 33-foot-long (10 m)

dinosaur was a relatively small member of the sauropods and is likely the same animal as the better-known *Pleurocoelus*.

"Astrodonius" (as-troh-**doh**-nee-us) Not a valid scientific name. Considered to be the same as "Astrodon."

"Atlantosaurus" (at-**lan**-toe-**sor**-uhss) Not a valid scientific name. See *Apatosaurus*.

Atlasaurus

at-luh-**sor**-uhss

NAMED AFTER: the Atlas Mountains, which were named for the Greek Titan Atlas

CLASSIFICATION: Saurischia, Sauropoda, Macronaria

LENGTH: 47 ft (14.3 m)

TIME: Middle Jurassic, 165 million years ago

PLACE: Morocco

DIET: plants

DETAILS: *Atlasaurus* was a four-legged plant-eater that resembled the later *Brachiosaurus,* though *Atlasaurus* was only half as long. A nearly complete *Atlasaurus* skeleton and skull have been found. The light skulls are rarely preserved because they were washed away by ancient streams.

Atlascopcosaurus

at-luh-scop-koh-**sor**-uhss

NAMED AFTER: Atlas Copco Company

CLASSIFICATION: Ornithischia, Hypsilophodontidae

LENGTH: 9 ft (2.7 m)

TIME: Early Cretaceous, 110 million years ago

PLACE: Australia

DIET: plants

DETAILS: This small, plant-eating dinosaur roamed Australia when *Atlascopcosaurus* that continent was within the Antarctic Circle. It lived in winter darkness and even saw snow. An *Atlascopcosaurus* weighed less than 250 pounds (113 kgs). It walked on its hind legs, much like other hypsilophodontids, a group of two-legged plant-eaters known worldwide at this time. *Atlascopcosaurus* looks most like the small American hypsilophodontid, *Zephyrosaurus*. Paleontologist Tom Rich named *Atlascopcosaurus* in 1989 to honor the Atlas Copco drilling company for its help in excavating this and other dinosaurs from the hard rock of southern Australia. *Atlascopcosaurus* was identified by its jaws and teeth.

"Aublysodon" (aw-**bliss**-oh-don) Not a valid scientific name. This dinosaur was one of the first dinosaurs named in North America. It was identified in 1868 from a few smooth teeth, lacking in serrations found on the edges of the teeth of other tyrannosaurs. Fossils called "Aublysodon" may be from young specimens of known tyrannosaurs.

"Augustia" (**aw**-guss-**tee**-a) Not a valid scientific name. See *Agustinia*.

"Austroraptor" (**aw**-strow-**rap**-tore) Not a valid scientific name for a fragmentary Australian dinosaur. See *Ozraptor*.

"Austrosaurus" (**aw**-stroh-**sor**-uhss) Not a valid scientific name. This large plant-eater was named for Australia's position within the Southern Hemisphere. Only teeth and a partial skull have been found. They may have belonged to a plant-eater about 50 feet long (15 m) that lived in the Late Cretaceous Period.

Avaceratops

ay-vuh-**sayr**-a-tops
NAMED AFTER: rancher Ava Cole
CLASSIFICATION: Ornithischia, Ceratopsia
LENGTH: 8 ft (2.4 m)
TIME: Late Cretaceous, 75 million years ago
PLACE: Montana, U.S.
DIET: plants
DETAILS: This small, frilled-horn dinosaur is one of the most complete ever found in Montana. Some scientists once thought this relatively tiny horned dinosaur was actually a young *Centrosaurus*. Now it is generally considered to be an adult. Like other horned dinosaurs, *Avaceratops* fed on low-growing plants. It was named in 1996 in honor of its discoverer, rancher Ava Cole.

Avaceratops

Avimimus

Avimimus

ay-vih-**my**-muss
NAME MEANS: "bird mimic"
CLASSIFICATION: Saurischia, Theropoda, Oviraptorosauria
LENGTH: 5 ft (1.5 m)
TIME: Late Cretaceous, 80 million years ago
PLACE: Mongolia, China
DIET: insects, reptiles, and possibly plants
DETAILS: New fossils of this poorly known dinosaur show that it was a small, long-legged, very birdlike animal. Early discoveries were so fragmentary that some scientists thought the material might be mixed-up bones of baby ornithomimid dinosaurs and other animals. Some experts think it may have had feathers because of its bird-like skeleton.

"Avipes" (**ay**-vih-peez) Not a valid scientific name. A tiny primitive meat-eater known from few fossils, "Avipes" may not have been a dinosaur, but more closely related to the ancestors of dinosaurs.

Azendohsaurus

ahz-**end**-oh-**sor**-uhss
NAMED AFTER: Azendoh village in Marrakesh, Morocco
CLASSIFICATION: Saurischia, Prosauropoda
LENGTH: 15 ft (4.6 m)
TIME: Late Triassic, 220 million years ago
PLACE: Morocco
DIET: plants
DETAILS: Perhaps the earliest large primitive plant-eater, *Azendohsaurus* is known from only a few teeth and parts of a jaw.

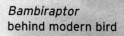

Bambiraptor
behind modern bird

Abelisauridae Ankylosauria basal Coelurosauria basal Iguanodontia Camarasauridae Carnosauria Ceratopsia Ceratosauria Dromaeosauridae Diplodocoidea Hadrosauridae Herrerasauridae Heterodontosauridae

Bactrosaurus

back-troh-**sor**-uhss

NAME MEANS: "club lizard," because of the shape of the high spines on its vertebrae

CLASSIFICATION: Ornithischia, Iguanodontia, Hadrosauridae

LENGTH: 20 ft (6.1 m)

TIME: Late Cretaceous, 80 million years ago

PLACE: China, Mongolia

DIET: plants

Bactrosaurus

DETAILS: *Bactrosaurus* is one of the earliest crested duckbills. Strong and sturdy, this primitive plant-eater was found in the 1920s by an expedition from the American Museum of Natural History. *Bactrosaurus* bears a striking resemblance to more recent duckbill dinosaurs from North America. Nearly identical duck-billed dinosaurs in both continents supports the theory that dinosaurs migrated between Asia and North America across a land connection that is now underwater.

Bagaceratops

bog-uh-**sayr**-uh-**tops**

NAME MEANS: "small horned face"

CLASSIFICATION: Ornithischia, Ceratopsia

LENGTH: 3 ft (0.9 m)

TIME: Late Cretaceous, 84 million years ago

PLACE: Mongolia

DIET: plants

DETAILS: This small, early horned dinosaur had a relatively small frill with tiny openings over its neck. *Bagaceratops* was smaller than other similar early horned dinosaurs. Skulls of this primitive plant-eater were discovered in the Gobi Desert on an expedition led by female Polish scientists.

Bagaceratops

Bagaraatan

bog-uh-**rah**-tahn

NAME MEANS: "small hunter" or "little predator"

CLASSIFICATION: Saurischia, Theropoda, basal Coelurosauria

LENGTH: 10 ft (3 m)

TIME: Late Cretaceous, 75 million years ago

PLACE: Mongolia

DIET: meat

DETAILS: This meat-eater was one of the smallest predators found in the Gobi Desert of southern Mongolia. It prowled Asia about 75 million years ago. *Bagaraatan* had a rigid tail with large spines on each tail vertebra.

"Bahariasaurus" (bah-hah-**ree**-yuh-**sor**-uhss) Not a valid scientific name. It was named after the Bahariŷa Oasis in northern Egypt, where its bones were discovered. The only known fossils of this predatory Late Cretaceous dinosaur were destroyed during World War II.

Bambiraptor

bam-bee-**rap**-tor

NAME MEANS: "bambi [baby] robber"

CLASSIFICATION: Saurischia, Theropoda, Deinonychosauria, Dromaeosauridae

LENGTH: 4 ft (1.2 m)

TIME: Late Cretaceous, 69 million years ago

PLACE: Montana, U.S.

DIET: meat

DETAILS: A skeleton of a young, small, long-clawed meat-eater was discovered by a 14-year-old boy and named in 2000. *Bambiraptor* was anatomically similar to *Archaeopteryx*, although it was nearly twice as large as that oldest known bird. *Bambiraptor* had a well-developed wishbone and extremely long forearms that could fold like a bird's wings. Compared with the size of its body, it had the largest brain of any known dinosaur. But that big-brain ratio might be related to the age of the dinosaur: immature animals have bigger heads compared with their bodies than do adults. Some scientists think *Bambiraptor* is not a new species, but an immature individual of *Saurornitholestes*, another dromaeosaur.

43

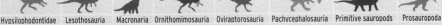

Barapasaurus

buh-**rah**-puh-**sor**-uhss

NAME MEANS: "big leg lizard"

CLASSIFICATION: Saurischia, Sauropoda, Primitive sauropods

LENGTH: 60 ft (18.3 m)

TIME: Early Jurassic, 190 million years ago

PLACE: India

DIET: plants

DETAILS: This early sauropod nipped at plants with its spoon-shape teeth. It walked on legs that were slender for a big four-legged dinosaur. Its name refers to the length of the dinosaur's five-foot-long (1.5 m) femur. This giant leg bone was one of the first *Barapasaurus* bones excavated in 1961. Remains of more than 300 individuals have since been found in the Godavari Valley of southern India.

Barosaurus

bear-oh-**sor**-uhss

NAME MEANS: "heavy lizard"

CLASSIFICATION: Saurischia, Sauropoda, Diplodocoidea

LENGTH: 89 ft (27.1 m)

TIME: Late Jurassic, 145 million years ago

PLACE: South Dakota, Colorado, Utah, U.S.; Tanzania

DIET: plants

DETAILS: This long, slim plant-eater walked on all fours. It had a long whip tail. Unlike many sauropods, remains of *Barosaurus* as a youngster have been found (though there are few fossil skeletons of this big animal). A *Barosaurus* skeleton was recently re-created rearing on its hind limbs in the lobby of New York's American Museum of Natural History. To make the skeleton of *Barosaurus* accomplish this acrobatic stunt, several vertebrae had to be broken and refitted on the cast. It is unlikely the animal ever stood in this position when it was alive.

"Barsboldia" (bars-**bold**-ee-uh) Possibly a valid scientific name. Named for the Mongolian paleontologist Rinchen Barsbold, this Mongolian crested, duck-billed dinosaur is not represented by a skull.

Baryonyx

bear-ee-**on**-iks

NAME MEANS: "heavy claw"

Baryonyx

CLASSIFICATION: Saurischia, Theropoda, Spinosauria

LENGTH: 30 ft (9.1 m)

TIME: Early Cretaceous, 121 million years ago

PLACE: England

DIET: meat, perhaps fish

DETAILS: This impressive meat-eater probably fished for food. Bipedal *Baryonyx* may have used its foot-long (30 cm) hooked thumb claws to spear fish. Its crocodile-like snout was full of sharp teeth. When a nearly complete skeleton was excavated, fish scales were discovered where its stomach had been. Its huge claw was unearthed in 1983 in a clay pit in Great Britain by an amateur fossil–hunter.

Becklespinax

beck-luh-**spy**-naks

NAME MEANS: "Beckles's spined one" after its discoverer, Samuel Husband Beckles

CLASSIFICATION: Saurischia, Theropoda, Spinosauria

LENGTH: 26 ft (7.9 m)

TIME: Early Cretaceous, 137 million years ago

PLACE: England

DIET: meat

DETAILS: Only three of its massive, high-spined vertebrae have been discovered, so little is actually known about this dinosaur. Comparison with vertebrae of other Jurassic meat-eating dinosaurs like South American *Piatnizkysaurus* suggests *Becklespinax* was a primitive animal with high spines on its back.

Barosaurus

Hypsilophodontidae Lesothosauria Macronaria Ornithomimosauria Oviraptorosauria Pachycephalosauria Primitive sauropods Prosauropoda Spinosauria Stegosauria Therizinosauridae Troodontidae Tyrannosauridae

heat. *Brachiosaurus* probably wasn't a swift runner, but it could easily access its food from the high forest canopies of the Late Jurassic Period.

This dinosaur was named in 1903, based on a fossil skeleton only 30% complete. *Brachiosaurus* remains are among the rarest skeletons of all large plant-eaters known from the North American West. It was originally discovered in Colorado, but another species has been found in Tanzania, Africa.

Brachyceratops

brack-ee-**sayr**-a-tops

NAME MEANS: "short horned face"
CLASSIFICATION: Ornithischia, Ceratopsia
LENGTH: 10 ft (3 m)
TIME: Late Cretaceous, 70 million years ago
PLACE: Montana, U.S.
DIET: plants
DETAILS: This small member of the horned dinosaur group had tiny brow horns and a nose horn with a slight upward curve. Smithsonian scientist Charles Gilmore originally found five small *Brachyceratops* near a sixth specimen twice their size in 1913. Perhaps these animals belonged to a group of youngsters of two different ages. Some paleontologists suggest that *Brachyceratops* may be the young of *Achelousaurus* or *Einiosaurus*. The horns and frills of horned dinosaurs changed dramatically as they grew up, so a juvenile's skull did not look as elaborately decorated as that of the adult. Adult *Brachyceratops* may have had longer horns than those of the juveniles found so far.

Brachyceratops

Brachylophosaurus

Brachylophosaurus

brack-ee-loaf-oh-**sor**-uhss

NAME MEANS: "short crest lizard"
CLASSIFICATION: Ornithischia, Hadrosauridae
LENGTH: 23 ft (7 m)
TIME: Late Cretaceous, 78 million years ago
PLACE: Montana, U.S.; Alberta, Canada
DIET: plants
DETAILS: This duck-billed dinosaur had a low, solid crest with a short spike behind and between its eyes. The spike may have been used in a *Brachylophosaurus* head-butting ritual, but it was more likely a sign to identify other members of the same species. This hadrosaur had longer front legs than most other duckbills.

"Brachypodosaurus" (**brack**-ee-**pod**-oh-**sor**-uhss) Not a valid scientific name. This dinosaur's name means "short-legged lizard" because its arm bones were short.

"Brachyrophus" (brack-**ear**-oh-fuss) Not a valid scientific name. See *Camptosaurus*.

"Bradycneme" (brad-ick-**nee**-mee) Not a valid scientific name. Originally identified as a giant owl, this is actually a small, carnivorous dinosaur. Its size is uncertain since only an end of a leg bone had been found by Lady Smith-Woodward in Transylvania in 1923.

Breviceratops

brev-ih-**sayr**-a-tops
NAME MEANS: "short horned face"
CLASSIFICATION: Ornithischia, Ceratopsia
LENGTH: 6.6 ft (1.8 m)
TIME: Late Cretaceous, 86 million years ago
PLACE: Mongolia, China
DIET: plants

Breviceratops

DETAILS: A thick snout and a small, flattened horn or hornlike bump on its nose are among the features of this protoceratopsid horned dinosaur. Many remains of *Breviceratops* babies have been recovered from rocks that are generally considered to be more recent than those in which the most famous member of its group, *Protoceratops,* has been found.

"Brontoraptor" (**bron**-toe-**rap**-tor) Not a valid scientific name. A supposed theropod not yet formally described.

"Brontosaurus" (**bron**-toe-**sore**-us) Not a valid scientific name. The famous "thunder lizard" long known by scientists as *Apatosaurus.*

"Bruhathkayosaurus" (broo-hut-**kah**-yuh-**sor**-uhss) Not a valid scientific name. Bones from a large meat-eater from India were jumbled with those of a giant plant-eater, leading to wildly mistaken

estimates of a carnivore three times the size of *T. rex.*

Bugenasaura

boo-jenn-a-**sor**-uh
NAME MEANS: "large cheek lizard"
CLASSIFICATION: Ornithischia, Hypsilophodontidae
LENGTH: 15 ft (4.6 m)
TIME: Late Cretaceous, 71 million years ago
PLACE: South Dakota, U.S.
DIET: plants

Bugenasaura

DETAILS: This two-legged plant-eater had massive ridges on its jawbones, suggesting that it may have had deep pouches on the sides of its face, similar to mammal cheeks. Its skull was originally identified as that of the closely related *Thescelosaurus.*

Byronosaurus

bye-ron-oh-**sor**-uhss
NAMED AFTER: Byron Jaffe, whose family supports paleontological research
CLASSIFICATION: Saurischia, Theropoda, Deinonychosauria, Troodontidae
LENGTH: 5 ft (1.5 m)
TIME: Late Cretaceous, 84 million years ago
PLACE: Mongolia
DIET: meat

DETAILS: *Byronosaurus* was one of the slender, agile troodontids that lived in both North America and Asia. Among the brainiest of all dinosaurs, *Byronosaurus* boasts one of the most well-preserved skulls of any member of that group discovered to date. The eight-inch-long (20 cm) skull had nasal passages similar to a bird's, and a jaw packed with small teeth without serrations. These smooth teeth are unlike most meat-eaters' teeth but very similar  to those of the flying bird *Archaeopteryx.* *Byronosaurus* was named in 2000.

Byronosaurus teeth

Camarasaurus adult and juvenile (t.), and *Coelurus* (b.)

Abelisauridae   Ankylosauria   basal Coelurosauria   basal Iguanodontia   Camarasauridae   Carnosauria   Ceratopsia   Ceratosauria   Dromaeosauridae   Diplodocoidea   Hadrosauridae   Herrerasauridae   Heterodontosauridae

Caenagnathasia

see-**nag**-na-**thay**-zhee-uh

NAME MEANS: "recent jaw from Asia"

CLASSIFICATION: Saurischia, Theropoda, Oviraptorosauria

LENGTH: 3 ft (0.9 m)

TIME: Late Cretaceous, 90 million years ago

PLACE: Uzbekistan

DIET: meat

DETAILS: This is the earliest known caenagnathid, a form of small, toothless, bipedal carnivore. It was a swift runner, like others of its kind known from East Asia and North America.

"**Caenagnathus**" (**see**-nag-**nay**-thuss) Not a valid scientific name. See *Chirostenotes,* a previously named, and probably identical, small meat-eater.

"**Calamosaurus**" (**kal**-a-moe-**sor**-uhss) Not a valid scientific name. See *Aristosuchus.*

"**Calamospondylus**" (**kal**-a-moe-**spon**-dill-us) Not a valid scientific name. See *Aristoscuchus.*

"**Callovosaurus**" (kal-**loh**-voh-**sor**-uhss) Not a valid scientific name. This dinosaur was identified from just an upper leg bone found in England, not enough for reliable naming.

Camarasaurus

cam-a-ruh-**sor**-uhss

NAME MEANS: "chambered lizard"

CLASSIFICATION: Saurischia, Sauropoda, Camarasauridae

LENGTH: 66 ft (20.1 m)

TIME: Late Jurassic, 145 million years ago

PLACE: Colorado, Utah, Wyoming, U.S.; Portugal

DIET: plants

DETAILS: *Camarasaurus* is one of the first known giant plant-eaters from the North American West. Its head was short and boxlike, with large nostrils above the snout and in front of the eyes. It was an animal with four large limbs of nearly equal length.

Many of the skeletons unearthed have belonged to young or juvenile camarasaurs. A rare sample of fossilized skin impression is known from a *Camarasaurus* discovered at Dinosaur National Monument in Utah. For many years, *Apatosaurus* was mistakenly reconstructed with the skull of the distantly related *Camarasaurus,* because the skull of *Camarasaurus* was discovered near the body bones of *Apatosaurus.*

Camelotia

cam-a-**loh**-tee-uh

NAMED AFTER: Camelot, the legendary home of King Arthur of England

CLASSIFICATION: Saurischia, Prosauropoda

LENGTH: 30 ft (9.1 m)

TIME: Late Triassic, 206 million years ago

PLACE: England

DIET: plants

DETAILS: This prosauropod was a large primitive plant-eater much like those known worldwide at this time. It was named after the English medieval court because its bones were found near the location of Camelot.

Camposaurus

camp-oh-**sor**-uhss

NAMED AFTER: American paleontologist Charles Lewis Camp

CLASSIFICATION: Saurischia, Theropoda, Ceratosauria

LENGTH: 65 ft (19.8 m)

TIME: Late Triassic, 210 million years ago

PLACE: Arizona, U.S.

DIET: meat

DETAILS: *Camposaurus* differs from other small early meat-eaters such as *Coelophysis* and *Syntarsus* because of its sturdier hind limbs. It was probably just as deadly as other bipedal hunters because of its agility and intelligence.

"**Camptonotus**" (camp-toe-**note**-uhss) Not a valid scientific name. This dinosaur is known as *Camptosaurus.*

Camptosaurus

camp-toe-**sor**-uhss

NAME MEANS: "flexible back lizard"

CLASSIFICATION: Ornithischia, basal Iguanodontia

LENGTH: 23 ft (7 m)

TIME: Late Jurassic, 145 million years ago

PLACE: Wyoming, South Dakota, Colorado, Utah, U.S.; England

DIET: plants

DETAILS: *Camptosaurus* is more advanced than the primitive two-legged plant-eating hypsilo-phodontids, but it is more primitive than hadrosaurs, the later duck-billed dinosaurs. It has most in common with the iguanodontids, other plant-eaters of the same time. *Camptosaurus* was small compared with iguanodontids or the later hadrosaurs. Its weight has been estimated at up to 1.7 tons.

Camptosaurus

"Campylodon" (camp-ee-**loh**-don) Not a valid scientific name. Now known as *Campylodoniscus*.

Campylodoniscus

camp-**pie**-loh-don-**iss**-cuss

NAME MEANS: "bent tooth"

CLASSIFICATION: Saurischia, Sauropoda, Macronaria

LENGTH: 50 ft (15.2 m)

TIME: Late Cretaceous, 65 million years ago

PLACE: Argentina

DIET: plants

DETAILS: A four-legged, browsing plant-eater, *Campylodoniscus* is known only from an incomplete upper jaw with a single tooth. This dinosaur is important because it belongs to one of the last sauropod groups that apparently thrived in South America, long after similar sauropods became nearly extinct in most of North America.

Campylodoniscus teeth

"Capitalsaurus" (**cap**-it-ul-**sor**-uhss) Not a valid scientific name. A fragment of a dinosaur named after Washington, D.C.

Carcharodontosaurus

car-care-oh-**don**-toe-**sor**-uhss

NAME MEANS: "shark-toothed lizard"

CLASSIFICATION: Saurischia, Theropoda, Carnosauria

LENGTH: 40 ft (12.2 m)

TIME: Late Cretaceous, 110 million years ago

PLACE: Algeria, Egypt, Morocco

DIET: meat

DETAILS: Recognized for a long time from only fragmentary remains, this giant allosaurlike predator has only recently been understood well enough to build a good reconstruction. It was one of the largest known land predators, almost as enormous as *Tyrannosaurus* and *Giganotosaurus* in length and mass. *Carcharodontosaurus*'s teeth were long and serrated, well suited for slicing through the flesh of large North African prey. Some specimens collected and brought to Germany were destroyed in World War II bombing raids. But scientists found a nearly complete *Carcharodontosaurus* skull in southwestern Morocco in the 1990s. That skull lacked a snout and was mistakenly elongated, resulting in a reconstructed skull as long as that of the largest *Tyrannosaurus*.

The *Carcharodontosaurus* specimen was not only smaller than the largest *T. rex* skull, it had a far smaller brain than *T. rex*. *Carcharodontosaurus* was much more closely related to *Giganotosaurus*, its larger cousin that lived at the same time in South America. Their similarities show that South America and North Africa were joined later in the Cretaceous Period than had been previously thought. Both *Carcharodontosaurus* and *Giganotosaurus* have more in common with the earlier allosaurs than the later tyrannosaurs of North America.

"Cardiodon" (car-**die**-o-don) Not a valid scientific name. Based on a single plant-eater's tooth, now identified as belonging to *Cetiosaurus*.

"Carnosaurus" (**car**-no-**sor**-uhss) Not a valid scientific name for assorted large meat-eater bones.

Carnotaurus

car-no-**tor**-uhss

NAME MEANS: "flesh bull" or "meat-eating bull"

CLASSIFICATION: Saurischia, Theropoda, Abelisauridae

Carcharodontosaurus (b.),
pterosaur, a flying reptile (t.)

Hypsilophodontidae | Lesothosauria | Macronaria | Ornithomimosauria | Oviraptorosauria | Pachycephalosauria | Primitive sauropods | Prosauropoda | Spinosauria | Stegosauria | Therizinosauridae | Troodontidae | Tyrannosauridae

Carnotaurus

Abelisauridae | Ankylosauria | basal Coelurosauria | basal Iguanodontia | Camarasauridae | Carnosauria | Ceratopsia | Ceratosauria | Dromaeosauridae | Diplodocoidea | Hadrosauridae | Herrerasauridae | Heterodontosauridae

LENGTH: 25 ft (7.6 m)
TIME: Late Cretaceous, 80 million years ago
PLACE: Argentina, Patagonia
DIET: meat
DETAILS: This snub-nosed predator is unusual in many ways. Hornlike projections on its skull inspired its "bull" name. It had a distinctive short, deep snout. Its forelimbs were stubby with extremely short lower arm bones. Rare skin impressions were found with *Carnotaurus* remains, indicating small bumps were scattered across this meat-eater's hide.

Carnotaurus was the villain in the animated Disney film *Dinosaurs*. The cartoon movie version made this dinosaur larger, meaner, and faster than it actually was. It also showed the dinosaur living in a later time period and more northern location than it actually did.

Caseosaurus

case-ee-oh-**sor**-uhss
NAMED AFTER: American paleontologist Ermine Cowles Case
CLASSIFICATION: Saurischia, Theropoda, Herrerasauridae
LENGTH: 15 ft (4.6 m)
TIME: Late Triassic, 221 million years ago
PLACE: Texas, U.S.
DIET: meat
DETAILS: *Caseosaurus* was named from a hipbone that resembled that of another early, large meat-eater, *Herrerasaurus,* a similar-size dinosaur from Argentina. In the Late Triassic Period, the earth was still a single continent, so it would not be unusual for the same or closely related kinds of dinosaurs to be found both in Texas and Argentina.

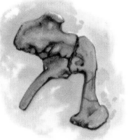
Caseosaurus hip bone

"Cathetosaurus" (**kath**-ee-toe-**sor**-uhss) Not a valid scientific name. According to the late digger "Dinosaur Jim" Jensen, who named "Cathetosaurus," the unique pelvis of this animal allowed it to rear up on its hind legs to reach for plants or to defend its young. The large, four-legged plant-eater's pelvis was tilted like those of two-legged dinosaurs. Tooth marks indicate that a number of scavengers of

Professor José Bonaparte has found and named more dinosaurs in South America than anyone else in history. Born in Argentina in the late 1920s, Professor Bonaparte has been digging dinosaurs for almost 50 years. His discoveries range from strange-spined plant-eaters such as *Amargasaurus* to odd meat-eaters like the tiny-armed *Carnotaurus.* Professor Bonaparte has excavated dinosaurs all across Argentina. He's a tireless researcher, a tough boss, and a fearless prospector. Bonaparte has even saddled up and ridden horseback high into the snowy slopes of the Andes Mountains in search of fossils.

José Bonaparte with Mussaurus *baby*

different sizes fed on the lifeless body of the first "Cathetosaurus" fossil discovered. "Cathetosaurus" is now widely considered to be a species of *Camarasaurus,* a Late Jurassic sauropod of western North America.

Caudipteryx

kaw-**dip**-tayr-iks
NAME MEANS: "tail feather"
CLASSIFICATION: Saurischia, Theropoda, basal Coelurosauria
LENGTH: 3 ft (1 m)
TIME: Early Cretaceous, 124 million years ago
PLACE: China
DIET: meat
DETAILS: This tiny meat-eater showed an unusual fan of large, symmetrical feathers on the end of its tail. *Caudipteryx* is one of the rare terrestrial, or flightless, dinosaurs known to have had feathery plumage.

"Cathetosaurus" also known as Camarasaurus

"Caudocoelus" (kaw-doh-**see**-luss) Not a valid scientific name. Now known as *Teinurosaurus.*

55

"Caulodon" (**kaw**-lo-don) Not a valid scientific name. Now known as *Camarasaurus*.

Cedarosaurus

see-duh-roh-**sor**-uhss

NAME MEANS: "cedar lizard"

CLASSIFICATION: Saurischia, Sauropoda, Macronaria

LENGTH: 46 ft (14 m)

TIME: Early Cretaceous, 125 million years ago

PLACE: Utah, U.S.

DIET: plants

DETAILS: *Cedarosaurus* was named for the Cedar Mountain Formation, where it and other dinosaurs such as the large "raptor" dromaeosaur *Utahraptor* were found. This medium-size sauropod was a late-surviving brachiosaur relative. Information about this dinosaur has not yet been widely published in great detail.

Cedarosaurus vertebra

Centrosaurus

senn-troh-**sor**-uhss

NAME MEANS: "spur frill lizard"

CLASSIFICATION: Ornithischia, Ceratopsia

LENGTH: 20 ft (6.1 m)

TIME: Late Cretaceous, 80 million years ago

PLACE: Alberta, Canada

DIET: plants

DETAILS: This horned dinosaur had hook-shape bone spurs that curve forward and downward from the top border of its frill. *Centrosaurus* was not fully understood when it was originally described by scientists. It was not until more specimens were discovered that paleontologists came to better identify the dinosaur's characteristics. Many bone beds of this dinosaur have been found in Dinosaur Provincial Park in Alberta, Canada. This suggests that *Centrosaurus* moved in herds that might have included thousands of individuals.

Ceratops

sayr-a-tops

NAME MEANS: "horned face"

CLASSIFICATION: Ornithischia, Ceratopsia

LENGTH: 30 ft (9.1 m)

TIME: Late Cretaceous, 80 million years ago

PLACE: Montana, U.S.

DIET: plants

DETAILS: One of the first ceratopsians found more than 100 years ago, this plant-eater was originally thought to be a close relative of the stegosaurs. Further research proved it belonged to a wholly new family of dinosaurs, the now well-known horned dinosaurs.

Ceratosaurus

ser-**rat**-o-**sor**-uhss

NAME MEANS: "horned lizard"

CLASSIFICATION: Saurischia, Theropoda, Ceratosauria

LENGTH: 30 ft (9.1 m)

TIME: Late Jurassic, 145 million years ago

PLACE: Colorado, U.S.; Tanzania

DIET: meat

DETAILS: This midsize meat-eater had several unusual features, including a large horn on the top of the snout just above the dinosaur's nasal passages. Scientists speculate that the horn may

Centrosaurus

Caudipteryx

Hypsilophodontidae   Lesothosauria   Macronaria   Ornithomimosauria   Oviraptorosauria   Pachycephalosauria   Primitive sauropods   Prosauropoda   Spinosauria   Stegosauria   Therizinosauridae   Troodontidae   Tyrannosauridae

have been brightly colored to attract a mate. Some have even suggested that the horn was used to help the newborn *Ceratosaurus* break out of its egg, much the way an egg tooth helps a baby chick break through its shell. This is unlikely, though, as the horn appears to be a bone that developed only in the adults. *Ceratosaurus* had four fingers, a primitive feature on the hands of dinosaurs; *T. rex*, one of the last and most advanced meat-eaters, had only two fingers. *Ceratosaurus* carried itself on two strong muscular hind legs and was likely capable of great bursts of speed. Its large eyes suggest it had excellent vision. The long, thin braincase suggests *Ceratosaurus* was not a particularly brainy dinosaur, but was more intelligent than the plant-eaters upon which it fed. Nineteenth-century Yale University paleontologist Othniel C. Marsh, who named *Ceratosaurus,* thought that its long, thin tail meant that it could swim. Today, most scientists agree that dinosaurs could swim but that they lived exclusively on land.

Ceratosaurus

Cetiosauriscus

see-tee-oh-sor-**riss**-cuss
NAME MEANS: "Cetiosaurus-like"
CLASSIFICATION: Saurischia, Sauropoda, Primitive sauropods
LENGTH: 50 ft (15.2 m)
TIME: Late Jurassic, 154 million years ago
PLACE: England
DIET: plants
DETAILS: *Cetiosauriscus* browsed for plants on four sturdy legs and probably used its whiplike tail as a defense against predators. It was originally misidentified as *Cetiosaurus,* another, larger sauropod with a shorter tail.

Cetiosaurus

see-tee-oh-**sor**-uhss
NAME MEANS: "whale-like lizard"
CLASSIFICATION: Saurischia, Sauropoda, Primitive sauropods
LENGTH: 59 ft (18 m)
TIME: Middle Jurassic, 164 million years ago
PLACE: England

DIET: plants
DETAILS: One of the earliest and most primitive sauropods ever discovered, *Cetiosaurus* was a large, bulky plant-eater with unusually long forelimbs. Fossil evidence suggests that *Cetiosaurus* may have thundered across the prehistoric beaches and lagoons of the Middle Jurassic. Sir Richard Owen named this dinosaur early in the 19th century, more than 35 years before its true nature was recognized. Owen first speculated that the bones of *Cetiosaurus* belonged to an aquatic reptile, a huge crocodile "with carnivorous habits." Owen's identification was later corrected by scientists at the Oxford Museum in England, who recognized the animal as a plant-eating dinosaur.

Chaoyangsaurus

chow-yong-**sor**-uhss
NAMED AFTER: Chaoyang in Liaoning Province, China
CLASSIFICATION: Ceratopsia
LENGTH: 7 ft (2.1 m)
TIME: Late Jurassic, 150 million years ago
PLACE: China
DIET: plants
DETAILS: This little dinosaur was one of the earliest, most primitive members of the protoceratopsian dinosaur family ever discovered. Based on an incomplete skeleton, scientists think *Chaoyangsaurus* had only a hint of a frill and no horns, and that it ran on two legs, unlike later and larger North American horned dinosaurs.

Charonosaurus

care-**roh**-no-**sor**-uhss
NAMED AFTER: Charon, the mythical Greek ferryman for the dead

Let's Call It a Dinosaur

Dinosaurs wouldn't be dinosaurs if it were not for Sir Richard Owen (1804–1892). In 1841, Owen decided to name a group of mysterious fossils of giant creatures *dinosaurs,* Greek for "terrible lizards." Owen was a famed British naturalist who began his career as a physician. He was a personal friend of England's Queen Victoria. Owen identified several dinosaurs, including the large British plant-eater *Cetiosaurus.*

Abelisauridae Ankylosauria basal Coelurosauria basal Iguanodontia Camarasauridae Carnosauria Ceratopsia Ceratosauria Dromaeosauridae Diplodocoidea Hadrosauridae Herrerasauridae Heterodontosauridae

CLASSIFICATION: Ornithischia, Hadrosauridae
LENGTH: 43 ft (13.1 m)
TIME: Late Cretaceous, 65 million years ago
PLACE: China
DIET: plants
DETAILS: *Charonosaurus* was an unusually large four-legged, crested duck-billed plant-eater with a long, backward-pointing hollow crest. Like other duckbills, its jaws held large batteries of grinding teeth behind a short cropping beak. *Charonosaurus* was scientifically described in 2000. It indicates that in Asia, as in North America, the crested duckbills survived until the end of the dinosaur era. It was named for Charon, the mythical ferryman, because the dinosaur's fossils were found on the bank of the Amur River dividing Russia from China.

Chaoyangsaurus partial upper jaw

Chasmosaurus

kaz-moe-**sor**-uhss
NAME MEANS: "wide-opening lizard"
CLASSIFICATION: Ornithischia, Ceratopsia
LENGTH: 26 ft (7.9 m)
TIME: Late Cretaceous, 75 million years ago
PLACE: Texas, U.S.; Alberta, Canada
DIET: plants
DETAILS: One look at the skull of *Chasmosaurus*, a four-legged plant-eater, explains its "wide-opening" name. There are two large holes on either side of the bony mass of its frill. Like other horned dinosaurs, *Chasmosaurus* has two brow horns, one over each eye, and a shorter, stocky horn on the snout. Fossilized skin impressions show several small, closely set bumps that increased in size to larger, rounder knobs along the animal's body.

"Chassternbergia" (chass-stern-**berg**-ee-uh) Not a valid scientific name, though an interesting one. This dinosaur was

named for the great dinosaur-finder Charles Sternberg. It may be a nodosaur, a clubless armored dinosaur. See *Edmontonia*.

Chialingosaurus

jyah-ling-oh-**sor**-uhss
NAMED AFTER: Jialing River of China
CLASSIFICATION: Ornithischia, Stegosauria
LENGTH: 12 ft (3.7 m)
TIME: Middle Jurassic, 165 million years ago
PLACE: China
DIET: plants
DETAILS: This Chinese discovery was a medium-size, plate-back stegosaur. It had a very slender skull, narrower than those of most other stegosaurs. Both plates and spines were arranged in two rows along its back, from the neck to the tail.

"Chiayusaurus" (**chyah**-yoo-**sor**-uhss) Not a valid scientific name. Based on a single Chinese tooth, this dinosaur may be the same as the giant plant-eating *Mamenchisaurus*, the longest necked of all dinosaurs.

"Chihuahuasaurus" (chih-**hwah**-hwah-**sor**-uhss) Not a valid scientific name. See *Sonorasaurus*.

59

Chasmosaurus

Chilantaisaurus

jee-**lon**-tie-**sor**-uhss

NAMED AFTER: Jilantai region in Inner Mongolia

CLASSIFICATION: Saurischia, Theropoda, Carnosauria

LENGTH: 43 ft (13.1 m)

TIME: Early Cretaceous, 120 million years ago

PLACE: China

DIET: meat

Chilantaisaurus claw

DETAILS: *Chilantaisaurus* may be a late-surviving relative of *Allosaurus* or a cousin of the even larger and later meat-eater *Carcharodontosaurus*.

Chindesaurus

chin-**dee**-**sor**-uhss

NAMED AFTER: Chinde Point in Petrified Forest National Park, Arizona

CLASSIFICATION: Saurischia, Theropoda, Herrerasauridae

LENGTH: 6.5 ft (2 m)

TIME: Late Triassic, 225 million years ago

PLACE: Arizona, New Mexico, U.S.

DIET: meat

DETAILS: Scientists think that this small, little-known early predator was close to the size of the earliest dinosaurs.

"Chingkankousaurus" (jing-**kan**-koh-**sor**-uhss) Not a valid scientific name. This meat-eater was named for the Jingankou village in Shandong Province, China.

"Chinshakiangosaurus" (chin-sha-**kiang**-oh-**sor**-uhss) This may have been the largest prosauropod but is not well represented by fossils.

Chirostenotes

kie-ro-**sten**-o-teez

NAME MEANS: "narrow hand"

CLASSIFICATION: Saurischia, Theropoda, Oviraptorosauria

LENGTH: 6 ft (1.8 m)

TIME: Late Cretaceous, 75 million years ago

PLACE: Alberta, Canada

DIET: meat

DETAILS: For more than 75 years, this small dinosaur was thought to be one of many forms of dinosaur, including dromaeosaurids. Recently, scientists have reexamined its remains and decided that it was most closely related to the odd-looking, mostly toothless oviraptorid dinosaurs. *Chirostenotes* appears to have taken two distinct forms, one more heavily built than the other. The larger animal may have been the female. This fast-moving, small meat-eater had a slender grasping hand that may have helped it catch small mammals and lizards.

Chirostenotes

"Chondrosteosaurus" (kon-**dross**-tee-oh-**sor**-uhss) Not a valid scientific name. A camarasaurid relative, this plant-eater was named for the soft cartilage thought to have filled hollow spaces in its bones.

"Chuandongocoelurus" (chwahn-**doong**-oh-see-**lure**-uhss) Not a valid scientific name. Named for Chuandong in Sichuan Province, China, its fossils were too incomplete for a full scientific analysis. This dinosaur may belong to the small meat-eaters, the coelurosaurs.

Chuanjiesaurus

chwahn-jeh-**sor**-uhss

NAMED AFTER: Chuanjie, a village in southern China

CLASSIFICATION: Saurischia, Sauropoda, Primitive sauropods

LENGTH: 60 ft (18.3 m)

TIME: Middle Jurassic, 170 million years ago

PLACE: China

DIET: plants

DETAILS: A large, four-legged browser, *Chuanjiesaurus* is thought to have been a member of the primitive, long-forearmed cetiosaurids known from China to England. Like most sauropod fossils, it lacks the scientifically important skull, which was too small and light to be preserved with the heavier body bones. It was named in 2000.

Chubutisaurus

chew-**boot**-ih-**sor**-uhss

NAMED AFTER: Chubut Province, Argentina

CLASSIFICATION: Saurischia, Sauropoda, Macronaria
LENGTH: 75.5 ft (23 m)
TIME: Early Cretaceous, 112 million years ago
PLACE: Argentina
DIET: plants
DETAILS: Once considered a brachiosaurid, *Chubutisaurus* may actually be a very primitive titanosaur, a giant, four-legged plant-eater with all four legs equal in length.

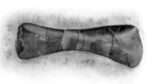

Chubutisaurus femur

Chungkingosaurus

choong-king-oh-**sor**-uhss
NAMED AFTER: Chongqing, China
CLASSIFICATION: Ornithischia, Stegosauria
LENGTH: 13 ft (4 m)
TIME: Late Jurassic, 145 million years ago
PLACE: China
DIET: plants
DETAILS: A spike-backed stegosaur, *Chungkingosaurus* lived at the same time as *Stegosaurus,* the North American plate-backed stegosaur that grew to twice its size.

Chungkingosaurus dermal spike

"Cionodon" (sigh-**oh**-no-don) Not a valid scientific name. Named for the columnlike shape and arrangement of its teeth, this duckbill is known only from fragments.

Citipati

chit-ee-**putt**-ee
NAME MEANS: "lord of the funeral pyre" in Buddhism
CLASSIFICATION: Saurischia, Theropoda, Oviraptorosauria
LENGTH: 7 ft (2.1 m)
TIME: Late Cretaceous, 80 million years ago
PLACE: Mongolia
DIET: meat
DETAILS: A very complete and newfound oviraptor, named in 2001. This large oviraptor is known not only from a complete skeleton, but from another

skeleton lying on a nest of eggs and from an embryo found in an egg. The skull of *Citipati* is unusually short and the neck bones are longer than those of other oviraptorids.

"Claorhynchus" (**clay**-oh-**rink**-uhss) Not a valid scientific name. This plant-eater, known only from a skull fragment, may have been either a duckbill or a horned dinosaur.

Claosaurus

clay-oh-**sor**-uhss
NAME MEANS: "broken lizard," after its crushed fossils
CLASSIFICATION: Ornithischia, basal Iguanodontia
LENGTH: 11.5 ft (3.5 m)
TIME: Late Cretaceous, 84 million years ago
PLACE: Kansas, U.S.
DIET: plants
DETAILS: *Claosaurus* is not a well-known animal, but appears to have been a small cousin of *Iguanodon* that lived later than other *Iguanodon* relatives.

"Clasmodosaurus" (**klaz**-moh-doh-**sor**-uhss) Not a valid scientific name. This sauropod is known only from its teeth.

"Clevelanotyrannus" (kleve-**lan**-oh-tir-**an**-uhss) Not a valid scientific name. An early, informal name for "Nanotyrannus."

Citipati

Hypsilophodontidae Lesothosauria Macronaria Ornithomimosauria Oviraptorosauria Pachycephalosauria Primitive sauropods Prosauropoda Spinosauria Stegosauria Therizinosauridae Troodontidae Tyrannosauridae

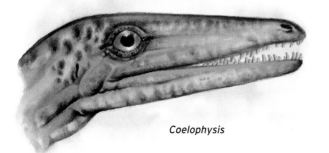

Coelophysis

Coelophysis

see-loh-**fie**-siss

NAME MEANS: "hollow form"
CLASSIFICATION: Saurischia, Theropoda, Ceratosauria
LENGTH: 10 ft (3 m)
TIME: Late Triassic, 220 million years ago
PLACE: Arizona, New Mexico, U.S.
DIET: meat
DETAILS: *Coelophysis* was a light, agile predator and perhaps a cannibal. This dinosaur is well-known, thanks to the many skeletons preserved in a large bone bed at Ghost Ranch, New Mexico. The rib cages of several skeletons were found to contain the bones of young *Coelophysis*. This was at first taken as evidence that *Coelophysis* gave birth to live young instead of laying eggs. Further study showed that the young were too well-developed to be embryos. They were probably eaten by the adult dinosaurs. This apparent cannibalism may not have been a regular practice. It may have been related to whatever natural catastrophe killed the *Coelophysis* group.

"Coelosaurus" (**see**-loh-**sor**-uhss) Not a valid scientific name. Now known as *Ornithomimus*.

Coelurus

see-**lure**-us

NAME MEANS: "hollow tail"
CLASSIFICATION: Saurischia, Theropoda, basal Coelurosauria
LENGTH: 6.5 ft (2 m)
TIME: Late Jurassic, 145 million years ago
PLACE: Wyoming, U.S.
DIET: meat
DETAILS: This small and little-known carnivore was named for the

Coelurus vertebra

thin-walled, hollow vertebrae in its back and tail.

"Coloradia" (col-oh-**rod**-ee-uh) Not a valid scientific name. This name had been already used for another animal when a dinosaur was given this name, so "Coloradia" was changed to *Coloradisaurus*.

Coloradisaurus

col-oh-**rod**-ih-**sor**-uhss

NAMED AFTER: Los Colorados Formation in Argentina
CLASSIFICATION: Saurischia, Prosauropoda
LENGTH: 13 ft (4 m)
TIME: Late Triassic, 210 million years ago
PLACE: Argentina
DIET: plants
DETAILS: *Coloradisaurus* may actually be the adult form of *Mussaurus,* for which no adult is positively known. *Coloradisaurus* was one of the smallest of the prosauropod plant-eaters that walked on four legs or just their hind legs.

Compsognathus

komp-**sog**-na-thus or **komp**-sog-**nay**-thus

NAME MEANS: "delicate jaw"
CLASSIFICATION: Saurischia, Theropoda, basal Coelurosauria
LENGTH: 3 ft (0.9 m)
TIME: Late Jurassic, 151 million years ago
PLACE: France, Germany
DIET: meat
DETAILS: One of the smallest known dinosaurs, the agile *Compsognathus* had large eyes, relatively powerful legs, and a lightweight build. This must have been a great advantage in hunting insects, small mammals, and lizards. For many years, *Compsognathus* was reconstructed with only two fingers on each hand. This suggested it may have been related to tyrannosaurs, much larger and later meat-eaters with two fingers on each hand. Recent fossil evidence, however, indicates that the tiny predator's hand had three clawed fingers, like those of most meat-eating dinosaurs. The best specimen is a juvenile, so this dinosaur may have grown considerably larger.

"Compsosuchus" (**comp**-so-**sook**-uhss) Not a valid scientific name. Remains are too fragmentary to fully identify this small meat-eater.

Compsognathus

Corythosaurus

Conchoraptor

conk-o-**rap**-tor

NAME MEANS: "shell plunderer"

CLASSIFICATION: Saurischia, Theropoda, Oviraptorosauria

LENGTH: 3 ft (1 m)

TIME: Late Cretaceous, 80 million years ago

PLACE: Mongolia

DIET: meat

DETAILS: *Conchoraptor* was named for its supposed diet of shellfish. The true function of its oddly shaped beak remains uncertain. It was one of the smallest members of the oviraptor family, which includes recently discovered giant oviraptors nearly 20 ft (6.1 m) long.

Conchoraptor

Corythosaurus

koh-**rith**-oh-**sor**-uhss

NAME MEANS: "Corinthian helmet lizard"

CLASSIFICATION: Ornithischia, Hadrosauridae

LENGTH: 33 ft (10.1 m)

TIME: Late Cretaceous, 80 million years ago

PLACE: Montana, U.S.; Alberta, Canada

DIET: plants

DETAILS: This duck-billed dinosaur, or hadrosaur, was a beaked plant-eater with hundreds of mashing teeth. It belonged to the crested, or lambeosaurine, hadrosaurs. It was named for the large, hollow crest atop its skull, which was shaped like the helmet of ancient soldiers from Corinth, Greece.

"Craspedodon" (crass-**ped**-oh-don) Not a valid scientific name. This dinosaur was identified as an iguanodontid from the shape of its teeth. Otherwise not enough is known to identify it as a separate kind of animal.

"Crataeomus" (krat-ee-**oh**-muss) Not a valid scientific name. See *Struthiosaurus*.

"Craterosaurus" (**cray**-terr-oh-**sor**-uhss) Not a valid scientific name. This may be a primitive stegosaur, but it is known only from part of a bone.

"Creosaurus" (**cree**-oh-**sor**-uhss) Not a valid scientific name. Now known as *Allosaurus*.

"Cristatusaurus" (kriss-**tay**-tuh-**sor**-uhss) Not a valid scientific name. It is named from fragmentary meat-eater fossils that may belong to either *Baryonyx* or *Suchomimus*.

Cryolophosaurus

kry-oh-loaf-oh-**sor**-uhss

NAME MEANS: "frozen crested lizard" because of its Antarctic location and shape of skull

CLASSIFICATION: Saurischia, Theropoda, Carnosauria

LENGTH: 20 ft (6.1 m)

TIME: Early Jurassic, 195 million years ago

PLACE: Antarctica

DIET: meat

DETAILS: One of the oldest known carnosaurs and the only theropod discovered so far in Antarctica, *Cryolophosaurus* was the first dinosaur from that continent to be scientifically named and described. Although it is frozen today, Antarctica was much warmer in the time of *Cryolophosaurus*. The dinosaur was found within 200 miles of the South Pole. An unusual curved, ridged bone projected upward from between its eyes. This dinosaur is nicknamed "Elvisaurus," after Elvis Presley, a rock-and-roll star whose hairstyle was similar to *Cryolophosaurus*'s crest.

Cryolophosaurus

"Cryptodraco" (**crip**-toe-**dray**-koh) Not a valid scientific name. The name originates from the same fragmentary fossils as "Cryptosaurus."

"Cryptosaurus" (**crip**-toh-**sor**-uhss) Not a valid scientific name. This may have been an armored Jurassic dinosaur.

"Cumnoria" (kum-**nohr**-ee-a) Not a valid scientific name. See *Camptosaurus*.

"Cylindricodon" (**sil**-in-**drik**-oh-don) Not a valid scientific name. See *Hylaeosaurus*.

Daspletosaurus (l.)
and juvenile Chasmosaurus (r.)

Abelisauridae   Ankylosauria   basal Coelurosauria   basal Iguanodontia   Camarasauridae   Carnosauria   Ceratopsia   Ceratosauria   Dromaeosauridae   Diplodocoidea   Hadrosauridae   Herrerasauridae   Heterodontosauridae

Dacentrurus

da-sen-**true**-russ

NAME MEANS: "very spiky tail"

CLASSIFICATION: Ornithischia, Stegosauria

LENGTH: 15 ft (4.6 m)

TIME: Late Jurassic, 150 million years ago

PLACE: England, Portugal, France

DIET: plants

Dacentrurus dermal spine

DETAILS: Though the plant-eating *Dacentrurus* had the same general proportions as the 25-foot-long (8 m) *Stegosaurus*, its plate and spike configuration was quite different. *Dacentrurus* carried two rows of small plates and two rows of long, paired spines along its back. Where the plates ended and the spikes began is uncertain, due to limited fossil evidence. A possible *Dacentrurus* egg was discovered in Portugal.

"**Dachongosaurus**" (dah-**choong**-oh-**sor**-uhss) Not a valid scientific name. Very little is known about this large plant-eater. It may have been a prosauropod or a sauropod.

"**Damalasaurus**" (**dam**-uh-luh-**sor**-uhss) Not a valid scientific name. Another large, plant-eating, four-legged sauropod, "Damalasaurus" was found in China.

"**Dandakosaurus**" (**dunn**-duh-koh-**sor**-uhss) Not a valid scientific name. "Dandakosaurus" is still little known. It reportedly is similar to *Sinosaurus*, a primitive 10-foot-long (3 m) meat-eater.

"**Danubiosaurus**" (day-**noo**-bee-oh-**sor**-uhss) Not a valid scientific name. Now called *Struthiosaurus*.

"**Daptosaurus**" (**dap**-toe-**sor**-uhss) Not a valid scientific name. See *Deinonychus*.

Daspletosaurus

dass-**plee**-toe-**sor**-uhss

NAME MEANS: "frightful lizard"

CLASSIFICATION: Saurischia, Theropoda, Tyrannosauridae

LENGTH: 30 ft (9.1 m)

TIME: Late Cretaceous, 72 million years ago

PLACE: Montana, U.S.; Alberta, Canada

DIET: meat

DETAILS: This big meat-eater may have been the direct ancestor of *Tyrannosaurus rex*. With its large head and low horns above its eyes, it had an especially ferocious appearance. *Daspletosaurus* had a heavier neck and trunk than *Albertosaurus*, another large tyrannosaur that lived in the same time and place. Perhaps they preyed upon two different kinds of dinosaurs. The daspletosaurs might have hunted slow and bulky-horned dinosaurs, while the quicker albertosaurs hunted the faster duck-billed dinosaurs. *Daspletosaurus* had the largest arms of any tyrannosaur, though they were still small by comparison with the arms of earlier giant meat-eaters such as *Allosaurus*.

Datousaurus

dah-toe-**sor**-uhss

NAME MEANS: "chieftain lizard" or "big head lizard"

CLASSIFICATION: Saurischia, Sauropoda, Primitive sauropods

LENGTH: 50 ft (15.2 m)

TIME: Middle Jurassic, 170 million years ago

PLACE: China

DIET: plants

DETAILS: *Datousaurus* was unusually heavy for a primitive sauropod. Its skull was large and heavy in comparison to other sauropod heads, with nostril openings in the front rather than on top. Its teeth were large and spoon-shaped. *Datousaurus* limbs were also heavy. Some researchers question if the head and body, which were found separately, actually belong to the same kind of dinosaur.

Datousaurus

Hypsilophodontidae   Lesothosauria   Macronaria   Ornithomimosauria   Oviraptorosauria   Pachycephalosauria   Primitive sauropods   Prosauropoda   Spinosauria   Stegosauria   Therizinosauridae   Troodontidae   Tyrannosauridae

Deinocheirus

die-no-**kie**-russ

NAME MEANS: "terrible hand"

CLASSIFICATION: Saurischia, Theropoda, Therizinosauridae?

LENGTH: 40 ft (12.2 m)

TIME: Late Cretaceous, 75 million years ago

PLACE: Mongolia

DIET: meat

DETAILS: The only parts of this animal that have been found so far are its record-size forelimb and sharp, strong claws on an arm eight feet (2.4 m) long. Based on the three long, slender fingers, *Deinocheirus* was probably a theropod of considerable size and power. But whether its giant arms were matched by a huge skull, body, or legs is unknown. The structure of the arms suggests to some paleontologists that this dinosaur was a gigantic relative of the ornithomimids, or ostrich-mimic dinosaurs. If so, it would have towered over all other known members of that group. Because the claws have some similarities to those of modern sloths, other scientists think *Deinocheirus* may have used its huge claws to pull down tree branches.

Deinocheirus forelimb

"Deinodon" (**dye**-nuh-don) Not a valid scientific name. This dinosaur may actually be made up of two or more kinds of dinosaurs. It was named in 1856 by famed paleontologist Joseph Leidy of Philadelphia, based on a scattering of carnivorous teeth.

Deinonychus

die-**non**-ih-cuss or dye-no-**nye**-cuss

NAME MEANS: "terrible claw"

CLASSIFICATION: Saurischia, Theropoda, Deinonychosauria, Dromaeosauridae

LENGTH: 10 ft (3 m)

TIME: Early Cretaceous, 119 million years ago

PLACE: Montana, Oklahoma, Wyoming, Utah, U.S.

DIET: meat

DETAILS: The discovery of *Deinonychus* in 1964 changed the direction of dinosaur science. It helped scientists understand the relationship between meat-eating dinosaurs and birds. It also changed the idea that dinosaurs were great, stupid, sluggish lizards. The deadly, razor-sharp claw on the second toe of *Deinonychus*'s hind foot showed that some

68

The Mystery of the Long-Armed Dinosaur

Dr. Halska Osmolska, born in the early 1930s, is a ruggedly independent Polish paleontologist. She was one of the three female leaders of an ambitious expedition through Mongolia in the 1960s. The team traveled the harsh desert terrain in huge trucks. They uncovered many new dinosaur fossils from the Late Cretaceous Period, including dome-headed dinosaurs and the mysterious giant-armed *Deinocheirus*. No one since has found more evidence of this strange giant.

dinosaurs must have been quick, agile hunters, maybe even warm-blooded and smart.

Deinonychus was a powerful 10-foot-long (3 m) predator. Long, muscular forelimbs and three-fingered hands gave it the ability to grip its prey. A long, stiff tail helped it to balance while running, kicking, or leaping. The ripping claw on the second toe of its back foot made *Deinonychus* a vicious killer. This five-inch-long (13 cm) talon was held off the ground while walking and could be deployed in a powerful slashing kick.

Deinonychus's strong, lean back legs were relatively short for a small theropod, and suggest that the dinosaur was not as fast as its smaller "raptor" relatives. *Deinonychus*'s hollow bones and the shape of its front limbs show the close relationship between dinosaurs and birds. Recent discoveries in related species suggest that *Deinonychus* may have had featherlike coverings or decoration. It possessed a light skeleton, large eyes, and a relatively big brain for a dinosaur.

Deinonychus left foot

Deinonychus might have hunted and fed in packs. In size and skull shape, it comes closest of all known "raptor" dinosaurs to the killer dinosaurs in *Jurassic Park,* which were called *Velociraptors.*

Deltadromeus

dell-ta-**droh**-mee-uhss

NAME MEANS: "delta runner"

CLASSIFICATION: Saurischia, Theropoda, basal Coelurosauria

LENGTH: 26 ft (7.9 m)

Deltadromeus (t.) chases a hypsilophodont family

TIME: Late Cretaceous, 90 million years ago
PLACE: Morocco
DIET: meat
DETAILS: This fearsome African meat-eater had powerful, yet unusually slim, hind limbs, suggesting that it was a swift and deadly killer. Named in 1996, *Deltadromeus* at first was estimated to be the size of an *Allosaurus*, roughly 30 feet (9 m) long. But the measurement has been revised downward. *Deltadromeus* was only half as heavily built in the legs as *Allosaurus*. It apparently lived in the same river delta environment and during the same time as *Carcharodontosaurus*, a huge meat-eater nearly twice its size.

"Denversaurus" (**den**-ver-**sor**-uhss) Not a valid scientific name. See *Edmontonia*.

Dianchungosaurus

dyen-joong-o-**sor**-uhss
NAMED AFTER: Central Yunnan, China
CLASSIFICATION: Ornithischia, Hypsilophodontidae
LENGTH: 5 ft (1.5 m)
TIME: Early Jurassic, 195 million years ago
PLACE: China

Dianchungosaurus fragmentary jaw

DIET: plants
DETAILS: Only fossil fragments have been found to help identify this early ornithischian, or bird-hipped, dinosaur. It appears to have been a small plant-eating dinosaur with a thin jaw. Its jaw was toothless in the front, but lined with small rounded teeth in the back.

Diceratops

die-**sayr**-a-tops
NAME MEANS: "two horned face" because of the pair of large horns over its eyes
CLASSIFICATION: Ornithischia, Ceratopsia
LENGTH: 30 ft (9.1 m)
TIME: Late Cretaceous, 65 million years ago
PLACE: Wyoming, U.S.
DIET: plants
DETAILS: An almost complete skull of *Diceratops* was found a century ago. It shows this plant-eater had a skull frill longer than that of *Triceratops*, but had no nose horn. Its frill also had many holes, which may have been the result of disease or injury. For a long time, scientists thought this dinosaur might have been a *Triceratops* without a nose horn. But *Diceratops* recently has been identified as a distinct kind of dinosaur.

Diceratops skull

"Diclonius" (die-**kloh**-nee-uhss) Not a valid scientific name. Edward Drinker Cope, the great 19th-century American paleontologist, named this plant-eating hadrosaur in 1876, based on a few teeth he found in Montana. He later incorrectly used the name "Diclonius" for the duck-billed dinosaur now called *Anatotitan*.

Dicraeosaurus

die-**kree**-oh-**sor**-uhss
NAME MEANS: "forked lizard"
CLASSIFICATION: Saurischia, Sauropoda, Diplodocoidea
LENGTH: 45 ft (13.7 m)
TIME: Late Jurassic, 156 million years ago
PLACE: Tanzania

Hypsilophodontidae Lesothosauria Macronaria Ornithomimosauria Oviraptorosauria Pachycephalosauria Primitive sauropods Prosauropoda Spinosauria Stegosauria Therizinosauridae Troodontidae Tyrannosauridae

Dicraeosaurus

DIET: plants

DETAILS: This medium-size sauropod had a short neck and slightly humped back. It fed on plants, like all sauropods, and had relatively short front legs, slightly more than half the length of its back legs. It had a long, tapering tail that it may have cracked like a bullwhip. The booming sound would have scared off predators.

"**Didanodon**" (die-**dan**-oh-don) Not a valid scientific name. This animal is known only from teeth that probably belong to *Lambeosaurus*.

Dilophosaurus
die-**loaf**-o-**sor**-uhss
NAME MEANS: "double-crested lizard"
CLASSIFICATION: Saurischia, Theropoda, Ceratosauria
LENGTH: 23 ft (7 m)
TIME: Early Jurassic, 195 million years ago
PLACE: Arizona, Connecticut, U.S.; China
DIET: meat
DETAILS: Made famous by Steven Spielberg's film *Jurassic Park,* this crested theropod was actually 20 ft (6.1 m) long. It did not have an umbrellalike neck frill, nor did it spit poison. It did have longer forelimbs than other meat-eaters of its time. Slender teeth and a relatively weak jaw suggest that *Dilophosaurus* did not go after very large prey. Trackways in Arizona and Connecticut suggest that *Dilophosaurus* may have traveled in packs.

"**Dimodosaurus**" (die-**moh**-doh-**sor**-uhss) Not a valid scientific name. Now called *Plateosaurus.*

Dinheirosaurus
deen-**yay**-roh-**sor**-uhss
NAMED AFTER: Porto Dinheiro, Portugal
CLASSIFICATION: Saurischia, Sauropoda, Diplodocoidea
LENGTH: 50 ft (15.2 m)
TIME: Late Jurassic, 150 million years ago
PLACE: Portugal
DIET: plants
DETAILS: In some ways, including the shape of its neck and back vertebrae, this sauropod resembled *Diplodocus.* Some experts say they are simply two different dinosaurs with similar traits.

Dinheirosaurus vertebra

"**Dinodocus**" (die-**nod**-oh-cuss) Not a valid scientific name. See *Pelorosaurus.*

"**Dinosaurus**" (die-no-**sor**-uhss) Not a valid scientific name. These bones were renamed "Gressylosaurus" for a meat-eater, many specimens of which were later discovered to be *Plateosaurus,* a prosauropod plant-eater.

"**Dinotyrannus**" (die-no-teer-**ran**-uhss) Not a valid scientific name. The skeleton of this meat-eater is probably a young *Tyrannosaurus* and not a separate genus.

Diplodocus
dip-**lod**-oh-cuss
NAME MEANS: "double beam"
CLASSIFICATION: Saurischia, Sauropoda, Diplodocoidea
LENGTH: 88 ft (26.8 m)
TIME: Late Jurassic, 145 million years ago
PLACE: Colorado, Utah, Wyoming, Montana, U.S.
DIET: plants
DETAILS: *Diplodocus* is one of the longest dinosaurs ever unearthed. A long neck helped it to feed widely on conifers, cycads, ginkgoes, and ferns. It had an elongated snout and nostrils on the top of its head. The peglike teeth at the front of its mouth were probably used like a comb to rake leaves from branches. *Diplodocus* had no grinding teeth in the back of its mouth. Instead, it

70

Abelisauridae   Ankylosauria   basal Coelurosauria   basal Iguanodontia   Camarasauridae   Carnosauria   Ceratopsia   Ceratosauria   Dromaeosauridae   Diplodocoidea   Hadrosauridae   Herrerasauridae   Heterodontosauridae

Dilophosaurus chasing pterosaur

Hypsilophodontidae Lesothosauria Macronaria Ornithomimosauria Oviraptorosauria Pachycephalosauria Primitive sauropods Prosauropoda Spinosauria Stegosauria Therizinosauroidae Troodontidae Tyrannosauridae

Diplodocus and young

Abelisauridae   Ankylosauria   basal Coelurosauria   basal Iguanodontia   Camarasauridae   Carnosauria   Ceratopsia   Ceratosauria   Dromaeosauridae   Diplodocoidea   Hadrosauridae   Herrerasauridae   Heterodontosauridae

swallowed rounded stones, which helped mash plant material inside its belly into easily digested pulp. *Diplodocus*'s neck and tail made up more than half its length. Muscles in its long, barrel-like midsection may have helped the mighty sauropod to lash its incredibly long, thin tail like a bullwhip at attacking predators. *Diplodocus* was named by Othniel C. Marsh, the famed 19th-century Yale University paleontologist.

"Diplotomodon" (dip-loh-**tom**-oh-don) Not a valid scientific name. This species was named by 19th-century paleontologist Joseph Leidy and replaced the prior genus "Tomodon." "Diplotomodon" was a large, meat-eating dinosaur with a strange, bladelike tooth. It was originally identified as the tooth of a marine reptile or plesiosaur, and later as that of a fish. Upon closer study, it became clear that the tooth most resembled those of tyrannosaurids, meat-eating dinosaurs.

"Diracodon" (die-**rack**-oh-don) Not a valid scientific name. Now called *Stegosaurus*.

"Dolichosuchus" (**dol**-ih-kuh-**sook**-uhss) Not a valid scientific name. Very little is known about this early meat-eater. Based on the only fossil find, a partial and imperfectly preserved hind leg almost a foot long, "Dolichosuchus" was probably a medium-size theropod.

"Doryphorosaurus" (doh-**riff**-oh-roh-**sor**-uhss) Not a valid scientific name. See *Kentrosaurus*.

Draconyx
drack-**on**-iks
NAME MEANS: "dragon claw"
CLASSIFICATION: Ornithischia, Ornithopoda, basal Iguanodontia
LENGTH: 16 ft (4.9 m)
TIME: Late Jurassic, 155 million years ago
PLACE: Portugal
DIET: plants
DETAILS: *Draconyx* was recently named but is known from only a few bones. It was probably most like *Camptosaurus*, a relatively small iguanodon relative from North America.

Dracopelta
drack-oh-**pelt**-uh
NAME MEANS: "dragon shield"
CLASSIFICATION: Ornithischia, Ankylosauria
LENGTH: 6.5 ft (2 m)
TIME: Late Jurassic, 150 million years ago
PLACE: Portugal
DIET: plants
DETAILS: Little, four-legged *Dracopelta* was the first Late Jurassic ankylosaur, or armored dinosaur, to be discovered. It was wide, stocky, and had at least five distinct kinds of armor on its body, ranging from very small bony bumps to longer plates, which ranged from 1 inch by 1 inch (2.5 cm by 2.5 cm) to 8 inches by 4 inches (20 cm by 10 cm).

Dracopelta dermal plates, ribs

Drinker
drink-er
NAMED AFTER: 19th-century paleontologist Edward Drinker Cope
CLASSIFICATION: Ornithischia, Heterodontosauridae
LENGTH: 6.5 ft (2 m)
TIME: Late Jurassic, 156 million years ago
PLACE: Wyoming
DIET: plants
DETAILS: *Drinker* was an ornithischian dinosaur with leaf-shape teeth. It may have been related to *Othnielia*, named for paleontologist Othniel C. Marsh. A team of four paleontologists named this small, little-known, and only recently discovered plant-eater. Its name honors one of two men (Marsh was the other) largely responsible for the onset of the dinosaur "bone wars" of the turn of the late 19th century. This was a time of fierce competition to collect and name dinosaur species.

Drinker

Dromaeosaurus
droh-mee-oh-**sor**-uhss
NAME MEANS: "running lizard" or "swift-foot lizard"
CLASSIFICATION: Saurischia, Theropoda, Deinonychosauria, Dromaeosauridae
LENGTH: 12 ft (3.7 m)

Edmontonia (f.)
and *Dromaeosaurus* (b.)

Abelisauridae   Ankylosauria   basal Coelurosauria   basal Iguanodontia   Camarasauridae   Carnosauria   Ceratopsia   Ceratosauria   Dromaeosauridae   Diplodocoidea   Hadrosauridae   Herrerasauridae   Heterodontosauridae

Echinodon

eh-**kie**-no-don

NAME MEANS: "prickly tooth"

CLASSIFICATION: Ornithischia, Ankylosauria

LENGTH: 2 ft (0.6 m)

TIME: Late Jurassic, 145 million years ago

PLACE: England

DIET: plants

DETAILS: A small plant-eater described in 1861, *Echinodon* may be related to the primitive armored dinosaur *Scutellosaurus*.

"**Echizensaurus**" (**etch**-ee-zen-**sor**-uhss) Not a valid scientific name. This is a yet-unpublished new ornithischian, a small plant-eater from the Late Cretaceous Period in Japan.

Edmarka

ed-**mark**-uh

NAMED AFTER: Dr. Bill Edmark, who helped discover these fossils

CLASSIFICATION: Saurischia, Theropoda, Carnosauria

LENGTH: 40 ft (12.2 m)

TIME: Late Jurassic, 145 million years ago

PLACE: Wyoming

DIET: meat

DETAILS: This huge meat-eater may have been as big as *Tyrannosaurus* but is incompletely known. It may be closely related to, if not the same as, *Torvosaurus*, which lived at around the same time in the same region.

Edmontonia

ed-mon-**toe**-nee-uh

NAMED AFTER: Edmonton Formation, Canada

CLASSIFICATION: Ornithischia, Ankylosauria

LENGTH: 23 ft (7 m)

TIME: Late Cretaceous, 68 million years ago

PLACE: Montana, South Dakota, Texas, U.S.; Alberta, Canada

DIET: plants

DETAILS: Like other nodosaurids, *Edmontonia* had hard, bony plates and nodules embedded in its skin as protection against the teeth and claws of predators. *Edmontonia* is the last, or youngest, clubless armored dinosaur yet known.

Edmontosaurus

ed-**mon**-toe-**sor**-uhss

NAMED AFTER: Edmonton Formation, Canada

CLASSIFICATION: Ornithischia, Hadrosauridae

LENGTH: 40 ft (12.2 m)

TIME: Late Cretaceous, 65 million years ago

PLACE: Colorado, North Dakota, South Dakota, Wyoming, Montana, Alaska, U.S.; Alberta, Saskatchewan, Canada

DIET: plants

DETAILS: This noncrested duck-billed hadrosaur was first described in 1917. *Edmontosaurus* was once known by the now invalid names "Trachodon" and "Anatosaurus." A remarkably well-preserved pair of fossils discovered in Wyoming show the skin had many bumps, or tubercles. Its feet were protected by fleshy pads, similar to those on the bottom of cat or dog paws. *Edmontosaurus* had a wide tail, first thought to be an aid in swimming, but now considered a feature useful for balance while running. *Edmontosaurus*'s skin impressions also show that these dinosaurs had frill-like ridges that formed a midline down their tails.

"**Efraasia**" (ef-**frah**-zee-uh) Not a valid scientific name. A small plant-eater, now known as *Sellosaurus*.

Edmontosaurus

Einiosaurus

Einiosaurus

eye-nee-oh-**sor**-uhss

NAME MEANS: "bison lizard" in the language of the Blackfeet, on whose reservation the fossils were found

CLASSIFICATION: Ornithschia, Centrosauria

LENGTH: 20 ft (6.1 m)

TIME: Late Cretaceous, 80 million years ago

PLACE: Montana, U.S.

DIET: plants

DETAILS: This frilled and horn-faced dinosaur featured an unusual nose horn that bent sharply forward. *Einiosaurus* was as large as a laundry truck. Some of the young featured curving horns. Others had small, straight horns. This may represent a difference between males and females.

Elaphrosaurus

el-a-froh-**sor**-uhss or el-**af**-roh-**sor**-uhss

NAME MEANS: "lightweight lizard"

CLASSIFICATION: Saurischia, Theropoda, Ceratosauria

LENGTH: 17 ft (5.2 m)

TIME: Late Jurassic, 155 million years ago

PLACE: North America; Tanzania

DIET: meat

DETAILS: This lightly built carnivore was scientifically described in 1920 based on incomplete remains. It was mistaken at one time for an ostrichlike dinosaur. Footprints found in Niger and in Jerusalem, Israel, may have been created by an *Elaphrosaurus*.

Elmisaurus

el-mee-**sor**-uhss

NAME MEANS: "hindfoot lizard"

CLASSIFICATION: Saurischia, Theropoda, Oviraptorosauria

LENGTH: 6.5 ft (2 m)

TIME: Late Cretaceous, 70 million years ago

PLACE: Mongolia; Alberta, Canada

DIET: meat

DETAILS: *Elmisaurus* was named in 1981 for the distinctive fusing of several bones in its long and narrow foot. Some scientists think that it is closely to *Chirostenotes*.

"Elopteryx" (el-**op**-tayr-iks) Not a valid scientific name. This fragmentary Transylvanian meat-eater, originally identified as a bird, may be a troodontid.

"Elosaurus" (el-oh-**sor**-uhss) Not a valid scientific name. Fossil material once assigned to this genus is now believed to belong to a juvenile *Apatosaurus*.

"Elvisaurus" (el-vis-**sor**-uhss) Not a valid scientific name. This was the informal pre-publication nickname for *Cryolophosaurus*.

Emausaurus

em-ow-**sor**-uhss

NAME MEANS: "E.M.A.U. lizard" after a German university site

CLASSIFICATION: Ornithischia, Ankylosauria

LENGTH: 6.5 ft (2 m)

TIME: Early Jurassic, 188 million years ago

PLACE: Germany

DIET: plants

DETAILS: This small dinosaur was a primitive armored dinosaur.

"Embasaurus" (em-bah-**sor**-uhss) Not a valid scientific name. Named for the Emba River in Kazakhstan. Only two broken vertebrae have been uncovered, so this animal cannot be identified scientifically.

Enigmosaurus

ee-**nig**-moh-**sor**-uhss

NAME MEANS: "enigma lizard"

CLASSIFICATION: Saurischia, Theropoda, Therizinosauroidea

LENGTH: 24.5 ft (7.5 m)

TIME: Late Cretaceous, 88 million years ago

PLACE: Mongolia

DIET: unknown

DETAILS: *Enigmosaurus* was named in 1983 for the puzzling and unusual shape of its pelvis. It is a considerably larger dinosaur than the related *Erlikosaurus*.

 ## Eobrontosaurus

ee-oh-bron-toe-**sor**-uhss

NAME MEANS: "dawn thunder lizard"
CLASSIFICATION: Saurischia, Sauropoda, Diplodocoidea
LENGTH: 80 ft (24.4 m)
TIME: Late Jurassic, 145 million years ago
PLACE: Wyoming, U.S.
DIET: plants
DETAILS: A recently discovered member of the giant sauropod dinosaur group, *Eobrontosaurus* was a primitive relative of *Apatosaurus*. Its forearms and front feet were more massive than any of the other large, western North American plant-eaters of its time.

"Eoceratops" (ee-oh-**sayr**-a-tops) Not a valid scientific name. This short-frilled horned dinosaur is now considered to be *Chasmosaurus*.

"Eohadrosaurus" (ee-oh-**had**-roh-**sor**-uhss) Not a valid scientific name. See *Eolambia*.

 ## Eolambia

ee-oh-**lam**-bee-uh

NAME MEANS: "dawn lambeosaurine" because it pre-dates other duckbills

Eolambia

CLASSIFICATION: Ornithischia, basal Iguanodontia
LENGTH: 30 ft (9.1 m)
TIME: Early Cretaceous, 100 million years ago
PLACE: Utah, U.S.
DIET: plants
DETAILS: Perhaps the earliest known hadrosaur, this plant-eater was going to be called "Eohadrosaurus" until it was discovered to have primitive features resembling those of the crested duckbills. *Eolambia* was named in 1998.

? Eoraptor

ee-oh-**rap**-tor

NAME MEANS: "dawn plunderer"
CLASSIFICATION: Saurischia, Theropoda, Herrerasauridae?
LENGTH: 3 ft (1 m)
TIME: Late Triassic, 228 million years ago
PLACE: Argentina

DIET: meat
DETAILS: This small early meat-eater may be the most primitive dinosaur yet known. *Eoraptor* may belong to primitive, very early dinosaurs that preceded a division into the two famous dinosaur groups, ornithischians and saurischians. Described in 1993, *Eoraptor* lacks several of the characteristics of

Eoraptor

other meat-eating dinosaurs, such as a joint in the middle of its jawbone. Its hand had a fifth digit. Most other meat-eating dinosaurs had only four or fewer fingers. Its front teeth were curved like meat-eaters' teeth.

Eotyrannus

ee-oh-tih-**ran**-uhss

NAME MEANS: "dawn tyrant"
CLASSIFICATION: Saurischia, Theropoda, Tyrannosauridae
SIZE: 16 ft (4.9 m) or more
TIME: Early Cretaceous, 130 million years ago
PLACE: Isle of Wight, Great Britain
DIET: meat
DETAILS: *Eotyrannus* may have been an early ancestor of *Tyrannosaurus rex*. Although its teeth and portions of its skull resemble the later tyrannosaurids, its long neck and long front limbs are unlike those of tyrannosaurs. This fast and light hunter could grab prey in its long hands. The only skeleton found, and recently named, belonged to a juvenile, so an adult animal would have grown much larger as an adult.

Epachthosaurus

eh-**pack**-thoh-**sor**-uhss

NAME MEANS: "heavy lizard"
CLASSIFICATION: Saurischia, Sauropoda, Macronaria
LENGTH: 65.5 ft (20 m)

Hypsilophodontidae Lesothosauria Macronaria Ornithomimosauria Oviraptorosauria Pachycephalosauria Primitive sauropods Prosauropoda Spinosauria Stegosauria Therizinosauroidea Troodontidae Tyrannosauridae

Erectopus
leg bones

TIME: Late Cretaceous, 92 million years ago
PLACE: Argentina
DIET: plants
DETAILS: This little-known, long-necked plant-eater may have belonged to the titanosaur group of huge sauropods. Although some of these giant plant-eaters had armor, *Epachthosaurus* probably did not.

"Epanterias" (ep-an-**teer**-ee-uhss) Not a valid scientific name. Originally classified as a sauropod, "Epanterias" appears to have been a meat-eater, almost certainly a giant specimen of *Allosaurus*.

Erectopus

ee-**reck**-toe-puss
NAME MEANS: "upright foot"
CLASSIFICATION: Saurischia, Theropoda, Carnosauria
LENGTH: 20 ft (6.1 m)
TIME: Early Cretaceous, 113 million years ago
PLACE: France, Egypt, Portugal
DIET: meat
DETAILS: *Erectopus* was a moderate-size meat-eating dinosaur. Its fossilized bones were first discovered in a well in northern France, and the animal was formally described in 1922.

Erlikosaurus

air-lick-oh-**sor**-uhss
NAMED AFTER: Erlik, the Buddhist King of the Dead
CLASSIFICATION: Saurischia, Theropoda, Therizinosauroidea
LENGTH: 20 ft (6.1 m)
TIME: Late Cretaceous, 88.5 million years ago
PLACE: Mongolia
DIET: plants?
DETAILS: This member of the strange, huge-clawed therizinosaur group is much like the larger and also poorly understood Mongolian meat-eater, *Segnosaurus*. *Erlikosaurus* has the best-preserved and most complete skull of any member of the therizinosaur group. Its skull has some of the features of birds and of a few advanced meat-eaters such as tyrannosaurs.

Erlikosaurus

Eshanosaurus

uh-**shah**-no-**sor**-uhss
NAMED AFTER: Eshan County, Yunnan Province, southern China
CLASSIFICATION: Saurischia, Theropoda, Therizinosauridae
LENGTH: 7 ft (2.1 m)
TIME: Early Jurrasic, 198 million years ago
PLACE: Yunnan Province, China
DIET: plants
DETAILS: *Eshanosaurus* is the earliest known therizinosaur. Unlike other theropods, therizinosaurs may have evolved as plant-eaters. They may have used their leaf-shaped teeth to snip plants or eat fish.

"Euacanthus" (**you**-uh-**can**-thuss) Not a valid scientific name. See *Polacanthus*.

"Eucamerotus" (**you**-cam-uh-**roh**-tuss) Not a valid scientific name. See *Pelorosaurus*.

"Eucentrosaurus" (you-**sen**-troh-**sor**-uhss) Not a valid scientific name. See *Centrosaurus*.

"Eucercosaurus" (you-**sayr**-ko-**sor**-uhss) Not a valid scientific name. Its fossil fragments were first thought to belong to an armored dinosaur, then to an ornithopod.

"Eucnemesaurus" (yook-**nee**-mee-**sore**-uhss) Not a valid scientific name. Known only from one leg bone; probably the same animal as *Euskelosaurus*.

Eucoelophysis

you-**see**-loh-**fie**-siss
NAME MEANS: "true hollow form"
CLASSIFICATION: Saurischia, Theropoda, Ceratosauria
LENGTH: 8 ft (2.4 m)
TIME: Late Triassic, 210 million years ago
PLACE: New Mexico, U.S.
DIET: meat
DETAILS: This small, agile theropod may have actually been the same animal as *Coelophysis*. If not, it was certainly a very close relative. It was identified from bones collected in 1881 and described by famed paleontologist Edward Drinker Cope and from fossils found in the 1990s.

Euhelopus

you-**hell**-oh-puss

NAME MEANS: "true marsh foot"

CLASSIFICATION: Saurischia, Sauropoda, Camarasauridae

LENGTH: 34 ft (10 m)

TIME: Late Jurassic, 150 million years ago

PLACE: Shandong, China

DIET: plants

DETAILS: This long-necked dinosaur was named and described in 1956. At the time, sauropods were generally considered to have been lizardlike marsh-dwellers, and *Euhelopus* received its name from that inaccurate perception of the group.

Euhelopus

Euoplocephalus

you-oh-ploh-**seff**-a-luss

NAME MEANS: "well-armored head"

CLASSIFICATION: Ornithischia, Ankylosauria

LENGTH: 17 ft (5.2 m)

TIME: Late Cretaceous, 76 million years ago

PLACE: Montana, U.S.; Alberta, Canada

DIET: plants

DETAILS: The best known of the armored dinosaurs, this ankylosaur's back and sides were covered in a dense protective layer of bony plates. Fossils of *Euoplocephalus*, described in 1910, provided the first evidence for the clublike

Euoplocephalus (b.), *Albertosaurus* (t.)

lump of bone found at the end of the stiff tails of ankylosaurs. This solid, heavily reinforced club might have been wielded like a knight's mace. It could have been a powerful weapon. Some researchers think, however, that these animals did not have the muscles to swing the end club. They think the club was more of a threat feature, or a weapon only if the dinosaur turned its body, or even, as one scientist has suggested, a radiator for cooling the dinosaur.

"Eureodon" (**yoo**-ree-a-**don**) Not a valid scientific name. Now considered to be *Tenontosaurus*.

"Euronychodon" (your-oh-**nick**-oh-don) Not a valid scientific name. This small, Late Cretaceous predator from Portugal is known only from teeth similar to those of the North American *Paronychodon*.

Euskelosaurus

you-skell-oh-**sor**-uhss

NAME MEANS: "good-legged lizard"

CLASSIFICATION: Saurischia, Prosauropoda

LENGTH: 30 ft (9.1 m)

TIME: Late Triassic, 215 million years ago

PLACE: Lesotho; South Africa; Zimbabwe

DIET: plants

DETAILS: *Euskelosaurus* was one of the earliest plant-eating dinosaurs. Described in 1866, this dinosaur was a prosauropod, the primitive relatives of the long-necked sauropod giants. Like other prosauropods, *Euskelosaurus* probably walked on all four legs, but could rear up on two legs to feed or to defend itself with its sharp foreclaws.

Euskelosaurus thigh bone

Eustreptospondylus

you-**strep**-toe-**spon**-dill-uhss

NAME MEANS: "well-curved vertebra"

CLASSIFICATION: Saurischia, Theropoda, Carnosauria

LENGTH: 23 ft (7 m)

TIME: Middle Jurassic, 165 million years ago

PLACE: England

DIET: meat

DETAILS: Named in 1964, this meat-eating dinosaur was identified from fossils that appear to be from a juvenile, under 20 feet (6 m) long. This animal had many features similar to *Allosaurus*. Its skull was more primitive, however, and when fully grown, may have been longer than that of *Allosaurus*.

Eustreptospondylus (b.), *Cetiosaurus* (t.)

Fabrosaurus (f.)
and a giant crocodilian (b.)

Abelisauridae   Ankylosauria   basal Coelurosauria   basal Iguanodontia   Camarasauridae   Carnosauria   Ceratopsia   Ceratosauria   Dromaeosauridae   Diplodocoidea   Hadrosauridae   Herrerasauridae   Heterodontosauridae

Fabrosaurus

fab-ruh-**sor**-uhss

NAMED AFTER: French geologist, Jean Fabre

CLASSIFICATION: Ornithischia, Lesothosauria

LENGTH: 3 ft (0.9 m)

TIME: Early Jurassic, 195 million years ago

PLACE: Africa

DIET: plants

DETAILS: Identified from a segment of the lower right jaw and three teeth, this small plant-eater was an early and primitive ornithischian dinosaur. Its teeth were tiny, less than one-tenth of an inch (25 mm) long, with narrow crowns and long, vertical roots. *Fabrosaurus* appears to have been closely related to *Lesothosaurus*. Some researchers suggest that the two may be members of the same genus.

"Frenguellisaurus" (fren-**gwell**-ee-**sor**-uhss) Not a valid scientific name. See *Herrerasaurus*.

Fukuiraptor

foo-**koo**-ee-**rap**-tor

NAME MEANS: "Fukui plunderer" after Fukui Prefecture, Japan

CLASSIFICATION: Saurischia, Theropoda, Carnosauria

LENGTH: 14 ft (4.3 m)

TIME: Early Cretaceous, 120 million years ago

PLACE: Japan

DIET: meat

DETAILS: This is the most complete dinosaur ever found in Japan, with parts of all major bones represented. It was dug from one of the world's largest dinosaur quarries. The excavation ran nearly 100 ft (30.5 m) down a cliff face. Named in 2000, this meat-eater was related to *Allosaurus*, but it was more like a "raptor" in appearance.

"Fukuisaurus" (foo-koo-ee-**sor**-uhss) Not a valid scientific name. This animal was described based on fragments of an iguanodontid dinosaur found in Fukui Prefecture of Japan.

"Fulengia" (foo-**len**-jee-uh) Not a valid scientific name. The name was derived from an anagram for "Lufeng," the region of the Yunnan Province of China where the fossil was discovered. See *Lufengosaurus*.

Fulgurotherium

fool-gur-o-**thee**-ree-um

NAME MEANS: "lightning beast," after Lightning Ridge in New South Wales

CLASSIFICATION: Ornithischia, Hypsilophodontidae

LENGTH: 5 ft (1.5 m)

Fulgurotherium femur

TIME: Early Cretaceous, 110 million years ago

PLACE: Australia

DIET: plants

DETAILS: Originally identified as a coelurosaur, a type of small theropod, this swift little dinosaur was later identified as a hypsilophodont, one of a worldwide group of plant-eaters.

"Futabasaurus" (**foo**-tah-bah-**sor**-uhss) Not a valid scientific name. Fossil bits found in Japan came from what may have been a tyrannosaur family member.

Fukuiraptors

83

Gallimimus

Gallimimus

gal-ih-**my**-muss

NAME MEANS: "chicken mimic"

CLASSIFICATION: Saurischia, Theropoda, Ornithomimosauria

LENGTH: 17 ft (5.2 m)

TIME: Late Cretaceous, 75 million years ago

PLACE: Mongolia

DIET: meat

DETAILS: *Gallimimus* was named for its neck structure, which was said to resemble that of a rooster. But this speedy, ostrichlike dinosaur was a great deal larger than a supermarket chicken and is known from many exceptionally well-preserved skulls and a skeleton. It had a long, beaklike snout, shaped like a shovel or a duck's bill: flat at the tip on both the bottom and the top of the jaw. One specimen of *Gallimimus* has been found with a comblike structure inside its beak. This suggests the dinosaur may have fed by filtering small animals from the water. Its eyes were located on the sides of its head to provide a wide-angle view, though perhaps not good depth perception. Its arms and fingers were weak. What *Gallimimus* did best was run. With its long legs and light, streamlined body, it could go as fast as 40 miles per hour (67 kmph) or more. Footprints and bone beds from other ornithomimids suggest, however, that these animals did live and run in groups.

"Galtonia" (gal-**tone**-ee-uh) Not a valid scientific name. An as-yet little-known ornithischian from Pennsylvania, recently named based on teeth.

Gargoyleosaurus

gar-**goy**-loh-**sor**-uhss

NAME MEANS: "gargoyle lizard" because of its resemblance to Gothic ornamental monster statues

CLASSIFICATION: Ornithischia, Ankylosauria

LENGTH: 10 ft (3 m)

TIME: Late Jurassic, 145 million years ago

PLACE: Wyoming, U.S.

DIET: plants

DETAILS: This plant-eater's body was protected by at least two spines jutting out from each shoulder. The long, narrow beak at the tip of its skull contains seven teeth, unlike any other ankylosaurs. These beak teeth disappeared in later armored dinosaurs, which usually had broad, flat mouths.

Gargoyleosaurus

Garudimimus

gah-**rood**-ih-**my**-muss

NAMED AFTER: Garuda, a bird of Asian mythology

CLASSIFICATION: Saurischia, Theropoda, Ornithomimosauria

LENGTH: 13 ft (4 m)

TIME: Late Cretaceous, 88.5 million years ago

PLACE: Mongolia, China

DIET: meat

DETAILS: Like the other ostrichlike ornithomimids, *Garudimimus* was long-legged and fleet-footed, and probably fed on small reptiles, mammals, or insects. It had a birdlike skull and skeleton. Its toes were shorter than those of most other theropods. *Garudimimus* had a short fourth toe on its foot, like many other meat-eaters, but unlike other three-toed ornithomimids.

Garudimimus skull

Gasosaurus

gas-oh-**sor**-uhss

NAME MEANS: "gas lizard," after both the Chinese natural gas prospectors who found the first fossils and the Chinese word for "make trouble"

CLASSIFICATION: Saurischia, Theropoda, Ceratosauria

Gasosaurus

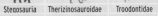

What a Gas!

Chinese paleontologist Dong Zhiming is expert at finding dinosaurs. He has probably found and named more dinosaurs than anyone else in the world. Born in 1937 in Tsingtao, eastern China, Dong first started digging up dinosaur bones when he was a young boy.

Dong Zhiming

Learning on the job without a professional degree, in 1962 Dong was appointed director of dinosaur paleontology for the Institute of Vertebrate Paleontology and Paleoanthropology. This put Dong in charge of all dinosaur fossil exploration in China—one of the world's richest dinosaur fossil lands. He held the position for nearly 30 years!

LENGTH: 12 ft (3.7 m)
TIME: Middle Jurassic, 163 million years ago
PLACE: China
DIET: meat
DETAILS: *Gasosaurus* was a midsize meat-eater found among many large plant-eaters. Perhaps it hunted in packs or was a ferocious predator. The Chinese word for gas can also mean "make trouble." Chinese paleontologist Dong Zhiming (see above) had this double meaning in mind when he named the dinosaur.

Gasparinisaura

gas-par-**ee**-nee-**sor**-uh
NAMED AFTER: Argentine paleontologist Dr. Zulma B. Gasparini
CLASSIFICATION: Ornithischia, basal Iguanodontia
LENGTH: 2.5 ft (0.8 m) (perhaps a juvenile)
TIME: Late Cretaceous, 84 million years ago
PLACE: Argentina
DIET: plants
DETAILS: This tiny iguanodontid lived in Patagonia. It could walk on two or all four feet. Scientists are puzzled that this primitive dinosaur would be found in the Late Cretaceous Period in Argentina, when iguanodontids are best known from earlier times and other parts of the world. Named for a female scientist, *Gasparinisaura* is one of the few dinosaurs with a "saura" (vs. "saurus") ending.

Gastonia

gas-**tone**-ee-uh
NAMED AFTER: fossil prospector Robert Gaston
CLASSIFICATION: Ornithischia, Ankylosauria
LENGTH: 20 ft (6.1 m)
TIME: Early Cretaceous, 121 million years ago
PLACE: Utah
DIET: plants
DETAILS: *Gastonia* exhibited a spectacular array of body armor, including large triangular plates projecting sideways along its tail. It is the most heavily armored of all known dinosaurs, but did not have a bony club at the tip of its tail. Its skull was broad and triangular with nasal openings in the front. The eyes were forward-facing for three-dimensional vision. The braincase was well protected to absorb shock in the event of collision with another dinosaur, perhaps including rivals of its own kind. Utah paleontologist Jim Kirkland named this medium-size early ankylosaur based on the discovery of more than 1,000 bones and bits of armor in Grand County, Utah. The bones appear to have belonged to four or five individuals.

Gastonia

Abelisauridae   Ankylosauria   basal Coelurosauria   basal Iguanodontia   Camarasauridae   Carnosauria   Ceratopsia   Ceratosauria   Dromaeosauridae   Diplodocoidea   Hadrosauridae   Herrerasauridae   Heterodontosauridae

Gasparinisaura

Hypsilophodontidae Lesothosauria Macronaria Ornithomimosauria Oviraptorosauria Pachycephalosauria Primitive sauropods Prosauropoda Spinosauria Stegosauria Therizinosauroidae Troodontidae Tyrannosauridae

Giganotosaurus

Abelisauridae Ankylosauria basal Coelurosauria basal Iguanodontia Camarasauridae Carnosauria Ceratopsia Ceratosauria Dromaeosauridae Diplodocoidea Hadrosauridae Herrerasauridae Heterodontosauridae

Genusaurus

jen-oo-sor-uhss

NAME MEANS: "knee lizard"

CLASSIFICATION: Saurischia, Theropoda, Ceratosauria

LENGTH: 13 ft (4 m)

TIME: Early Cretaceous, 112 million years ago

PLACE: France

DIET: meat

DETAILS: Thought to be the latest known ceratosaur, *Genusaurus* was probably a powerful predator. It was a meat-eater with four-fingered, grasping hands. This dinosaur's name refers to its crested knee bones.

"Genyodectes" (**jen**-ee-oh-**deck**-teez) Not a valid scientific name. A poorly known South American meat-eater that may be *Carnotaurus*.

"Geranosaurus" (**jer**-an-oh-**sor**-uhss) Not a valid scientific name. Known only from parts of a skull, this dinosaur may be a type of small plant-eating heterodontosaur.

Giganotosaurus

jig-a-not-oh-**sor-**uhss

NAME MEANS: "giant southern lizard"

CLASSIFICATION: Saurischia, Theropoda, Carnosauria

LENGTH: 42 ft (12.5 m)

TIME: Late Cretaceous, 100 million years ago

PLACE: Argentina

DIET: meat

DETAILS: This gigantic South American meat-eater is currently the largest known predatory dinosaur. *Giganotosaurus* is seven feet (2 m) longer and perhaps more than a ton heavier than the biggest known specimens of the other meat-eating giants, *Tyrannosaurus* and *Carcharodontosaurus*. This immense theropod had flattened, serrated, daggerlike teeth for slashing and slicing. *Giganotosaurus* may have hunted in packs, attacking sauropods much larger than itself, including the armored titanosaurs. This behavior is suggested for a close and as yet unnamed relative of *Giganotosaurus* found in the same region of western Patagonia. This new fossil find shows seven individuals. One was a youngster; another was an adult at least as large as the single well-known skeleton of *Giganotosaurus*. All seven were killed in an apparent flood. Their fossils suggest these dinosaurs were living, and perhaps hunting, in a group.

"Gigantosaurus" (jie-**gan**-toe-**sor**-uhss) Not a valid scientific name. One of the first giant browsing dinosaurs named was based on just a few British sauropod fossils, which may belong to *Pelorosaurus*, *Brachiosaurus*, or *Ischyrosaurus*. An African sauropod was mistakenly given the same name; this second dinosaur is now considered to be *Tornieria*.

"Gigantoscelus" (jie-gan-**toss**-kell-us) Not a valid scientific name. This animal is known from only part of a single bone.

Gilmoreosaurus

gill-more-oh-**sor-**uhss

NAMED AFTER: American paleontologist Charles Whitney Gilmore

CLASSIFICATION: Ornithischia, Hadrosauridae

LENGTH: 26 ft (8 m)

TIME: Late Cretaceous, 80 million years ago

PLACE: China

DIET: plants

DETAILS: *Gilmoreosaurus* has been called an evolutionary link between the iguanodontid plant-eaters and the later hadrosaurids, or duckbills. The ends of its toes are hooflike, as are those of iguanodontids. Its limbs, though, are more solid, like those of the duck-billed dinosaurs. *Gilmoreosaurus* may have been quick and agile, running on its hind legs. It was discovered in 1923 by an American Museum of Natural History expedition, but wasn't properly named until 1979. Bones of many members of this primitive, flat-headed hadrosaur species have been found in a bone bed in northern China, suggesting that *Gilmoreosaurus* traveled in herds.

Gilmoreosaurus

"Ginnareemimus" (**gin**-ah-**ree**-my-muss) Not a valid scientific name. This as-yet undescribed ornithomimid from the Early Cretaceous Period of Thailand may be the earliest known ostrich-mimic dinosaur but is so far based on only a few vertebrae and a foot bone.

"Giraffatitan" (jih-**raff**-uh-**tie**-ton) Not a valid scientific name. This giant plant-eater from Africa is named for the long-necked giraffe and considered by most paleontologists to be a type of *Brachiosaurus*.

Glyptodontopelta

glip-to-don-to-**pell**-tuh

Glyptodontopelta armor fragment

NAME MEANS: "glyptodont shield" as its armor resembles that of an Ice Age armored mammal
CLASSIFICATION: Ornithischia, Ankylosauria
LENGTH: 20 ft (6.1 m)
TIME: Late Cretaceous, 70 million years ago
PLACE: Western North America
DIET: Plants
DETAILS: This armored dinosaur was large in size for its kind, judging from its only known fossils, large pieces of armor that coincidentally look like the armor of giant Ice Age armadillos from South America.

Gojirasaurus

go-**jeer**-uh-**sor**-uhss

NAME MEANS: "Gojira lizard" ("Gojira" is the original Japanese name for the movie monster Godzilla)
CLASSIFICATION: Saurichia, Theropoda, Ceratosauria
LENGTH: 20 ft (6.1 m)
TIME: Late Triassic, 220 million years ago
PLACE: New Mexico, U.S.
DIET: meat

Gojirasaurus leg bone

DETAILS: *Gojirasaurus* was perhaps the largest meat-eater known from the Triassic Period and enormous for its time. A serrated tooth, four ribs, four backbones, and a few other bones have been uncovered. Denver Museum of Natural History

paleontologist Ken Carpenter is a big fan of the Japanese movie *Godzilla*. So in 1997 he named this remarkable theropod after the famous movie monster. *Gojirasaurus* is, however, considerably smaller than Godzilla.

Gondwanatitan

gond-**wah**-nuh-**tie**-ton

NAME MEANS: "Gondwana titan," after Gondwana, the continent that made up the modern southern continents and India during the Jurassic Period
CLASSIFICATION: Saurischia, Sauropoda, Macronaria
LENGTH: 24 ft (7.3 m)
TIME: Late Cretaceous, 70 million years ago

It's Alive!

Dinosaurs may have been extinct for 65 million years, but their fame lives on. These strange, huge creatures have scared us in films, entertained us as toys, and decorated our T-shirts.

Dinosaurs were first re-created as sculptures by British artist Waterhouse Hawkins in 1854 to great success at Britain's Crystal Palace Exhibition. One of the earliest cartoons ever made featured "Gertie" the dinosaur. These primitive black-and-white animations date from 1912.

Movies are a popular way for us to imagine what dinosaurs were like when they were alive (big and threatening always seems to be a crowd-pleaser).

Dinosaurs moved from

Godzilla *film still*

supporting roles in movies such as *King Kong* (1933) to star billing in movies like the *Godzilla* films from the 1960s and the *Jurassic Park* movies today. Along the way, movie dinosaurs got a makeover, too. They evolved as movie stars from slow, dumb, lumbering beasts to fast, clever villains. And they remain everybody's favorite real-life monsters!

Gondwanatitan
vertebra

PLACE: Brazil
DIET: plants
DETAILS: An incomplete skeleton of this lightly built sauropod was found in Brazil. Its limb bones are slender and long. Its tail vertebrae have an unusual heart shape. *Gondwanatitan* may be the same animal as *Aeolosaurus*.

"Gongbusaurus" (goong-boo-**sor**-uhss) Not a valid scientific name. It is known from a few teeth.

Gongxianosaurus

goong-shyen-oh-**sor**-uhss
NAMED AFTER: Gongxian region of China
CLASSIFICATION: Saurischia, Sauropoda, Primitive sauropods
LENGTH: 46 ft (14 m)
TIME: Early Jurassic, 180 million years ago
PLACE: China
DIET: plants
DETAILS: The skeleton of this large dinosaur was found nearly complete. The early giant plant-eater was bulky for its length. Its front legs were roughly 75% as large as its hind limbs. Belly ribs were also found with this skeleton—a primitive anatomical feature unknown in most sauropods. *Gongxianosaurus* had a snout with a sloping, rounded appearance. It was named in 1998.

Gorgosaurus

gore-go-**sor**-uhss
NAME MEANS: "fierce lizard"
CLASSIFICATION: Saurischia, Theropoda, Tyrannosauridae
LENGTH: 29.5 ft (9 m)
TIME: Late Cretaceous, 71 million years ago
PLACE: Montana, U.S; Alberta, Canada
DIET: meat
DETAILS: This large tyrannosaurid was an ancestor of *T. rex* and among the largest and last of all meat-eating giants. In recent years, the Royal Tyrrell Museum of Palaeontology in Drumheller, Alberta, Canada, has collected a number of skulls and skeletons belonging to both meat-eating dinosaurs. With more than 30 skeletons collected in Alberta alone, *Gorgosaurus* may be the most common fossil tyrannosaur known.

Goyocephale

go-yoh-**seff**-a-lee
NAME MEANS: "adorned head" because of the many bumps on its thick skull
CLASSIFICATION: Ornithischia, Pachycephalosauria
LENGTH: 10 ft (3 m)
TIME: Late Cretaceous, 80 million years ago
PLACE: Mongolia
DIET: plants
DETAILS: Like other pachycephalosaurs, *Goyocephale* had a thickened mass of protective bone surrounding its brain. But unlike most other "thick-headed" dinosaurs, the top of this dinosaur's skull was almost flat, making it perhaps the second "flat-headed" pachycephalosaur known after *Homalocephale*. The back edge of *Goyocephale*'s skull featured a number of small knobs and spikes. Both the upper and lower jaws of the animal were lined with large teeth suitable for snipping plants. Other parts of its skeleton are also known, a rare discovery among pachycephalosaurs.

Goyocephale
skull fragment

Goyocephale
recreated skull

91

Gorgosaurus

Graciliceratops

Graciliceratops

gra-sil-i-**sayr**-a-tops

NAME MEANS: "light horned face"

CLASSIFICATION: Ornithischia, Ceratopsia

SIZE: 3 ft (0.9 m)

TIME: Late Cretaceous, 80 million years ago

PLACE: China

DIET: Plants

DETAILS: This tiny protoceratopsian was recently named from fossils formerly thought to have belonged to *Microceratops*.

Gravitholus

grav-ih-**thoh**-luss

NAME MEANS: "heavy dome"

CLASSIFICATION: Ornithischia, Pachycephalosauria

LENGTH: 10 ft (3 m)

TIME: Late Cretaceous, 75 million years ago

PLACE: Alberta

DIET: plants

DETAILS: A thick-headed plant-eater, *Gravitholus* had a very large, wide, highly curved skull, with no ornamental head bumps or nodes. Because only the skull of *Gravitholus* has been found, the details of its body remain a mystery.

"Gresslyosaurus" (**gress**-lee-oh-**sor**-uhss) Not a valid scientific name. Now called *Plateosaurus*.

Gryposaurus

grip-oh-**sor**-uhss

NAME MEANS: "hook-nose lizard"

CLASSIFICATION: Ornithischia, Hadrosauridae

LENGTH: 30 ft (9.1 m)

TIME: Late Cretaceous, 76 million years ago

PLACE: Alberta, Canada

DIET: plants

DETAILS: This duck-billed dinosaur had a large, narrow skull. Its most distinctive feature was a hump of bone on its snout. This protruding bump was covered with skin and probably was inflated to attract a suitable mate or to intimidate rivals. Fossilized skin impressions give us an idea of how *Gryposaurus* looked when fleshed out. Smooth, polygonal scales about 0.25 inch (6 mm) in diameter covered its neck, sides, and abdomen. It also had cone-shape plates nearly as small on its tail. Only the shape of its teeth and snout distinguish *Gryposaurus* from *Kritosaurus*. In fact, some experts still believe that they are the same animal, although *Gryposaurus* is known only from Alberta, Canada, and *Kritosaurus* is from New Mexico.

? Guaibasaurus

gwie-bah-**sor**-uhss

NAMED AFTER: Rio Guaiba, Brazil

CLASSIFICATION: Saurischia, Theropoda?, Guaibasauridae?

LENGTH: 4 ft (1.2 m)

TIME: Late Triassic, 227 million years ago

PLACE: Brazil

DIET: meat?

DETAILS: This primitive dinosaur was closely related to the earliest representatives of both the meat-eaters and the plant-eating prosauropods. Unfortunately, the skeleton found was missing its fragile skull. Based on study of vertebrae, ribs, an incomplete scapula, a hind leg with a nearly complete foot, and other scattered fossils, it is clear that *Guaibasaurus* was anatomically more primitive than many early meat-eaters such as *Herrerasaurus*.

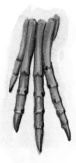

Guaibasaurus right foot bones

"Gyposaurus" (**jip**-oh-**sor**-uhss) Not a valid scientific name. Now called *Anchisaurus*.

Gryposaurus

Hypsilophodontidae | Lesothosauria | Macronaria | Ornithomimosauria | Oviraptorosauria | Pachycephalosauria | Primitive sauropods | Prosauropoda | Spinosauria | Stegosauria | Therizinosauroidae | Troodontidae | Tyrannosauridae

Harpymimus

Abelisauridae Ankylosauria basal Coelurosauria basal Iguanodontia Camarasauridae Carnosauria Ceratopsia Ceratosauria Dromaeosauridae Diplodocoidea Hadrosauridae Herrerasauridae Heterodontosauridae

"Hadrosauravus" (**had**-ro-**sore**-uh-vuss) Not a valid scientific name. Considered to be *Gryposaurus*.

Hadrosaurus

had-roh-**sor**-uhss

NAME MEANS: "bulky lizard"

CLASSIFICATION: Ornithischia, Hadrosauridae

LENGTH: 25 ft (7.6 m)

TIME: Late Cretaceous, 76 million years ago

PLACE: New Jersey, U.S.

DIET: plants

DETAILS: *Hadrosaurus* was a midsize duck-billed dinosaur. Its nearly complete skeleton was discovered in a pit in Haddonfield, New Jersey. *Hadrosaurus* was one of the first dinosaurs in the world named from a nearly complete skeleton, and one of the earliest North American dinosaurs to be named. It is the state dinosaur of New Jersey. Philadelphia paleontologist Joseph Leidy studied its fossils in 1858. Leidy at first believed that *Hadrosaurus* alternated between browsing for plants on land and swimming. He pioneered the idea that *Hadrosaurus* and many other dinosaurs walked on two legs in an upright position.

Hadrosaurus

"Halticosaurus" (**hal**-tick-oh-**sor**-uhss) Not a valid scientific name. Little is known about this small meat-eater from Europe.

Haplocanthosaurus

hap-loh-**can**-thoh-**sor**-uhss

NAME MEANS: "simple-spine lizard"

CLASSIFICATION: Saurischia, Sauropoda, Camarasauridae

LENGTH: 70 ft (21.3 m)

TIME: Late Jurassic, 145 million years ago

PLACE: Colorado, U.S.

DIET: plants

DETAILS: One of the most primitive sauropods known from North America, *Haplocanthosaurus* was the length of two school buses. A pair of well-preserved specimens was unearthed more than 100 years ago near Canon City, Colorado. Famed bone hunter John Bell Hatcher studied the larger of the two. The Cleveland Museum of Natural History excavated and mounted a third specimen found in the same area in 1954. This individual may have been as much as 50% larger than the first two specimens discovered. Originally called "Haplocanthus" ("simple spine"), the dinosaur's name was changed to *Haplocanthosaurus* when scientists realized that the original name had already been used to describe a prehistoric fish.

Haplocanthosaurus

"Haplocanthus" (**hap**-lo-**kan**-thus) Not a valid scientific name. Now known as *Haplocanthosaurus*.

Harpymimus

harp-ee-**my**-muss

NAMED AFTER: the Greek mythological monsters, the Harpies

CLASSIFICATION: Saurischia, Theropoda, Ornithomimosauria

LENGTH: 12 ft (3.7 m)

TIME: Early Cretaceous, 97.5 million years ago

PLACE: Mongolia

DIET: insects, reptiles, and plants

DETAILS: *Harpymimus* was one of the most primitive ostrichlike dinosaurs. Like all of the ornithomimosaurs, *Harpymimus* had delicate, three-fingered hands, long-shinned, slender legs adapted for speed, and a beaklike snout with a mostly toothless jaw. These features resemble those of modern-day flightless birds. Unlike most ornithomimids, *Harpymimus* did have six small teeth located in the front of its jaw. It also had foot bones shaped more like those of meat-eaters with teeth. These features suggest that *Harpymimus* may have been an evolutionary bridge between less specialized meat-eaters and more typical ostrich-mimics like *Gallimimus* and *Ornithomimus*. Like other ornithomimids, *Harpymimus* may have eaten a variety of foods, including meats, insects, fruits, and nuts.

"Hecatasaurus" (**heck**-uh-tuh-**sor**-uhss) Not a valid scientific name. Now called *Telmatosaurus*.

"Heishansaurus" (hay-shahn-**sor**-uhss) Not a valid scientific name. Too poorly known from just a few fossils to identify what kind of dinosaur this was.

"Helopus" (**hell**-oh-puss) Not a valid scientific name. This name was already in use for another animal; see *Euhelopus*.

"Heptasteornis" (hep-**tass**-tee-**or**-niss) Not a valid scientific name. Found in Transylvania, this small meat-eater is known only from fragmentary leg bones. The bones were originally identified as those of a huge prehistoric owl. Its misnaming is one of the most remarkable bloopers in science.

Herrerasaurus

hay-**rare**-uh-**sor**-uhss
NAME MEANS: "Herrera's lizard," after Argentine rancher Don Victorino Herrera
CLASSIFICATION: Saurischia, Theropoda, Herrerasauridae
LENGTH: 16.5 ft (5 m)
TIME: Late Triassic, 225 million years ago

Herrerasaurus

PLACE: Argentina
DIET: meat
DETAILS: Probably the earliest known theropod, *Herrerasaurus* was much more primitive than later predators. The largest of the early meat-eating dinosaurs, it may have weighed about 400 pounds (181 kilograms). Double-hinged jaws allowed *Herrerasaurus* to grip its prey and to swallow huge chunks of meat. Serrated teeth helped it slice the flesh from a fresh kill. Evidence of its primitive nature includes such anatomical features as the rectangular shape of its nearly complete skull fossil.

Heterodontosaurus

het-uh-roh-**don**-toe-**sor**-uhss
NAME MEANS: "different-toothed lizard"
CLASSIFICATION: Ornithischia, Heterodontosauridae
LENGTH: 3 ft (1 m)
TIME: Early Jurassic, 200 million years ago
PLACE: South Africa
DIET: plants

Heterodontosaurus

DETAILS: This small plant-eater was named for the surprising difference between its unusually long and sharp canine teeth and plant-snipping cheek teeth. It could run on either two or four legs and had very large eyes. Its slender hind legs were well adapted for quick bursts of speed; it used its tail for balance during those short sprints. The dinosaur's long, slender fingers may have been used for grasping or tearing. Some scientists suggest that only the males of this genus had enlarged canine tusks.

"Heterosaurus" (**het**-uh-roh-**sor**-uhss) Not a valid scientific name. Probably the same as *Iguanodon*.

"Hierosaurus" (**hie**-uh-roh-**sor**-uhss) Not a valid scientific name.

96

Histriasaurus

his-tree-uh-**sor**-uhss

NAMED AFTER: Istria region of Croatia

CLASSIFICATION: Saurischia, Sauropoda, Diplodocoidea

LENGTH: 50 ft (15.2 m)

TIME: Early Cretaceous, 127 million years ago

PLACE: Croatia

DIET: plants

DETAILS: Found in limestone near the village of Bale in Croatia, this four-legged plant-eater was named from a nearly complete backbone at the base of the animal's back. It is probably related to *Rebacchisaurus,* but is considered to be anatomically more primitive.

Homalocephale

hom-uh-loh-**seff**-a-lee

NAME MEANS: "level head"

CLASSIFICATION: Ornithischia, Pachycephalosauria

LENGTH: 10 ft (3 m)

TIME: Late Cretaceous, 70 million years ago

PLACE: Mongolia

DIET: plants

DETAILS: This small pachycephalosaur is one of the best-known members of the flat-headed dinosaurs. It was named for its flat-roofed skull. This skull was 5.5 inches (14 cm) wide and 4.5 inches (11 cm) high. Small bony knobs ran along the edges of its armored skull. Researchers once thought that *Homalocephale* might have used its flattened skull for head-butting displays, much as bighorn sheep do today. That theory is now rejected by many scientists, who think head-butting was too difficult and dangerous a behavior for these animals.

Homalocephale

Hoplitosaurus

hop-**lite**-oh-**sor**-uhss

NAME MEANS: "shield-carrier lizard"

CLASSIFICATION: Ornithischia, Ankylosauria

LENGTH: 8 ft (2.4 m)

TIME: Early Cretaceous, 119 million years ago

PLACE: South Dakota, U.S.

DIET: plants

DETAILS: *Hoplitosaurus* stood about four feet (1.2 m) tall at the hip. This sturdy little plant-eater was covered in a highly varied protective layer of bone. This armor includes thin, flat rectangles; round spikes; thick button-shape spikes; triangular plates; and spiny scutes. However, where the scattered plates were located on the dinosaur's body is uncertain. Scientists first thought *Hoplitosaurus* was a stegosaur, but revised their thinking as more information became available. *Hoplitosaurus* is now known to be an ankylosaur. Some researchers think that it is the same animal as *Polacanthus.*

Hoplitosaurus seen from above

"Hoplosaurus" (**hop**-loh-**sor**-uhss) Not a valid scientific name.

"Hortalotarsus" (**hort**-uh-loh-**tar**-suss) Not a valid scientific name. See *Massospondylus.*

? Huabeisaurus

hwah-bay-**sor**-uhss

NAMED AFTER: Huabei administrative region of China

CLASSIFICATION: Saurischia, Sauropoda, Macronaria

LENGTH: 65 ft (19.8 m)

TIME: Late Cretaceous, 71 million years ago

PLACE: China

DIET: plants

DETAILS: *Huabeisaurus* was a large sauropod and one of the last giant plant-eaters known to have lived in Asia. It resembles *Opisthocoelicaudia,* also from Asia late in dinosaur time. Experts disagree as to whether this four-legged browser was a member of the titanosaur or camarasaur family. Perhaps it belonged to its own as yet unknown family. Titanosaurs are well known worldwide from this time, but not camarasaurs. *Huabeisaurus* was named in 2000.

Huayangosaurus

Huayangosaurus

hwah-yong-oh-**sor**-uhss

NAMED AFTER: Huayang or Sichuan area of China

CLASSIFICATION: Ornithischia, Stegosauria

LENGTH: 13.5 ft (4 m)

TIME: Middle Jurassic, 170 million years ago

PLACE: China

DIET: plants

DETAILS: This plant-eating dinosaur is one of the most primitive and best-represented of all the stegosaurs. It was adorned with two rows of small, paired heart-shape plates on its back and narrow spikes at the shoulders. Scientists have placed it in its own family, apart from other plate-backed dinosaurs.

Hudiesaurus

hoo-dyeh-**sor**-uhss

NAME MEANS: "butterfly lizard," because of the shape of its backbone

CLASSIFICATION: Saurischia, Sauropoda, Camarasauridae

LENGTH: 80 ft (24.4 m)

TIME: Late Jurassic, 145 million years ago

PLACE: China

DIET: plants

DETAILS: *Hudiesaurus* is one of the largest sauropods known from China. Four serrated, flattened teeth suggest that *Hudiesaurus* may have resembled *Mamenchisaurus* although *Hudiesaurus* was the larger dinosaur. It was discovered by a team of Chinese and Japanese scientists.

Hudiesaurus right foot

Hulsanpes

hool-sahn-peez

NAME MEANS: "Khulsan foot," after Khulsan, Mongolia

CLASSIFICATION: Saurischia, Theropoda, Deinonychosauria, Dromaeosauridae

LENGTH: 5 ft (1.5 m)

TIME: Late Cretaceous, 77 million years ago

PLACE: Mongolia

DIET: meat

Hulsanpes foot bones

DETAILS: Known only from its slender, incompletely preserved foot, *Hulsanpes* was a three-toed meat-eater that may have been a "raptor" dromaeosaurid. Unlike other dromaeosaurs, the claw on the second toe of its foot was smaller than the other two toe claws. *Hulsanpes* was scientifically described in 1982.

"Hunhosaurus" (**hoo**-no-sor-**uhss**) Not a valid scientific name. See *Yandusaurus*.

Hylaeosaurus

hie-**lee**-oh-**sor**-uhss

NAME MEANS: "woodland lizard" or "Wealden lizard," after quarry where its bones were found

CLASSIFICATION: Ornithischia, Ankylosauria

LENGTH: 13 ft (4 m)

TIME: Early Cretaceous, 135 million years ago

PLACE: England

DIET: plants

Hylaeosaurus

DETAILS: This medium-size and early armored dinosaur was one of the first three animals identified as dinosaurs. (The other two were *Iguanodon* and *Megalosaurus*.) It is the first known armored dinosaur and was described by Dr. Gideon Mantell, the physician who in 1824 identified *Iguanodon* from fossils found in the same stone quarry as *Hylaeosaurus*.

Hypacrosaurus

high-**pack**-roh-**sor**-uhss

NAME MEANS: "near-topmost lizard"

Hypacrosaurus

CLASSIFICATION: Ornithischia, Hadrosauridae
LENGTH: 30 ft (9.1 m)
TIME: Late Cretaceous, 70 million years ago
PLACE: Montana, U.S.; Alberta, Canada
DIET: plants
DETAILS: The shape of this duck-billed hadrosaur's head crest was similar to that of *Corythosaurus*. The head crest of *Hypacrosaurus,* however, was less rounded and positioned farther forward than that of *Corythosaurus*. *Hypacrosaurus* had a distinctive ridged back with very long spines atop its backbones. American fossil finder Barnum Brown gave *Hypacrosaurus* its name because he thought this plant-eater stood as tall as any duck-billed dinosaur. In recent years, excavations in Alberta and Montana have yielded eggs containing the bones of *Hypacrosaurus* embryos.

Hypselosaurus

hip-sell-oh-**sor**-uhss
NAME MEANS: "high lizard"
CLASSIFICATION: Saurischia, Sauropoda, Macronaria
LENGTH: 40 ft (12.2 m)
TIME: Late Cretaceous, 65 million years ago
PLACE: France and Spain
DIET: plants
DETAILS: *Hypselosaurus* was relatively small for a sauropod. It was originally described as an aquatic animal, possibly a large crocodilian. *Hypselosaurus* eggs found in 1860 were the first dinosaur eggs ever discovered. Scientists at the time were not sure whether the heavy fossilized eggs had belonged to a dinosaur or to a very large bird. In 1992, a single *Hypselosaurus* egg was sold at auction for $11,000 — a record price for a dinosaur egg and an upsetting development for the many scientists (and this author) who strongly oppose commercial sales of fossils, which are rare and valuable for scientific study.

"Hypsibema" (**hip**-si-**bee**-muh) Not a valid scientific name. See *Hadrosaurus*.

Hypselosaurus egg

Hypsilophodon

hip-sih-**loaf**-oh-don
NAME MEANS: "high-crested tooth"
CLASSIFICATION: Ornithischia, Hypsilophodontidae
LENGTH: 7.5 ft (2.3 m)
TIME: Early Cretaceous, 115 million years ago
PLACE: England, Spain, Portugal
DIET: plants
DETAILS: The long fingers and toes of this small, fast-moving plant-eater, discovered in 1849 on the Isle of Wight, have led one scientist to propose that *Hypsilophodon* may have been an agile tree-climber. Limb bones suggesting the presence of powerful hind leg muscles were once thought to support this climbing theory, but they may have provided the small dinosaur with quick bursts of ground speed instead. Armor found near *Hypsilophodon* fossils may have belonged to the dinosaur, but most paleontologists do not believe that the bones and the armor came from the same animal. *Hypsilophodon* was named for a type of iguana (*Hypsilophus*), because it was thought to be similar to *Iguanodon*.

"Hypsirophus" (hip-**sear**-oh-fuss) Probably not a valid scientific name. See *Stegosaurus*, though one researcher contends this is a different animal from *Stegosaurus*.

Hypsilophodon

Hypsilophodontidae Lesothosauria Macronaria Ornithomimosauria Oviraptorosauria Pachycephalosauria Primitive sauropods Prosauropoda Spinosauria Stegosauria Therizinosauridae Troodontidae Tyrannosauridae

Iguanodon

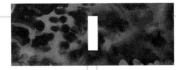

Iguanodon

igg-**wah**-no-don

NAME MEANS: "Iguana tooth"

CLASSIFICATION: Ornithischia, basal Iguanodontia

LENGTH: 33 ft (10.1 m)

TIME: Early Cretaceous, 110 million years ago

PLACE: South Dakota, Utah, U.S.; Europe

DIET: plants

DETAILS: One of the most famous dinosaurs and a more primitive relative of the duck-billed hadrosaurs, *Iguanodon* featured a large thumb-spike used for scraping up plants or perhaps for defense. There were many related forms of *Iguanodon* around the world. Most were shorter than 30 feet (9 m) long.

Iguanodon was the second dinosaur discovered and identified by scientists. According to dinosaur legend, it was found in 1822 by Mary Ann Mantell, the wife of doctor and amateur geologist Gideon Mantell. Mrs. Mantell supposedly found the remains in the gravel of a driveway of a home where her husband was making a house call. In truth, Dr. Mantell had the gravel delivered to his house from the Tilgate Forest quarries expressly so that he could search for mysterious prehistoric teeth and bones. When Mantell named *Iguanodon* in 1825, however, he was sure that the teeth he'd found belonged to a giant plant-eating reptile. When better fossil material was uncovered in the mid-1800s, Sir Richard Owen reconstructed *Iguanodon* as a sprawling, lizardlike creature with a horn on its nose.

Ilokelesia

ee-low-kay-**lay**-see-uh

NAME MEANS: "Flesh-eating lizard" in Mapuche Indian language

CLASSIFICATION: Saurischia, Theropoda, Ceratosauria, Abelisauridae

SIZE: 20 ft (6.1 m)

PLACE: Argentina

TIME: Late Cretaceous, 95 million years ago

DIET: meat

DETAILS: This newly named dinosaur was a primitive relative of the abelisaur meat-eaters that dominated Late Cretaceous South America. It was possibly a close relative of *Carnotaurus,* a peculiarly short-limbed and bulldog-faced meat-eater.

"**Iliosuchus**" (**ill**-ee-oh-**sue**-cuss) Not a valid scientific name. Based only on a small ilium bone from England.

Indosaurus

in-doh-**sor**-uhss

NAME MEANS: "Indian lizard"

CLASSIFICATION: Saurischia, Theropoda, Ceratosauria, Abelisauridae

LENGTH: 30 ft (9.1 m)

TIME: Late Cretaceous, 65 million years ago

PLACE: India

DIET: meat

DETAILS: This large meat-eater may have had horns over its eyes. Argentine researchers have found many similarities between *Indosaurus* and South American meat-eaters such as the horned *Carnotaurus* and *Abelisaurus.* The similarities between these carnivores suggests that there may once have been a land connection between India and South America.

Indosaurus

Indosuchus

in-doh-**sue**-cuss

NAME MEANS: "Indian crocodile"

CLASSIFICATION: Saurischia, Theropoda, Ceratosauria

LENGTH: 25 ft (7.6 m)

TIME: Late Cretaceous, 65 million years ago

PLACE: India

DIET: meat

DETAILS: *Indosuchus,* a large meat-eater, was discovered together with *Indosaurus.* The two may have been related species.

Ingenia

ing-**gay**-nee-a

NAMED AFTER: Ingeni, a region of southern Mongolia

CLASSIFICATION: Saurischia, Theropoda, Oviraptorosauria

LENGTH: 6 ft (1.8 m)

TIME: Late Cretaceous, 70 million years ago

PLACE: Mongolia

DIET: meat

DETAILS: *Ingenia* was a small meat-eater similar to *Oviraptor* but had stubbier, more powerful hands. Its thumbs were large compared with its two other fingers.

Ingenia

"Inosaurus" (**in**-oh-**sor**-uhss) Not a valid scientific name.

Irritator

ear-ih-**tay**-tor

NAME MEANS: "irritator"

CLASSIFICATION: Saurischia, Theropoda, Spinosauria?

LENGTH: 26 ft (8 m)

TIME: Early Cretaceous, 99 million years ago

PLACE: Brazil

DIET: meat

DETAILS: *Irritator* was a theropod with an unusual crest at the rear of its head. It was probably a fish-eater. Commercial fossil collectors made its snout longer than in life in hopes of making the fossils appear more complete and valuable. Reconstructing the dinosaur's original features proved frustrating for researchers, and so it was named *Irritator.* This dinosaur's species name is *challengeri,* in honor of the fictional Professor Challenger from Arthur Conan Doyle's novel *The Lost World.*

Isanosaurus

ee-sah-no-**sor**-uss

NAMED FOR: The Isan region of northeastern Thailand

CLASSIFICATION: Saurischia, Sauropoda, Primitive sauropods

SIZE: 40 ft (12.2 m)

PLACE: Thailand

TIME: Late Triassic, 208 million years ago

DIET: plants

DETAILS: This is the earliest of all known sauropods. Only a portion of a half-grown adolescent animal has been found so far. Fully grown, this was the largest dinosaur from the Triassic Period.

Isanosaurus thigh bone

"Ischisaurus" (**iss**-chee-**sor**-uhss) Not a valid scientific name. Now called *Herrerasaurus.*

"Ischyrosaurus" (is-**kie**-roh-**sor**-uhss) Not a valid scientific name. Probably the same dinosaur as *Pelorosaurus.*

Itemirus

ee-teh-**mee**-russ

NAMED AFTER: Itemir, a site in Uzbekistan

CLASSIFICATION: Saurischia, Theropoda, Dromaeosauridae, Deinonychosauria

LENGTH: 5 ft (1.5 m)

TIME: Late Cretaceous, 90 million years ago

PLACE: Uzbekistan

DIET: meat

DETAILS: This little-known meat-eater probably had unusually well-developed senses of sight and hearing. Scientific ideas about *Itemirus*'s senses are based on the discovery of its fossil braincase, which had unusually well-preserved inner ear canals. Scientists think these ear structures helped the animal maintain its balance. *Itemirus* may also have had exceptional vision. Its braincase is similar to those of small predatory dinosaurs like the "raptor" *Dromaeosaurus.*

Itemirus braincase

"Iuticosaurus" (**you**-tick-oh-**sor**-us) Not a valid scientific name.

Irritator

Jaxartosaurus

Abelisauridae | Ankylosauria | basal Coelurosauria | basal Iguanodontia | Camarasauridae | Carnosauria | Ceratopsia | Ceratosauria | Dromaeosauridae | Diplodocoidea | Hadrosauridae | Herrerasauridae | Heterodontosauridae

"Jainosaurus" (jie-no-sor-us) Not a valid scientific name. The fossils of this Late Cretaceous giant plant-eater, named for Indian paleontologist Sohan Lal Jain, may be a specimen of *Titanosaurus*.

Janenschia

yah-**nen**-she-uh

NAMED AFTER: German paleontologist Werner Janensch

CLASSIFICATION: Saurischia, Sauropoda, Macronaria

LENGTH: 60 ft (18.3 m)

TIME: Late Jurassic, 156 million years ago

PLACE: Tanzania

DIET: plants

DETAILS: Perhaps the earliest known titanosaurid, a form of giant sauropod, this massive quadruped may have stretched as long as 130 feet (39.6 m) from its snout to the end of its tail. Its hind thighbone alone was just under 5 feet (1.5 m) high — about as tall as an average 10-year-old child.

Janenschia
right foot

Jaxartosaurus

yack-**sar**-tuh-**sor**-uhss

NAMED AFTER: Jaxartes (or Syr Darya) River in Kazakhstan

CLASSIFICATION: Ornithischia, Hadrosauridae

LENGTH: 30 ft (9.1 m)

TIME: Late Cretaceous, 91 million years ago

PLACE: Kazakhstan, China

DIET: plants

DETAILS: The first fossil discovery of this important duckbill showed no crest. Later discoveries revealed that this animal did have a helmet-shape crest. Like other duck-billed dinosaurs, *Jaxartosaurus* had a series of hinges and joints in its skull that gave it the most flexible and advanced jaws for grinding plants of any large animals ever known.

? Jeholosaurus

juh-**hole**-o-**sor**-uss

NAMED AFTER: Jehol, an old name for a region of northeastern China

CLASSIFICATION: Saurischia, Ornithopoda?

LENGTH: 2.5 ft (76.2 cm)

PLACE: China

TIME: Early Cretaceous, 130 million years ago

DIET: plants

DETAILS: This tiny primitive ornithopod is known from two nearly complete skulls, and was recently named. However, scientists have yet to determine where *Jeholosaurus* belongs among the ornithopods.

Jeholosaurus

"Jenghizkhan" (jen-giss-con) Not a valid scientific name. A large Mongolian meat-eater named for Genghis Khan, the world's greatest conqueror. Only recently suggested by scientists as a name.

Jingshanosaurus

jing-shah-no-**sor**-uhss

NAMED AFTER: Jingshan, a town in Yunnan Province, China

CLASSIFICATION: Saurischia, Prosauropoda

LENGTH: 32 ft (9.8 m)

TIME: Late Triassic, 206 million years ago

PLACE: China

DIET: plants

DETAILS: This giant prosauropod, a primitive ancestor of even more enormous four-legged plant-eaters, may have been an unusually large specimen of *Yunnanosaurus*.

Jobaria (t.) and
a large carnivore (b.)

Abelisauridae　Ankylosauria　basal Coelurosauria　basal Iguanodontia　Camarasauridae　Carnosauria　Ceratopsia　Ceratosauria　Dromaeosauridae　Diplodocoidea　Hadrosauridae　Herrerasauridae　Heterodontosauridae

Jinzhousaurus

jeen-joe-**sor**-uss

NAMED AFTER: Jinzhou, a city in Liaoning Province, northern China

CLASSIFICATION: Ornithischia, Ornithopoda, basal Iguanodontia

SIZE: 30 ft (9.1 m)

TIME: Early Cretaceous, 130 million years ago

PLACE: China

DIET: plants

DETAILS: This large dinosaur has typical iguanodont-like teeth and beak, but many other features in its body are more like those of the later duckbills. This is the first large dinosaur found in the lake bottom rocks of Liaoning. This site has produced many spectacularly well-preserved fossils of small dinosaurs and birds, including feather impressions on both dinosaurs and birds.

Jinzhousaurus

Northward, Ho!

Some plant-eating dinosaurs lived in huge herds that were often on the move. They had to be. If the herd stayed in one place, they might have eaten all the plants and starved.

Trackways suggest dinosaurs may have migrated a thousand miles or more in a single year. *Edmontosaurus* may have migrated from southern Canada all the way to northern Alaska each summer. Why? To feed on plants that grew huge during the long, sunlit Arctic days.

Other dinosaurs also walked a long way for food. A huge "dinosaur highway" of millions of footprints of plant-eating dinosaurs stretches north and south through the American West. It must have been a spectacular—and *smelly* parade—when thousands of hungry dinosaurs marched to new feeding grounds.

Jobaria

joe-**bar**-ee-uh

NAMED AFTER: Jobar, a mythical creature of the Tuareg people of North Africa

CLASSIFICATION: Saurischia, Sauropoda, Camarasauridae

LENGTH: 70 ft (21.3 m)

TIME: Early Cretaceous, 132 million years ago

PLACE: Niger

DIET: plants

DETAILS: The primitive, relatively short-necked sauropod *Jobaria* was named in 1999 by a team of paleontologists. A completely articulated adult skeleton and a partial skeleton and skull have allowed paleontologists to reconstruct about 95% of the animal. The rounded skull is smaller than that of *Camarasaurus* and has a short snout and spoon-shape teeth. It has been reconstructed standing on its hind legs, but few paleontologists think that this posture was likely for the four-legged plant-eater.

"**Jubbulpuria**" (juh-bull-**poor**-ee-uh) Not a valid scientific name.

"**Jurassosaurus**" (**joo**-rass-oh-**sor**-uhss) Not a valid scientific name for a Jurassic Period armored dinosaur recently found in China. Named for the film *Jurassic Park,* this dinosaur was already known as *Tianchisaurus*.

Kentrosaurus (b.)
and a *Ceratosaurus* (t.)

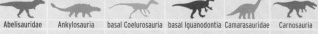

Abelisauridae   Ankylosauria   basal Coelurosauria   basal Iguanodontia   Camarasauridae   Carnosauria   Ceratopsia   Ceratosauria   Dromaeosauridae   Diplodocoidea   Hadrosauridae   Herrerasauridae   Heterodontosauridae

Kangnasaurus tooth

"**Kagasaurus**" (**kag**-a-**sor**-uhss) Not a valid scientific name. A meat-eater based on just a few Japanese fossils.

Kaijiangosaurus

kie-**jyong**-oh-**sor**-uhss

NAMED AFTER: Kai River, Sichuan Province in southern China

CLASSIFICATION: Saurischia, Theropoda, Carnosauria

LENGTH: 20 ft (6.1 m)

TIME: Middle Jurassic, 175 million years ago

PLACE: China

DIET: meat

DETAILS: *Kaijiangosaurus* was a meat-eater with large slicing teeth and narrow shoulder bones. *Gasosaurus* was found in the same fossil bed. Some experts think that they may be the same animal.

Kakuru

kack-oo-roo

NAME MEANS: "ancestral rainbow serpent" of the Guyani tribe of southern Australia

CLASSIFICATION: Saurischia, Theropoda, Troodontidae

LENGTH: 8 ft (2.4 m)

TIME: Late Cretaceous, 99 million years ago

PLACE: Australia

DIET: meat

Kakuru opalized leg bone

DETAILS: *Kakuru* is known from only a single leg bone called a tibia. Through a rare and unusual process, the bone was converted to semiprecious opal gemstone during fossilization. The opalized tibia was purchased by a gem shop in 1973 along with a foot claw that might have come from the same animal. This small meat-eater had long, slender legs. Its ankle was higher and narrower than those of most other swift theropods. *Kakuru* was formally named in 1980.

Kangnasaurus

kong-nuh-**sor**-uhss

NAME MEANS: "Kangna lizard"

CLASSIFICATION: Ornithischia, basal Iguanodontia

LENGTH: 11 ft (3.4 m)

TIME: Early Cretaceous, 115 million years ago

PLACE: South Africa

DIET: plants

DETAILS: *Kangnasaurus* was a small primitive plant-eater. The dinosaur was at first mistaken for *Iguanodon*. But the hind leg, anklebone, and three-toed clawed feet clearly belong to a dryosaurid, a smaller but related animal. The long, tapering teeth were much like the ridged teeth of *Hypsilophodon*. *Kangnasaurus* was discovered on a farm in Little Bushmanland, South Africa.

"**Kelmayisaurus**" (kull-**my**-ih-**sor**-uhss) Not a valid scientific name. This large Chinese plant-eater is too poorly known to fully identify.

Kentrosaurus

ken-troh-**sor**-uhss

NAME MEANS: "sharp point lizard"

CLASSIFICATION: Ornithischia, Stegosauria

LENGTH: 17 ft (5.2 m)

TIME: Late Jurassic, 156 million years ago

PLACE: Tanzania

DIET: plants

DETAILS: The large spikes along the back and tail of *Kentrosaurus* inspired this dinosaur's name. *Kentrosaurus* had hoof-shape toe claws and may have weighed more than two tons. *Kentrosaurus* appears to have been closely related to the British stegosaur, *Lexovisaurus*. Europe, North America, and East Africa were apparently united at this time, so stegosaurs from all three continents have many similarities.

"**Kentrurosaurus**" (ken-**troo**-roh-**sor**-uhss) Not a valid scientific name. See *Kentrosaurus*.

Khaan

🦖 Khaan

kahn
NAME MEANS: "ruler" in Mongolian
CLASSIFICATION: Saurischia, Theropoda, Oviraptorosauria
LENGTH: 4 ft (1.2 m) long
TIME: Late Cretaceous, 80 million years ago
PLACE: Mongolia
DIET: meat, plants, insects, eggs, fruits, nuts
DETAILS: This newly named medium-size oviraptor is known from a number of complete skeletons recently found in Mongolia. Its skull did not have a crest as several other oviraptorids did.

"Kitadanisaurus" (kit-a-**dah**-nee-**sahr**-uss) Not a valid scientific name. A Japanese meat-eater named from an arm bone and tail vertebra is most likely *Fukuiraptor*.

🦕 Klamelisaurus

klah-**may**-lee-**sor**-uhss
NAMED AFTER: the Klameli Mountains of northwestern China
CLASSIFICATION: Saurischia, Sauropoda, Camarasauridae
LENGTH: 56 ft (17 m)
TIME: Middle Jurassic, 159 million years ago
PLACE: China
DIET: plants
DETAILS: This little-known sauropod may be the adult form of *Bellusaurus*.

Koparion

koh-**pare**-ee-on
NAME MEANS: "scalpel"
CLASSIFICATION: Saurischia, Theropoda, Deinonychosauria, Troodontidae
LENGTH: 1.6 ft (48.8 cm)
TIME: Late Jurassic, 151 million years ago
PLACE: Utah, U.S.
DIET: meat
DETAILS: The name *Koparion* refers to this tiny theropod's small, knifelike teeth. Little else is known about this meat-eater, which may have been an early *Troodon* relative. It was one of the smallest of all dinosaurs.

Koparion tooth

Psssst! Check This Out!

A fellow passenger on a train ride through Wyoming in 1868 showed Othniel Charles Marsh (1831–1899) something unusual: an incredibly large bone. This helped set off the famous 19th-century "bone wars." Marsh, a well-known paleontologist at Yale University, began financing dinosaur-hunting expeditions in the American West and Midwest. He supervised many of the expeditions in search of Late Jurassic dinosaurs himself. Marsh was fiercely competitive with another fossil finder, Edward Drinker Cope (see page 27). Their workers hid dinosaur bones from each other and even shot at their rivals. Professor Marsh named several of the best-known of all dinosaurs, including "Brontosaurus" and *Apatosaurus*.

Othniel Charles Marsh

Abelisauridae Ankylosauria basal Coelurosauria basal Iguanodontia Camarasauridae Carnosauria Ceratopsia Ceratosauria Dromaeosauridae Diplodocoidea Hadrosauridae Herrerasauridae Heterodontosauridae

Kotasaurus

koh-tuh-**sor**-uhss

NAMED AFTER: Kota Formation in India

CLASSIFICATION: Saurischia, Sauropoda, Camarasauridae

LENGTH: 30 ft (9.1 m)

TIME: Early Jurassic, 188 million years ago

PLACE: India

DIET: plants

DETAILS: The skeleton of the very primitive sauropod *Kotasaurus* displays characteristics of both the giant sauropods and their smaller, more primitive ancestors, the prosauropods.

This dinosaur had weak, spoon-shape teeth like those of *Camarasaurus,* a much later sauropod. Its backbones were also shaped like those of sauropods. But its hips were more like those of prosauropods.

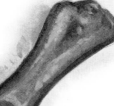

Kotasaurus front limb bone

Kritosaurus

kritt-oh-**sor**-uhss

NAME MEANS: "separated lizard"

CLASSIFICATION: Ornithischia, Hadrosauridae

LENGTH: 30 ft (9.1 m)

TIME: Late Cretaceous, 80 million years ago

PLACE: New Mexico, U.S.

DIET: plants

DETAILS: This little-known duckbill may have had a wide, flat head with a bump over its snout. It has a very confusing naming history. *Kritosaurus* was named in 1910 by Barnum Brown, a famous bone collector on assignment for New York's American Museum of Natural History. But Brown reconstructed his fossil find based on the skull of "Trachodon," unaware of the true shape of *Kritosaurus*'s snout. The name "separated lizard"

Big, Bigger, Biggest!

The biggest of all dinosaurs is *Argentinosaurus,* which weighed up to 100 tons (90.7 t). The longest is *Seismosaurus,* up to 150 feet (45.7 m) long. The longest-necked is *Mamenchisaurus* or perhaps the newfound *Sauroposeidon,* each with necks about 33 feet (10.1 m) long. At 47 feet (14.3 m) long, *Giganotosaurus* is the largest named meat-eater. *T. rex* is the still the smartest, nastiest, and most powerful of all the giant meat-eaters, however.

probably originated from Brown's incorrect theory that the cheekbones of *Kritosaurus* fit together in an unusual way, with two bones completely separated. "Trachodon" and *Gryposaurus* have at times in the past been identified as *Kritosaurus*. *Kritosaurus* skulls have also been called *Naashoibitosaurus* and "Anasazisaurus," names that other scientists have questioned.

Kulceratops

cool-**sayr**-a-tops

NAME MEANS: "lake horned face"

CLASSIFICATION: Ornithischia, Ceratopsia

LENGTH: 6 ft (1.8 m)

TIME: Early Cretaceous, 125 million years ago

PLACE: Uzbekistan

DIET: plants

DETAILS: This is a primitive and poorly known protoceratopsian, or hornless relative of the large-horned North American dinosaurs. It is among the few fossils of this group of dinosaurs known from Central Asia; the only area besides North America and Mongolia where horned dinosaurs have been discovered.

"Kunmingosaurus" (koon-**ming**-oh-**sor**-uhss) Not a valid scientific name. This large Chinese plant-eater has not been formally described.

111

Lambeosaurus

Abelisauridae Ankylosauria basal Coelurosauria basal Iguanodontia Camarasauridae Carnosauria Ceratopsia Ceratosauria Dromaeosauridae Diplodocoidea Hadrosauridae Herrerasauridae Heterodontosauridae

? Labocania

lah-boh-**kah**-nee-uh

NAMED AFTER: La Bocana Roja in Baja California, Mexico

CLASSIFICATION: Saurischia, Theropoda, Tyrannosauridae?

LENGTH: 20 ft (6.1 m)

TIME: Late Cretaceous, 73 million years ago

PLACE: California, U.S.; Mexico

DIET: meat

DETAILS: Only fragmentary fossil remains of this heavy-skulled meat-eater have been uncovered. Its skull was unusually thick for a member of the group of large carnivorous theropods. *Labocania* resembled both primitive Asian carnosaurs and North American tyrannosaurs, suggesting that these landmasses were connected during the Cretaceous.

Labocania

"Labrosaurus" (**lab**-roh-**sor**-uhss) Not a valid scientific name. See *Allosaurus*.

"Laelaps" (**lee**-laps) Not a valid scientific name. This dinosaur was going to be named after a mythical leaping hunting dog, but "Laelaps" was already being used for another animal. The dinosaur is now known as *Dryptosaurus*.

"Laevisuchus" (**lee**-vih-**sue**-cuss) Not a valid scientific name. Little is known about this Indian meat-eater.

Lambeosaurus

lam-bee-oh-**sor**-uhss

NAMED AFTER: Canadian paleontologist Lawrence Morris Lambe

CLASSIFICATION: Ornithischia, Hadrosauridae

LENGTH: 50 ft (15.2 m)

TIME: Late Cretaceous, 72 million years ago

PLACE: Montana, U.S.; Alberta, Canada; Mexico

DIET: plants

DETAILS: Best known for the high, plowlike crest at the top of its head, *Lambeosaurus* is a large member of the plant-eating duck-billed dinosaurs. The shape of its crest may have varied with age and gender. *Lambeosaurus* crests were hollow and contained paired canals that connected to the nostrils. Whether these canals helped the animal sniff odors or make noise is a matter of scientific debate. Certainly they helped identify the animals. By blowing through their canals, these and other crested duckbills might have communicated within their large herds or intimidated rivals and predators. Fossilized skin impressions show that *Lambeosaurus* was covered with polygon-shape scales.

Lambeosaurus

"Lametasaurus" (luh-**may**-tuh-**sor**-uhss) Not a valid scientific name. A few fossils of an armored dinosaur found in India are the basis of its name.

"Lanasaurus" (**lay**-na-**sor**-uhss) Not a valid scientific name. See *Lycorhinus*.

"Lancanjiangosaurus" (lahn-kahn-**jyong**-oh-**sor**-uhss) Not a valid scientific name. There is little fossil evidence for this giant Chinese Jurassic Period plant-eater.

"Laosaurus" (**lay**-oh-**sor**-uhss) Not a valid scientific name. See *Othnielia, Dryosaurus,* and perhaps *Orodromeus,* any one of which might have been the small plant-eating dinosaur to which the fragmentary fossils of "Laosaurus" truly belong.

Laplatasaurus

lah-**plot**-uh-**sor**-uhss

NAMED AFTER: La Plata, a region in eastern Argentina

CLASSIFICATION: Saurischia, Sauropoda, Macronaria

LENGTH: 60 ft (18.3 m)

TIME: Late Cretaceous, 65 million years ago

PLACE: Argentina, Madagascar, India

DIET: plants

113

Hypsilophodontidae | Lesothosauria | Macronaria | Ornithomimosauria | Oviraptorosauria | Pachycephalosauria | Primitive sauropods | Prosauropoda | Spinosauria | Stegosauria | Therizinosauridae | Troodontidae | Tyrannosauridae

DETAILS: Slimmer than most of the giant titanosaurids, *Laplatasaurus,* a primitive sauropod, may have been armored, as some other titanosaurids were. Rare skin impressions found in South America show armored plates.

Lapparentosaurus

la-pah-**rent**-oh-**sor**-uhss
NAMED AFTER: French paleontologist Albert de Lapparent
CLASSIFICATION: Saurischia, Sauropoda, Macronaria
LENGTH: 50 ft (15.2 m)
TIME: Middle Jurassic, 169 million years ago
PLACE: Madagascar
DIET: plants

Lapparentosaurus

DETAILS: Based on the remains of a juvenile, this dinosaur was first thought to belong to the genus of the English sauropod *Bothriospondylus.* Closer examination, however, revealed that *Lapparentosaurus* was a more primitive species, featuring a short snout, shortened tail, and front legs at least as long as the rear ones. *Lapparentosaurus* appears to have been closely related to *Brachiosaurus.*

Leaellynasaura

lee-**ell**-in-uh-**sor**-uh
NAMED AFTER: Leaellyn Rich, daughter of Australian paleontologists Thomas and Patricia Rich
CLASSIFICATION: Ornithischia, Hypsilophodontidae
LENGTH: 10 ft (3 m)
TIME: Early Cretaceous, 110 million years ago
PLACE: Australia
DIET: plants

DETAILS: This primitive little plant-eater was no bigger than a baby kangaroo. *Leaellynasaura* bore ridges on both sides of its upper cheek teeth, a distinctive feature shared only with *Othnielia.* *Leaellynasaura* had an unusually big brain for a dinosaur of its size, and its large eyes suggest that it had keen

Leaellynasaura

vision. Since it lived while Australia was within the Antarctic Circle, good eyesight would have helped this dinosaur survive in the long winter darkness. In the late 1970s, two-year-old Leaellyn Rich asked her paleontologist parents in Melbourne, Australia, to name a dinosaur after her. Years later, she got her wish.

"Leipsanosaurus" (lipe-**san**-oh-**sor**-uhss) Not a valid scientific name. See *Struthiosaurus.*

Leptoceratops

lept-oh-**sayr**-a-tops
NAME MEANS: "small horned face"
CLASSIFICATION: Ornithischia, Ceratopsia
LENGTH: 10 ft (3 m)
TIME: Late Cretaceous, 65 million years ago
PLACE: Wyoming, U.S.; Alberta, Canada
DIET: plants

DETAILS: *Leptoceratops* had a beaklike mouth and a small neck frill, but no nose horn or brow horns. It may have walked on two legs or on all fours, or switched between the two, depending upon need. Perhaps the most primitive of known

Can I Have a Dinosaur, Dad?

Leaellyn and Tim Rich are lucky kids. Their parents are Australian paleontologists. Thomas and Patricia Rich have found many dinosaur remains and named two new animals, *Leaellynasaura* and *Timimus,* after their two children.

The Riches have dug for many years into rocky cliffs to expose the relatively few and small dinosaur fossils Australia has. Tom Rich has also excavated for dinosaurs in the cold north of Alaska. To dig out the

Thomas and Patricia Rich at the dedication of a new Melbourne Science Center in Australia that Patricia helped found.

dinosaurs, the Riches had to use dynamite in the hard cliffs. Teams of workers hauled out the rocks and searched for dinosaur bones in the exposed tunnels and shafts.

Abelisauridae Ankylosauria basal Coelurosauria basal Iguanodontia Camarasauridae Carnosauria Ceratopsia Ceratosauria Dromaeosauridae Diplodocoidea Hadrosauridae Herrerasauridae Heterodontosauridae

protoceratopsids, this small plant-eating dinosaur lived at the same time as the larger horned dinosaurs. *Leptoceratops* was named in 1914 by famed fossil hunter "Mr. Dinosaur" Barnum Brown of New York's American Museum of Natural History.

"Leptospondylus" (**lept**-oh-**spon**-dill-us) Not a valid scientific name. See *Massospondylus*.

Lesothosaurus

luh-**soh**-toe-**sor**-uhss

NAMED AFTER: Lesotho, a region of South Africa

CLASSIFICATION: Ornithischia, Lesothosauria

LENGTH: 3 ft (1 m)

TIME: Early Jurassic, 200 million years ago

PLACE: South Africa

DIET: plants

DETAILS: This small plant-eater was one of the earliest known ornithischians, or bird-hipped dinosaurs. It was slender, lightly built, and quick. Its large eyes were set in a four-inch-long (10.2 cm) skull. Its long snout with a beaklike, horn-covered tip was ideal for cropping vegetation. *Lesothosaurus* had short forelimbs with a partially opposable thumb, suggesting that it had superior grasping power. Though it is generally thought to have been a plant-eater, *Lesothosaurus* may also have fed on insects or scavenged meat.

Lesothosaurus

Lessemsaurus

less-um-**sor**-uhss

NAMED AFTER: author and dinosaur philanthropist "Dino" Don Lessem

CLASSIFICATION: Saurischia, Prosauropoda

LENGTH: 20 ft (6.1 m)

TIME: Late Triassic, 208 million years ago

PLACE: Argentina

DIET: plants

DETAILS: This large and primitive plant-eater was

recently found and then named for this book's author, honoring his contributions to the establishment of dinosaur-related charities. *Lessemsaurus* was a prosauropod, one of the ancestors of the largest plant-eaters, the sauropods. Judging by the distinctive shape of its vertebrae, it was among the most advanced of prosauropods. The sauropod-style vertebrae inspired the species name, *sauropoides*.

Lessemsaurus

Lexovisaurus

lek-**so**-vih-**sor**-uhss

NAMED AFTER: the Lexovii, an ancient Celtic people

CLASSIFICATION: Ornithischia, Stegosauria

LENGTH: 17 ft (5.2 m)

TIME: Middle Jurassic, 169 million years ago

PLACE: England; France

DIET: plants

DETAILS: The back plates on this stegosaur were almost twice as high as they were wide. Its shoulder spines were exceptionally large, up to 10.5 inches (26.7 cm) high and more than a yard (91.4 cm) long. Some scientists think that the enormous size of these plates suggests that they were decorations. The plates also may have helped regulate the dinosaur's body temperature by providing a large surface for release of excess heat.

Lexovisaurus back plate

115

Liaoningosaurus

leeow-**ning**-oh-**sor**-uss

NAMED FOR: Liaoning Province of northern China

CLASSIFICATION: Ornithischia, Ankylosauria

LENGTH: 13 inches (33 cm) juvenile

TIME: Early Cretaceous, 130 million years ago

PLACE: northeastern China

DIET: plants

DETAILS: Only lately known from a skeleton of a very small and young but well-preserved animal, this

little armored dinosaur had highly unusual armor plates along its belly and hind feet. This armor appears to form a single sheet, which would mean *Liaonighosaurus* had to walk splay-legged, unlike other dinosaurs. Its teeth and tail resemble those of the clubless armored nodosaurs. Scientists speculate it may belong to a family of armored dinosaurs distinct from all others now known.

Liliensternus

Ligabueino

lee-gah-**boo**-ay-**ee**-no
NAME MEANS: "Ligabue's little one," after Italian businessman and dinosaur research supporter Giancarlo Ligabue
CLASSIFICATION: Saurischia, Theropoda, Ceratosauria, Abelisauridae
LENGTH: 30 in. (76.2 cm)
TIME: Early Cretaceous, 127 million years ago
PLACE: Argentina
DIET: meat
DETAILS: This tiny hunter was discovered in Neuquén Province of Patagonia in western Argentina. It is possibly related to *Noasaurus,* an unusual meat-eater with "raptor"-like claws, though the animals are not closely related to the North American and Asian "raptor" dromaeosaurids.

Ligabueino pelvis

"Likhoelesaurus" (**lick**-hoh-li-**sor**-uhss) Not a valid scientific name. A name taken from a little-known and small collection of South African fossils.

Liliensternus

lill-ee-en-**stern**-us
NAMED AFTER: German paleontologist Hugo Ruehle von Lilienstern
CLASSIFICATION: Saurischia, Theropoda, Ceratosauria
LENGTH: 16 ft (4.9 m)
TIME: Late Triassic, 222 million years ago
PLACE: Germany

DIET: meat
DETAILS: This early carnivorous dinosaur had a long neck and tail and shortened forelimbs. It may have resembled *Dilophosaurus* and *Coelophysis*. Its hands still had five fingers, a primitive feature of early dinosaurs.

Lirainosaurus

lee-**rye**-noh-**sor**-uhss
NAME MEANS: "slender lizard"
CLASSIFICATION: Saurischia, Sauropoda, Macronaria
LENGTH: 50 ft (15.2 m)
TIME: Late Cretaceous, 80 million years ago
PLACE: Spain
DIET: plants

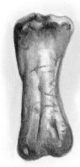

Lirainosaurus leg bone

DETAILS: The small titanosaur, discovered in the Basque region of Spain, was identified based on remains from both adults and juveniles. These fossils included a fragment of a skull, complete with pencil-like teeth. Skin armor was also found. A lightly built leg bone of *Lirainosaurus* is one of the most slender on a sauropod, the most heavily built of all dinosaurs.

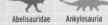

"Loncosaurus" (**long**-koh-**sor**-uhss) Not a valid scientific name.

"Longosaurus" (**long**-oh-**sor**-uhss) Not a valid scientific name. See *Coelophysis*.

Lophorhothon

loaf-oh-**roh**-thon
NAME MEANS: "crested nose"
CLASSIFICATION: Ornithischia, Hadrosauridae
LENGTH: 15 ft (4.6 m)
TIME: Late Cretaceous, 73 million years ago
PLACE: Alabama, U.S.
DIET: plants
DETAILS: A flat-headed duck-billed dinosaur, *Lophorhothon* had a deep skull with wide eye sockets and a short snout. A triangular horn or crest rose above this dinosaur's nose, much like the horn decorations of *Prosaurolophus*. But *Lophorhothon*'s horn is placed farther forward on the snout. Still, some scientists think *Lophorhothon* may actually be a juvenile *Prosaurolophus*.

Lophorhothon

"Loricosaurus" (**lore**-ick-oh-**sor**-uhss) Not a valid scientific name. See *Neuquensaurus*.

Losillasaurus

Loh-**seel**-yah-**sor**-uhss
NAMED AFTER: Losilla, a town in Valencia Province, Spain
CLASSIFICATION: Saurischia, Sauropoda, Diplodocoidea
LENGTH: 77 ft (23.5 m)
TIME: Late Jurassic, 145 million years ago
PLACE: Spain
DIET: plants
DETAILS: This huge sauropod, with a very long neck, was located recently in eastern Spain. In time, appearance, and size it was much like *Diplodocus* of the western United States.

Lourinhanosaurus

loh-reen-**yah**-no-**sor**-uhss
NAMED AFTER: the Lourinha region in Portugal
CLASSIFICATION: Saurischia, Theropoda, Carnosauria
LENGTH: 14 ft (4.3 m)
TIME: Late Jurassic, 145 million years ago
PLACE: Portugal
DIET: meat

Lourinhanosaurus pelvis

DETAILS: This carnivore is based on an incomplete skeleton without a skull discovered in west-central Portugal. Scientists think *Lourinhanosaurus* was a modest-size meat-eater. The shape of its pelvis and hind limbs suggest that it was a relative of allosaurs, which lived in North America at the same time. Thirty-two stomach stones called gastroliths were found in the animals' rib cage. Gastroliths were used by some dinosaurs to grind food into easily digested pulp. The presence of stomach stones in meat-eaters is uncommon but not unheard of. The first observation of gastroliths in large theropods came in 1835, when scientists found up to 10 of the polished stones in the belly region of *Poekilopleuron*.

Lourinhasaurus

loh-**reen**-yah-**sor**-uhss
NAME MEANS: "Lourinha lizard"
CLASSIFICATION: Saurischia, Sauropoda, Camarasauridae
LENGTH: 75 ft (22.9 m)

Nature Calls

Octavio Mateus is not a household name . . . yet! While still a student of paleontology at Lisbon University, Mateus (b. 1975) has named many dinosaurs in his native Portugal. He has excavated eggs and embryos of small meat-eating dinosaurs in the coastal village of Lourinha, north of Lisbon. Actually, his mother first discovered them. She was walking with Octavio's young sister. When the little girl stopped to go to the bathroom, the mother spotted the fossils. Mateus's discoveries indicate that dinosaurs in Europe looked much like those of North America in the Late Jurassic Period, 145 million years ago.

Hypsilophodontidae | Lesothosauria | Macronaria | Ornithomimosauria | Oviraptorosauria | Pachycephalosauria | Primitive sauropods | Prosauropoda | Spinosauria | Stegosauria | Therizinosauridae | Troodontidae | Tyrannosauridae

Lufengosaurus

Abelisauridae Ankylosauria basal Coelurosauria basal Iguanodontia Camarasauridae Carnosauria Ceratopsia Ceratosauria Dromaeosauridae Diplodocoidea Hadrosauridae Herrerasauridae Heterodontosauridae

TIME: Late Jurassic, 145 million years ago

PLACE: Portugal

DIET: plants

DETAILS: *Lourinhasaurus* was a long-necked sauropod assigned first to *Apatosaurus,* then to *Camarasaurus*. It is now considered a separate genus, though closely related to Late Jurassic North American giant plant-eaters.

"Lucianosaurus" (**loo**-shan-oh-sor-uhss) Not a valid scientific name. A possible ornithischian dinosaur about which little is known.

"Lufengocephalus" (loo-**fung**-oh-**seff**-a-luss) Not a valid scientific name. See *Lufengosaurus*.

Lufengosaurus

loo-**fung**-oh-**sor**-uhss

NAMED AFTER: Lufeng Basin region of southern China

CLASSIFICATION: Ornithischia, Prosauropoda

LENGTH: 20 ft (6.1 m)

TIME: Early Jurassic, 200 million years ago

PLACE: China

DIET: plants

DETAILS: *Lufengosaurus* was a large early plant-eater. It appears to have been closely related to the prosauropod *Plateosaurus*. Its skull was small with large eyes and a jaw containing serrated teeth. Like most prosauropods, this dinosaur's neck was long, its tail was massive, and its legs were thick and sturdy. The thumb and back toe of *Lufengosaurus* were especially powerful.

? Lukousaurus

loo-koh-**sor**-uhss

NAMED AFTER: Lukou Bridge, China

CLASSIFICATION: Saurischia, Theropoda

LENGTH: 6.5 ft (2 m)

TIME: Early Jurassic, 194 million years ago

PLACE: China

DIET: meat

DETAILS: Only a partial skull of this meat-eater has been found. It contained 15 flattened,

Lukousaurus

backward-pointing teeth. This dinosaur's muzzle was slender, its eye sockets were well-rounded, and the nasal openings were toward the front of its snout. It has been suggested that *Lukousaurus* may not be a dinosaur at all, but rather a related form of archosaur.

Lurdusaurus

loor-duh-**sor**-uhss

NAME MEANS: "heavy lizard"

CLASSIFICATION: Ornithischia, basal Iguanodontia

LENGTH: 29.5 ft (9 m)

TIME: Early Cretaceous, 112 million years ago

PLACE: Niger

DIET: plants

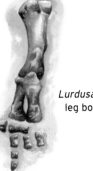

Lurdusaurus leg bones

DETAILS: Originally known as *Gravisaurus, Lurdusaurus* was a bulky, powerful iguanodontid with features similar to those of the giant ground sloth. Estimated to have weighed about 5.5 tons (5 t), *Lurdusaurus* was probably a slow mover. When it stood on all four legs, its underbelly may have hung only two feet (61 cm) above the ground. Its skull was small compared to its body.

"Lusitanosaurus" (loo-si-**tan**-uh-**sor**-uhss) Not a valid scientific name for a fragmentary possible jaw of an early armored dinosaur from Portugal.

Lycorhinus

like-oh-**rye**-nuss

NAME MEANS: "wolf snout"

CLASSIFICATION: Ornithischia, Heterodontosauria

LENGTH: 4 ft (1.2 m)

TIME: Early Jurassic, 200 million years ago

PLACE: South Africa

DIET: plants

Lycorhinus lower jaw section

DETAILS: Distinguished by its large canine teeth, *Lycorhinus* belonged to a group of primitive, two-legged plant-eaters. At one time, it was mistaken for a cynodont, a mammal-like reptile. *Lycorhinus* is now known to have been among the smallest of all dinosaurs.

Hypsilophodontidae   Lesothosauria   Macronaria   Ornithomimosauria   Oviraptorosauria   Pachycephalosauria   Primitive sauropods   Prosauropoda   Spinosauria   Stegosauria   Therizinosauridae   Troodontidae   Tyrannosauridae

Maiasaura

"Macrodontophion" (**mack**-roh-don-**toh**-fee-on) Not a valid scientific name. Based upon a single Ukranian tooth, this animal was identified as a large megalosaur but may not be a dinosaur at all.

"Macrophalangia" (**mack**-roh-fa-**lan**-jee-uh) Not a valid scientific name. See *Chirostenotes*.

Macrurosaurus

mack-**roor**-oh-**sor**-uhss
NAME MEANS: "long-tailed lizard"
CLASSIFICATION: Saurischia, Sauropoda, Macronaria
LENGTH: 50 ft (15.2 m)
TIME: Early Cretaceous, 138 million years ago
PLACE: England
DIET: plants
DETAILS: One of the first titanosaurs

Macrurosaurus
tail vertebra

ever found, this four-legged plant-eater is known mostly from fossilized tail vertebrae. Famed 19th-century British paleontologist Harry Govier Seeley estimated that the tail of this giant dinosaur may have been more than 15 feet (4.8 m) long.

"Magnosaurus" (**mag**-noh-**sor**-uhss) Not a valid scientific name. Little is known about this large Jurassic Period meat-eater from Britain.

Magyarosaurus

mag-yar-o-**sor**-uhss
NAMED AFTER: the Magyar people of Hungary
CLASSIFICATION: Saurischia, Sauropoda, Macronaria
LENGTH: 20 ft (6.1 m)
TIME: Late Cretaceous, 65 million years ago
PLACE: Hungary, Romania
DIET: plants
DETAILS: A member of the titanosaurids, a group of large, sometimes armored, sauropods. Like other Late Cretaceous European dinosaurs, it is unusually small and primitive for its group and time period. This "dwarfing" may be the result of the isolation of

these animals in what was then a group of islands and peninsulas. Scientists know little about the creature. Fossils assigned to this dinosaur may belong to several different kinds of dinosaur, all found in Transylvania.

Magyarosaurus
vertebrae fragments

Maiasaura

may-uh-**sor**-uh
NAME MEANS: "good-mother lizard"
CLASSIFICATION: Ornithischia, Hadrosauridae
LENGTH: 30 ft (9.1 m)
TIME: Late Cretaceous, 73 million years ago
PLACE: Montana, U.S.
DIET: plants
DETAILS: Judging from its many fossils, *Maiasaura* was a rather plain-looking duck-billed dinosaur, with a wide face and a short beak but no crest. Its skull was large, about 32 inches (81.3 cm) long. But *Maiasaura* was remarkable for the information its fossils provided regarding dinosaur behavior and parental care. Dr. John R. Horner found the skeletal remains of 11 *Maiasaura* babies, each just over three ft (91.4 cm) long, together in a nestlike setting. He discovered four more babies just seven feet (2.2 m) from the nest. Horner also found thousands of fragments of fossilized eggshell as well as unhatched *Maiasaura* eggs.

　　Maiasaura lived in huge herds or nesting groups.

121

Proud Parents

Scientists now think that many dinosaurs, such as *Maiasaura*, may have taken care of their newborn young. Just as most birds look after their hatchlings, dinosaurs may have fed their tiny babies. Plant-eating dinosaurs may have brought crushed plants to their helpless nestlings. Meat-eaters may have fed bits of prechewed meat to their youngsters. The newly hatched offspring of some dinosaurs, however, may have been born capable of walking, feeding, and caring for themselves.

Just 13 inches (33 cm) long when they hatched, young *Maiasaura* reached a length of 10 feet (3 m) by the end of their first year. Their rapid growth suggests a metabolism like that of warm-blooded animals such as modern birds. Because the tiny hatchlings had soft bone tips, they may have been unable to move around on their own. Parents or siblings may have cared for the youngsters until they were able to leave the nest and join the herd. The study of *Maiasaura* has revolutionized our view of how dinosaurs lived and grew.

"Majungasaurus" (mah-**joong**-gah-**sor**-uhss) Not a valid scientific name. Now known as *Majungatholus*.

Majungatholus

mah-**joong**-gah-**thoh**-luss
NAME MEANS: "Majunga dome"
CLASSIFICATION: Saurischia, Theropoda, Ceratosauria, Abelisauridae
LENGTH: 30 ft (9.1 m)
TIME: Late Cretaceous, 71 million years ago
PLACE: Madagascar
DIET: meat
DETAILS: This large meat-eater features a prominent domelike forehead with bony bumps and grooves. When it was discovered, *Majungatholus* was judged to be a giant member of the dome-headed pachycephalosaurs; those plant-eaters often have such fancy skull decorations. The recent unearthing of a second, more complete skull, as well as a skeleton, revealed that this was actually a meat-eating dinosaur. *Majungatholus* appears to have been an abelisaur, a large meat-eater related to dinosaurs of South America such as *Carnotaurus* and *Abelisaurus*. The function of its unusual forehead bone remains a mystery.

Majungatholus

Malawisaurus

mah-**lah**-wee-**sor**-uhss
NAMED AFTER: Malawi, the African nation

Skull and Bones

Soft-spoken Dr. Elizabeth Gomani, still in her thirties, is the only dinosaur scientist in her African country Malawi. She is also the leading researcher on Malawi's most significant dinosaur discovery, *Malawisaurus*. While studying computers, chemistry, and geology at the University of Malawi, Dr. Gomani participated in the excavation of *Malawisaurus*'s skeleton. Dinosaurs are hard to find in southeast Africa. Dr. Gomani led research into the find of the dinosaur named for her country. She is now researching several other dinosaur finds in Malawi, including discoveries that date back more than 70 years.

CLASSIFICATION: Saurischia, Sauropoda, Macronaria
LENGTH: 45 ft (13.7 m)
TIME: Early Cretaceous, 110 million years ago
PLACE: Malawi
DIET: plants
DETAILS: *Malawisaurus* was a long-necked primitive titanosaur, one of a worldwide group of giant plant-eaters. Few skulls of titanosaurs have ever been found, but a skull and nearly complete skeleton of a young *Malawisaurus* were discovered in the 1990s.

Malawisaurus jaw fragment

"Maleevosaurus" (mal-**yay**-ev-oh-**sor**-uhss) Not a valid scientific name. Researchers now think it was a young *Tarbosaurus,* a close Asian cousin of the North American *Tyrannosaurus rex*.

Maleevus

mal-**yay**-ev-us
NAMED AFTER: Russian paleontologist Evgenii Aleksandrovich Maleev
CLASSIFICATION: Ornithischia, Ankylosauria
LENGTH: 20 ft (6.1 m)
TIME: Late Cretaceous, 97.5 million years ago
PLACE: Mongolia
DIET: plants
DETAILS: This little-known armored dinosaur was once thought to be *Pinacosaurus*.

Abelisauridae | Ankylosauria | basal Coelurosauria | basal Iguanodontia | Camarasauridae | Carnosauria | Ceratopsia | Ceratosauria | Dromaeosauridae | Diplodocoidea | Hadrosauridae | Herrerasauridae | Heterodontosauridae

Mamenchisaurus

mah-**munch**-ih-**sor**-uhss

NAMED AFTER: Mamenchi, a ferry crossing in southern China

CLASSIFICATION: Saurischia, Sauropoda, Camarasauridae

LENGTH: 68 ft (20.7 m)

TIME: Late Jurassic, 160 million years ago

PLACE: China

DIET: plants

DETAILS: This is the longest-necked dinosaur yet known, with the possible exception of the less complete and recently discovered *Sauroposeidon*. *Mamenchisaurus*'s immensely long and thin neck made up almost half of its entire body length. Its neck alone was as long as a school bus. It also had the smallest head compared with its body of any animal, making it the most pea-headed of all creatures. *Mamenchisaurus* is similar in appearance to members of the giant, whip-tailed diplodocid family. The bones of its foot and ankle resemble those of *Tienshanosaurus*; its skull is unlike that of any other known dinosaur.

"Mandschurosaurus" (man-**chew**-roh-**sor**-uhss)
Not a valid scientific name. This dinosaur is named from many bones found in mass bone beds without any skulls. It is not clear which or how many

Mamenchisaurus

species of duck-billed dinosaur produced these fossils. It is the first dinosaur fossil found in China, discovered early in the 20th century in Manchuria.

"Marmarospondylus" (**mar**-mar-oh-**spon**-dill-uhss) Not a valid scientific name. Now called *Bothriospondylus*.

Marshosaurus

marsh-oh-**sor**-uhss

NAME MEANS: "Marsh's lizard"
CLASSIFICATION: Saurischia, Theropoda, Carnosauria
LENGTH: 17 ft (5.2 m)
TIME: Late Jurassic, 145 million years ago
PLACE: Utah, Colorado, U.S.
DIET: meat
DETAILS: This dinosaur was found in the same rocks that produced fossils of *Allosaurus*. It appears to have had a number of advanced features different from *Allosaurus*. Without additional remains, however, further classification will be difficult. *Marshosaurus* was named in 1976 in honor of the pioneering American dinosaur paleontologist Othniel C. Marsh of Yale University.

Masiakasaurus

muh-**shee**-uh-kuh-**sor**-uss

NAME MEANS: "vicious lizard"
CLASSIFICATION: Saurischia, Theropoda, Ceratosauria, Abelisauridae
LENGTH: 6 ft (1.8 m)
TIME: 66 million years ago
PLACE: Madagascar
DIET: meat
DETAILS: This is one of the strangest-looking of all meat-eaters. Spikelike teeth with hooked tips projected from the front of its jaws. In many other skeletal features, *Masiakasaurus* appears similar to the abelisaur meat-eaters of South America. This close relationship indicates that Madagascar was closely linked to South America as well as Africa (which lies between these areas) during the Cretaceous Period. Its species name, *knopfleri*, honors musician Mark Knopfler from the band Dire Straits,

Masiakasaurus

Mega Appetite!

The first person to scientifically describe a dinosaur was British minister William Buckland (1784–1856). Buckland, also a professor of geology at Oxford University, published a description of *Megalosaurus* in 1824, based on a toothed jawbone and scattered vertebrae, limb bones, and ribs. The professor was inspired in his studies by the work of British physician Gideon Mantell (1790–1852), who named *Iguanodon* around the same time. Buckland's *Megalosaurus* bones can still be seen at the Oxford University Museum.

William Buckland

Professor Buckland was a brilliant man, but he had strange tastes and hobbies. He kept a bear for a pet. Buckland also liked to eat zoo animals, which he raised and dined on at fancy banquets.

whose music was played often at the dig site while this dinosaur was uncovered.

Massospondylus

mass-oh-**spon**-dill-uhss

NAME MEANS: "elongated vertebra"
CLASSIFICATION: Saurischia, Prosauropoda
LENGTH: 20 ft (6.1 m)
TIME: Early Jurassic, 194 million years ago
PLACE: South Africa; Arizona, U.S.
DIET: plants

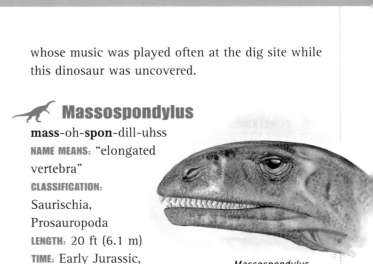
Massospondylus

DETAILS: *Massospondylus* had a small head with large, almost circular eye sockets, and relatively large teeth and nostrils. This slender prosauropod was named by famed scientist Sir Richard Owen in 1854. The first fossil found of this animal was destroyed in World War II bombings, but many more *Massospondylus* have since been identified.

"Megadontosaurus" (**meg**-a-**dont**-o-**sor**-uhss) Not a valid scientific name. A mixture of *Microvenator* and *Deinonychus* fossils.

Megalosaurus

meg-a-loh-**sor**-uhss
NAME MEANS: "great lizard"
CLASSIFICATION: Saurischia, Theropoda, Carnosauria
LENGTH: 33 ft (10 m)
TIME: Middle Jurassic, 155 million years ago
PLACE: England, France, Portugal
DIET: meat
DETAILS: *Megalosaurus* was the first dinosaur ever named. A jawbone with teeth was uncovered in England in the 1820s. When *Megalosaurus* was reconstructed and named in 1824, the dinosaur's body length was estimated at more than 60 feet (18.3 m), a great exaggeration. Once researchers removed bones that turned out not to have belonged to the original animal, its size was revised to a more realistic but still impressive 26 feet (7.9 m). *Megalosaurus* had long, powerful jaws and sharp, double-edged teeth. Unfortunately, as a complete skeleton has yet to be recovered, much remains to be learned about this famous dinosaur.

Megaraptor

meg-a-**rap**-tore
NAME MEANS: "big plunderer"
CLASSIFICATION: Saurischia, Theropoda, basal Coelurosauria
LENGTH: 26 ft (7.9 m)
TIME: Late Cretaceous, 86 million years ago
PLACE: Argentina
DIET: meat

Megaraptor claw

DETAILS: This puzzling and frightening predator is known from a single partial skeleton. Its most amazing feature is a huge 15-inch-long (38.1 cm) claw. The enormous slashing claw, twice the size of the toe claw of the biggest "raptor" dromaeosaurid, suggests that this animal was a fierce hunter. How it developed this claw is a mystery. *Megaraptor* was

apparently not closely related to the dromaeosaurid "raptors," which lived only in the Northern Hemisphere. Yet its claw is very similar in shape, a remarkable coincidence. Without a skull and more fossils, it is difficult for scientists to know what *Megaraptor*'s relationship is to other dinosaurs.

Melanorosaurus

mel-a-nor-oh-**sor**-uhss
NAME MEANS: "Black Mountain lizard"
CLASSIFICATION: Saurischia, Prosauropoda
LENGTH: 40 ft (12.2 m)
TIME: Late Triassic, 219 million years ago
PLACE: South Africa
DIET: plants
DETAILS: Unlike most prosauropods, this dinosaur probably walked on all fours. *Melanorosaurus* is considered to have been one of the heaviest prosauropods and resembles the larger sauropods because of its small head, long neck and tail, powerful legs, and sturdy skeleton.

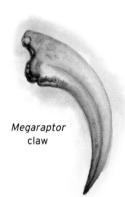

Melanorosaurus

Making Tracks

What kinds of hands and feet did dinosaurs have? Just check out their fossils and tracks. Meat-eating dinosaurs often left three-toed footprints, similar to today's bird tracks, only larger. Plant-eaters made three-toed or four-toed marks. The giant plant-eaters had feet like elephants', broad and rounded with thick pads at the base to support their great weight. Some plant-eaters' tracks are so wide and deep that two kids could take a bath in just one footprint!

Iguanodon had a big, thick thumb spike. Other dinosaurs had their own peculiar foot and hand gear. *Megaraptor* from Argentina had the largest killing claws, each more than 15 inches (40 cm) long. Large meat-eaters such as *T. rex* had four toes. The first toe had a tiny fourth claw that didn't even reach the ground.

Metriacanthosaurus

met-ree-uh-**can**-thoh-**sor**-uhss

NAME MEANS: "moderate-spine lizard"

CLASSIFICATION: Saurischia, Theropoda, Carnosauria

LENGTH: 26 ft (7.9 m)

TIME: Late Jurassic, 160 million years ago

PLACE: England

DIET: meat

DETAILS: This large carnivore appeared to be so similar to *Megalosaurus* that at first it was thought to be a new species of that dinosaur. But *Metriacanthosaurus* is unique because the shape of its high backbone spines. These spines were about 10 inches (25.4 cm) long,

Metriacanthosaurus leg bone

twice as high as the vertebrae themselves. When the animal was alive, these backbones would have been covered with muscle tissue and skin. The spiny bones would have given the dinosaur a distinctive ridge-back appearance.

"Microceratops" (mike-roh-**sayr**-a-tops) Not a valid scientific name. A tiny horned dinosaur whose fossils are now mostly thought to belong to *Gracileratops*.

"Microcoelus" (mike-ro-**see**-luhss) Not a valid scientific name. See *Saltasaurus*.

"Microhadrosaurus" (mike-roh-**had**-roh-**sor**-uhss) Not a valid scientific name. This Chinese dinosaur was named from a jaw fragment and tiny teeth that may have belonged to a young, flat-headed duckbill.

Micropachycephalosaurus

mike-roh-**pack**-ee-**seff**-a-low-**sor**-uhss

NAME MEANS: "small pachycephalosaurid"

CLASSIFICATION: Ornithischia, Pachycephalosauria

LENGTH: 2 ft (61 cm)

TIME: Late Cretaceous, 73 million years ago

PLACE: China

DIET: plants

DETAILS: A tiny thick-skulled plant-eater discovered in China, this specimen is one of only two pachycephalosaur species yet known from that country. Although it is one of the smallest known dinosaurs, *Micropachycephalosaurus* has the longest scientific name of any dinosaur.

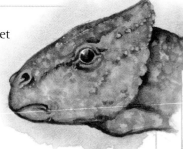

Micropachycephalosaurus

Microraptor

my-kroh-**rap**-tor

NAME MEANS: "small thief"

SIZE: 22 inches (55.9 cm)

PLACE: Liaoning Province, southern China

TIME: Early Cretaceous, 124 million years ago

CLASSIFICATION: Theropoda, Deinonychosauria, Dromaeosauridae

DIET: small animals; maybe insects, fish, shellfish

DETAILS: *Microraptor* is the smallest known theropod dinosaur. It had a featherlike covering and curved claws that it may have used to climb trees. Most scientists think *Microraptor* may be a close relative of the small, and as yet unknown, dinosaurs that many scientists think evolved into birds. Birds already existed at the time of *Microraptor*.

This dinosaur's fossils were found in China. Part of its tail was once mistakenly glued onto a bird fossil and called "Archaeoraptor." Scientists later proved that "Archaeoraptor" was created by combining part of *Microraptor*'s fossil with a bird fossil.

"Microsaurops" (mike-ro-**sore**-ops) Not a valid scientific name; an accidental misspelling of *Microcoelus*.

Microvenator

mike-roh-vee-**nay**-tore

NAME MEANS: "small hunter"

CLASSIFICATION: Saurischia, Theropoda, Oviraptorosauria

LENGTH: 10 ft (3 m)

TIME: Early Cretaceous, 113 million years ago

PLACE: Montana, U.S.

DIET: meat

DETAILS: This small and lightly built carnivore probably weighed less than 15 pounds (6.8 kg). It is known from the skeleton of a youngster just four feet (1.2 m) long. It may have been closely related to caenagnathid meat-eaters and the ostrichlike dinosaurs.

Microvenator

"**Mongolosaurus**" (**mong**-go-loh-**sor**-uhss) Not a valid scientific name. Based upon teeth alone, this is probably a Mongolian sauropod, a giant plant-eater, though some researchers think it may be a therizinosaur, a mysterious member of the meat-eater group.

Monkonosaurus

mong-**cone**-oh-**sor**-uhss

NAMED AFTER: Monko, a county in Tibet

CLASSIFICATION: Ornithischia, Stegosauria

LENGTH: 17 ft (5.2 m)

TIME: Early Cretaceous, 138 million years ago

PLACE: Tibet

DIET: plants

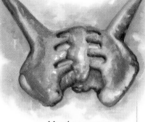

Monkonosaurus hips

DETAILS: First thought to be a bone-headed or pachycephalosaur dinosaur, *Monkonosaurus* was later identified as a medium-size stegosaur. *Monkonosaurus*, found in 1976, was Tibet's first dinosaur discovery.

127

Minmi

min-me

NAMED AFTER: Minmi Crossing, Queensland, Australia

CLASSIFICATION: Ornithischia, Ankylosauria

LENGTH: 10 ft (3 m)

TIME: Early Cretaceous, 113 million years ago

PLACE: Australia

DIET: plants

DETAILS: Unusually small for a clubless armored dinosaur, this sturdy four-legged plant-eater had bony armor beneath the skin on its belly. It is the only nodosaur known with this feature. *Minmi* is also the only armored dinosaur yet known from Australia. *Minmi* is the shortest dinosaur name.

"**Mochlodon**" (**mok**-loh-don) Not a valid scientific name. See *Rhabdodon*.

"**Monoclonius**" (mon-oh-**clone**-ee-us) Not a valid scientific name. This dinosaur, famous for its single horn, was most likely a juvenile specimen of the horned dinosaur *Centrosaurus*.

Monolophosaurus

mon-oh-**lofe**-oh-**sor**-uhss

NAME MEANS: "single-crest lizard"

CLASSIFICATION: Saurischia, Theropoda, Carnosauria

LENGTH: 16 ft (4.9 m)

TIME: Middle Jurassic, 170 million years ago

PLACE: China

DIET: meat

DETAILS: This medium-size meat-eater had a large skull with a distinctive half-circle crest above the snout and eyes. Some paleontologists suggest that this unusual structure served as a display to attract

Mononykus

Abelisauridae Ankylosauria basal Coelurosauria basal Iguanodontia Camarasauridae Carnosauria Ceratopsia Ceratosauria Dromaeosauridae Diplodocoidea Hadrosauridae Herrerasauridae Heterodontosauridae

Monolophosaurus

mates or to help protect territory. Such crests may have been brightly colored on the living dinosaurs.

"Mononychus" (mo-**non**-ick-us) Not a valid scientific name. See *Mononykus*.

Mononykus

mo-**non**-ick-us or **mon**-oh-**nye**-cuss
NAME MEANS: "one claw"
CLASSIFICATION: Saurischia, Theropoda, basal Coelurosauria
LENGTH: 3 ft (1 m)
TIME: Late Cretaceous, 70 million years ago
PLACE: Mongolia
DIET: insects?
DETAILS: *Mononkyus* was a wingless, birdlike animal whose short, stubby arms each ended in a powerful, curved claw. The unique claws and heavily muscled arms of this dinosaur may have been used for digging or for tearing bark to reach a hidden meal of insects. Some researchers originally believed *Mononykus* was closely related to birds. However, there is a consensus now that *Mononykus* was a dinosaur that coincidentally developed birdlike features.

Montanoceratops

mon-**tan**-oh-**sayr**-a-tops
NAME MEANS: "Montana horned face"
CLASSIFICATION: Ornithischia, Ceratopsia
LENGTH: 6 ft (1.8 m)
TIME: Late Cretaceous, 70 million years ago
PLACE: Montana, U.S.; Alberta, Canada
DIET: plants
DETAILS: This small horned dinosaur resembles the more primitive *Protoceratops*, its Asian relative. Compared with that dinosaur, *Montanoceratops* had a larger, stockier snout equipped with a small nose horn, longer forelimbs, and a thicker skeleton. It is considered to be more advanced than *Protoceratops*. The presence of protoceratopsians like *Montanoceratops* in North America indicates that these animals crossed between Asia and North America.

"Morinosaurus" (**more**-in-oh-**sor**-uhss) Not a valid scientific name, based on a single tooth of a large plant-eater.

"Morosaurus" (**more**-oh-**sor**-uhss) "Stupid reptile" Not a valid scientific name. See *Camarasaurus*.

Montanoceratops

Hypsilophodontidae | Lesothosauria | Macronaria | Ornithomimosauria | Oviraptorosauria | Pachycephalosauria | Primitive sauropods | Prosauropoda | Spinosauria | Stegosauria | Therizinosauridae | Troodontidae | Tyrannosauridae

Mussaurus

moo-**sor**-uhss

NAME MEANS: "mouse lizard"

CLASSIFICATION: Saurischia, Prosauropoda, Plateosauridae

LENGTH: 20 ft (6.1 m)

TIME: Late Triassic, 215 million years ago

PLACE: Argentina

DIET: plants

DETAILS: This spectacularly well-preserved 16-inch (40 cm) hatchling prosauropod was described from one of the smallest baby dinosaur skeletons discovered so far. The individual was very young and had probably died not long after hatching. The skull of this young *Mussaurus* was only about 1¼ inches (3.2 cm) long, roughly the size of a quarter. When Argentine scientist José Bonaparte broke open a ball of rock, he found the tiny dinosaur skeleton curled up within it.

Mussaurus juvenile fossil

130

Dig Right In

When a part of a dinosaur skeleton is unearthed, researchers look for more bones beneath the ground in the same area. They use shovels, crowbars, hammers, picks—and muscle!—to remove the rocks that lie on top of the bones. Once the researchers get closer to the layer of rock with the bones embedded in it, they switch to much smaller tools. Using awls and screwdrivers and sometimes even toothbrushes, they scrape rock away from bone. When the bones are finally exposed, they are coated with protective liquid and then wrapped in plaster casts like the one you'd get if you broke your arm. Then these plaster-coated heavy bones in plaster, and the rock surrounding them, are brought back to the laboratory for months of fine cleaning with tiny tools. Computers play little role in this 100-year-old process, though X rays can help distinguish bone from rock.

Muttaburrasaurus

mutt-uh-**burr**-uh-**sor**-uhss

NAMED AFTER: Muttaburra, Queensland, Australia

CLASSIFICATION: Ornithischia, basal Iguanodontia

LENGTH: 24 ft (7.3 m)

TIME: Early Cretaceous, 97.5 million years ago

PLACE: Australia

DIET: plants

DETAILS: This animal was a large *Iguanodon* relative with a large bump on its nose and unusually shaped shearing teeth. Some researchers suggest that *Muttaburrasaurus* may have actually been a camptosaurid, one of a group of plant-eaters slightly smaller than the iguanodontids that lived at the same time in North America. Its presence in Australia indicates that *Iguanodon*-like and camptosaur-like dinosaurs were a widespread success.

Muttaburrasaurus

Mymoorapelta

my-moor-uh-**pell**-tuh

NAME MEANS: "Mygatt Moore shield," after the landowners for whom the quarry site is named

CLASSIFICATION: Ornithischia, Ankylosauria

LENGTH: 9 ft (2.7 m)

TIME: Late Jurassic, 151 million years ago

PLACE: Colorado, U.S.

DIET: plants

DETAILS: *Mymoorapelta* was an early small club-tailed armored dinosaur. It is the most complete ankylosaur known from the Jurassic Period and the first armored dinosaur identified from the Late Jurassic Period in North America. As long as a tiger and far heavier, it was still tiny compared to many dinosaurs. It lived in the same environment and time period as huge plant-eaters such as *Apatosaurus, Diplodocus, Barosaurus, Camarasaurus,* and *Brachiosaurus*.

Mymoorapelta (b.) and a Utahraptor (t.)

Hypsilophodontidae Lesothosauria Macronaria Ornithomimosauria Oviraptorosauria Pachycephalosauria Primitive sauropods Prosauropoda Spinosauria Stegosauria Therizinosauridae Troodontidae Tyrannosauridae

Nedcolbertia

Abelisauridae · Ankylosauria · basal Coelurosauria · basal Iguanodontia · Camarasauridae · Carnosauria · Ceratopsia · Ceratosauria · Dromaeosauridae · Diplodocoidea · Hadrosauridae · Herrerasauridae · Heterodontosauridae

Naashoibitosaurus

nah-ah-show-ee-**bee**-to-**sor**-uhss

NAME MEANS: "lizard-creek lizard," from Navajo word

CLASSIFICATION: Ornithischia, Hadrosauridae

LENGTH: 33 ft (10 m)

TIME: Late Cretaceous, 65 million years ago

PLACE: New Mexico, U.S.

DIET: plants

DETAILS: Paleontologist Jack Horner assigned this fossil find to the genus *Kritosaurus* in 1992. But two New Mexico paleontologists think that the fossil skull came from a new kind of duckbill because of the unusual arch in its nose.

"Nanosaurus" (**nan**-uh-**sor**-uhss) Not a valid scientific name. This small but apparently fully grown plant-eating dinosaur was described and named based on the discovery of an incomplete jawbone in a sandstone slab. Named by Yale University paleontologist Othniel C. Marsh in 1877, this would be one of the smallest known adult dinosaurs if there were more fossil information to confirm it.

"Nanotyrannus" (**nan**-oh-tie-**ran**-us) Perhaps a valid scientific name. This 15-foot-long (4.8 m) "pygmy tyrannosaur" was named after a reexamination of a *Gorgosaurus*-labeled skull that had been fitted with plaster horns. Further research indicates this may not have been a different kind of animal but likely a juvenile of *Tyrannosaurus rex* or at least a closely related species.

Nanshiungosaurus

non-shyoong-oh-**sor**-uhss

NAMED AFTER: Nanxiong, China

CLASSIFICATION: Saurischia, Theropoda, Therizinosauridae

LENGTH: 13 ft (4 m)

TIME: Late Cretaceous, 75 million years ago

PLACE: China

DIET: plants?

DETAILS: This bizarre-looking bipedal dinosaur was

Nanshiungosaurus pelvis

originally thought to be a small sauropod. It is now recognized as a theropod dinosaur with a horny beak and toothless front jaw. Like other therizinosaurs, this mysterious dinosaur had big claws but a skull more like that of a plant-eater.

Nanyangosaurus

non-**yong**-oh-**sor**-uhss

NAME MEANS: "Nanyang lizard," named for the city of Nanyang, China

CLASSIFICATION: Ornithischia, basal Iguanodontia

LENGTH: 15 ft (4.6 m)

TIME: Late Cretaceous, 99 million years ago

PLACE: China

DIET: plants

Nanyangosaurus

DETAILS: Named in 2000, this flat-headed iguanodontid seems to be a link between iguanodontids and the later duck-billed plant-eaters. Like both iguanodontids and hadrosaurids, *Nanyangosaurus* was a browser, nipping plants and grinding them between its massive batteries of hundreds of teeth. It is among the smallest iguanodontids known.

Nedcolbertia

ned-cole-**bear**-tee-uh

NAMED AFTER: paleontologist Dr. Edwin Harris "Ned" Colbert

CLASSIFICATION: Saurischia, Theropoda, basal Coelurosauria

LENGTH: 10 ft (3 m)

TIME: Early Cretaceous, 127 million years ago

PLACE: Colorado, Utah, U.S.

DIET: meat

DETAILS: *Nedcolbertia* may have resembled *Ornitholestes,* another small meat-eater from Late Jurassic North America. But its hand claws were more powerful than those of *Ornitholestes,* and its feet differed as well. Clearly a swift runner, it lacked the slashing toe-claw of "raptor" dromaeosaurids and troodontids. *Nedcolbertia* was described in 1998 based on three partial skeletons. These skeletons of

133

Hypsilophodontidae Lesothosauria Macronaria Ornithomimosauria Oviraptorosauria Pachycephalosauria Primitive sauropods Prosauropoda Spinosauria Stegosauria Therizinosauroidea Troodontidae Tyrannosauridae

a juvenile *Nedcolbertia* and two adults were too incomplete to provide a strong comparison with better-known small theropods.

Nemegtosaurus

nay-**meg**-toe-**sor**-uhss

NAMED AFTER: Mongolia's Nemegt Basin

Nemegtosaurus

CLASSIFICATION: Saurischia, Sauropoda, Diplodocoidea

LENGTH: about 50 ft (15.2 m)

TIME: Late Cretaceous, 70 million years ago

PLACE: Mongolia

DIET: plants

DETAILS: This huge plant-eater may have been a member of the whip-tailed diplodocid branch of the sauropod dinosaurs. It was discovered in the Gobi Desert with its skull almost complete, one of only two skulls ever found of Late Cretaceous sauropods in Asia. Based on that discovery, scientists think *Nemegtosaurus* had large eyes, a light lower jaw, and pencil-shape teeth.

"Neosaurus" (**nee**-oh-**sor**-uhss) Not a valid scientific name. See *Parrosaurus*.

"Neosodon" (nee-**oh**-so-don) Not a valid scientific name. Named in 1885 from a single tooth found in France, this dinosaur may be a brachiosaur-like plant-eater.

Neovenator

nee-oh-veh-**nay**-tore

NAME MEANS: "new hunter"

CLASSIFICATION: Saurischia, Theropoda, Carnosauria

LENGTH: 25 ft (7.6 m)

TIME: Early Cretaceous, 112 million years ago

PLACE: England

DIET: meat

DETAILS: This large meat-eater's skeleton shows similarities to *Allosaurus* from North America and *Sinraptor* from China. These similarities reflect a close association between all the landmasses of the Northern Hemisphere at this time. Named in 1996, *Neovenator* is the first member of the allosaur family identified in Europe. It was discovered on the Isle of Wight in England.

Neuquensaurus

nay-oo-ken-**sor**-uhss

NAMED AFTER: Neuquén Province in Patagonia, Argentina

CLASSIFICATION: Saurischia, Sauropoda, Macronaria

LENGTH: 50 ft (15.2 m)

TIME: Late Cretaceous, 85 million years ago

PLACE: Argentina

DIET: plants

Neuquensaurus dermal plate

DETAILS: A giant four-legged, plant-eating titanosaur, *Neuquensaurus* was armored, unlike what is known for most sauropods. Its skin showed rounded plates and bony bumps. This armor helped the animal to defend itself from the teeth and claws of predatory dinosaurs. *Neuquensaurus*'s fossilized armor led scientists initially to mistake it for an ankylosaur. Neuquén Province, for which this dinosaur is named, is where the largest plant-eating and meat-eating dinosaurs have lately been found. Neuquen also happens to be a palindrome, a word that is spelled the same backward or forward.

"Ngexisaurus" (guh-shee-ei-**sor**-uhss) Not a valid scientific name. A small meat-eater never scientifically described.

Nigersaurus

nee-zhayr-**sor**-uhss or **nye**-jer-**sor**-uhss

NAMED AFTER: Niger, the African nation

CLASSIFICATION: Saurischia, Sauropoda, Diplodocoidea

LENGTH: 50 ft (15.2 m)

TIME: Early Cretaceous, 127 million years ago

PLACE: Niger

DIET: plants

DETAILS: *Nigersaurus* had a wide, squared-off snout similar to that of South America's *Antarctosaurus*. Its teeth formed a straight, comblike row across its upper and lower jaws. About 140 of these pencil-shape teeth are exposed along the front edge of its jaw, but replacement teeth are arranged beneath them in rows up to seven teeth deep, for a total of nearly 600 teeth. Some scientists say that the many replacement teeth indicate that

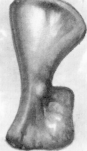

Nigersaurus scapule

Neovenator

Hypsilophodontidae Lesothosauria Macronaria Ornithomimosauria Oviraptorosauria Pachycephalosauria Primitive sauropods Prosauropoda Spinosauria Stegosauria Therizinosauridae Troodontidae Tyrannosauridae

Nigersaurus browsed on rough vegetation, which would quickly wear down teeth. This relatively primitive sauropod was first described in 1999. The skeleton was particularly well preserved.

Niobrarasaurus

nye-oh-**brah**-ruh-**sor**-uhss

NAMED AFTER: Niobrara Chalk Formation of Kansas

CLASSIFICATION: Ornithischia, Anklyosauria

LENGTH: 16.5 ft (5 m)

TIME: Late Cretaceous, 71 million years ago

PLACE: Kansas, U.S.

DIET: plants

DETAILS: *Niobrarasaurus* was a clubless armored dinosaur. It was midsize for an armored dinosaur; several other armored dinosaurs of its time grew to nearly twice its size.

Nipponosaurus

nip-**on**-oh-**sor**-uhss

NAME MEANS: "Japanese lizard"

CLASSIFICATION: Ornithischia, Hadrosauridae

LENGTH: 25 ft (7.6 m)

TIME: Late Cretaceous, 88 million years ago

PLACE: Russia

DIET: plants

Nipponosaurus partial skull of juvenile

DETAILS: What little is known about this hollow-crested duckbill named in 1936 is based on the incomplete skeleton of a juvenile. The crest is relatively modest in size. Lambeosaur crests appear to have grown significantly as these dinosaurs neared adult age. *Nipponosaurus*, uncovered on Sakhalin Island, near Japan, was one of very few dinosaur discoveries made on Pacific islands.

Noasaurus

no-ah-**sor**-uhss

NAME MEANS: "northwestern Argentina lizard"

CLASSIFICATION: Saurischia, Theropoda, Ceratosauria, Abelisauridae

LENGTH: 10 ft (3 m)

TIME: Late Cretaceous, 65 million years ago

PLACE: Argentina

DIET: meat

Noasaurus claw

DETAILS: This small abelisaur presents an amazing case of convergence – the development of similar features in animals not closely related. In this little predator, the convergent feature is a small "raptor"-like killing claw on each limb. The second toe of the *Noasaurus*'s hind foot had a sickle-claw adapted for slashing and tearing. This claw appears to have evolved separately from the similar switchblade talon seen in the dromaeosaurs and troodontids of North America and Asia. The small size of this dinosaur's teeth and hind feet suggests that it may have preyed on smaller animals, such as birds or young sauropods, rather than on large plant-eaters. Named in 1980, *Noasaurus* is the first small theropod ever found in South America.

Nodocephalosaurus

no-doh-**seff**-a-loh-**sor**-uhss

NAME MEANS: "knob-headed lizard"

CLASSIFICATION: Ornithischia, Ankylosauria

LENGTH: 15 ft (4.6 m)

TIME: Late Cretaceous, 71 million years ago

PLACE: New Mexico, U.S.

DIET: plants

Nodocephalosaurus skull

DETAILS: Named for the many bulb-shape lumps on its skull, this medium-size armored dinosaur had very unusual decorations on its skull. *Nodocephalosaurus* was a primitive armored dinosaur, perhaps similar to the Asian *Saichania*. It was named in 1999, from incomplete remains.

Nodosaurus

no-doh-**sor**-uhss

NAME MEANS: "knob lizard"

CLASSIFICATION: Ornithischia, Ankylosauria

LENGTH: 20 ft (6.1 m)

TIME: Early Cretaceous, 113 million years ago

PLACE: Wyoming, Kansas, U.S.

DIET: plants

DETAILS: The first nodosaurid to be identified, *Nodosaurus* was described in 1889 by famed Yale University paleontologist Othniel C. Marsh. Bony armor plates covered this dinosaur's sides and were arranged in a series of rows with interwoven patterns. A squat and bulky dinosaur, *Nodosaurus* walked on four stubby legs ending in powerful, clawed hands and feet. Like all other nodosaurs, it had no tail club.

Nodosaurus

Nomingia

no-**ming**-ee-uh

NAMED AFTER: Nomingian region of the Gobi Desert, Mongolia

CLASSIFICATION: Saurischia, Theropoda, Oviraptorosauria

LENGTH: 5.6 ft (1.7 m)

TIME: Cretaceous, 80 million years ago

PLACE: Mongolia

DIET: meat

DETAILS: *Nomingia* is the first oviraptor known to have a pygostyle — a tail with fused bones that is a feature of modern birds. *Nomingia* had 22 vertebrae in its tail, the last 11 of which were fused.

Nomingia
fused vertebrae
from the tail end

Nothronychus

noh-**thron**-ik-uhss or noth-roh-**nye**-cuss

NAME MEANS: "slothlike claw"

CLASSIFICATION: Saurischia, Theropoda, Therizinosauridae

LENGTH: 20 ft (6.1 m)

TIME: Late Cretaceous, 92 million years ago

PLACE: New Mexico, U.S.

DIET: plants and insects?

DETAILS: Named in 2001, this is the first North American representative yet known of the strange therizinosaur dinosaurs. These slothlike dinosaurs had long necks and long arms with huge sickle-shape claws. Like sloths, they may have used these claws to scrape the ground or trees for insects or plants, even though their ancestors were meat-eaters.

The scientist who discovered *Nothronychus* thinks it may have had some kind of feathers, since a feathered covering has been found on a similar dinosaur from China.

"Notoceratops" (**note**-oh-**sayr**-a-tops) Not a valid scientific name. Based on just a fragment of jaw, "Notoceratops" was thought to be the only horned dinosaur known from South America. However, it may actually be a duckbill.

Notohypsilophodon

note-oh-hip-sih-**loaf**-oh-don

NAME MEANS: "southern hypsilophodont"

CLASSIFICATION: Ornithischia, Hypsilophodontia

LENGTH: 3 ft (1 m) (probably a juvenile)

TIME: Late Cretaceous, 90 million years ago

PLACE: Argentina

DIET: plants

DETAILS: Perhaps the first ornithopod dinosaur ever discovered in South America, *Notohypsilophodon* is known only from a partial, headless skeleton that may have belonged to a youngster. *Notohypsilophodon* was named in 1998.

Nqwebasaurus

en-**kweb**-buh-**sor**-uhss

NAMED AFTER: Nqweba region of South Africa

CLASSIFICATION: Saurischia, Theropoda, basal Coelurosauria

LENGTH: 3 ft (1 m)

TIME: Early Cretaceous, 140 million years ago

PLACE: South Africa

DIET: meat

DETAILS: This newly named dinosaur was a fast-running and lightly built meat-eater. Its long hands had nimble fingers that could grasp prey. Stones, called gastroliths, found in the gut area of its skeleton helped to digest foods, a feature of many plant-eaters and some other meat-eaters.

Nqwebasaurus
stomach stones

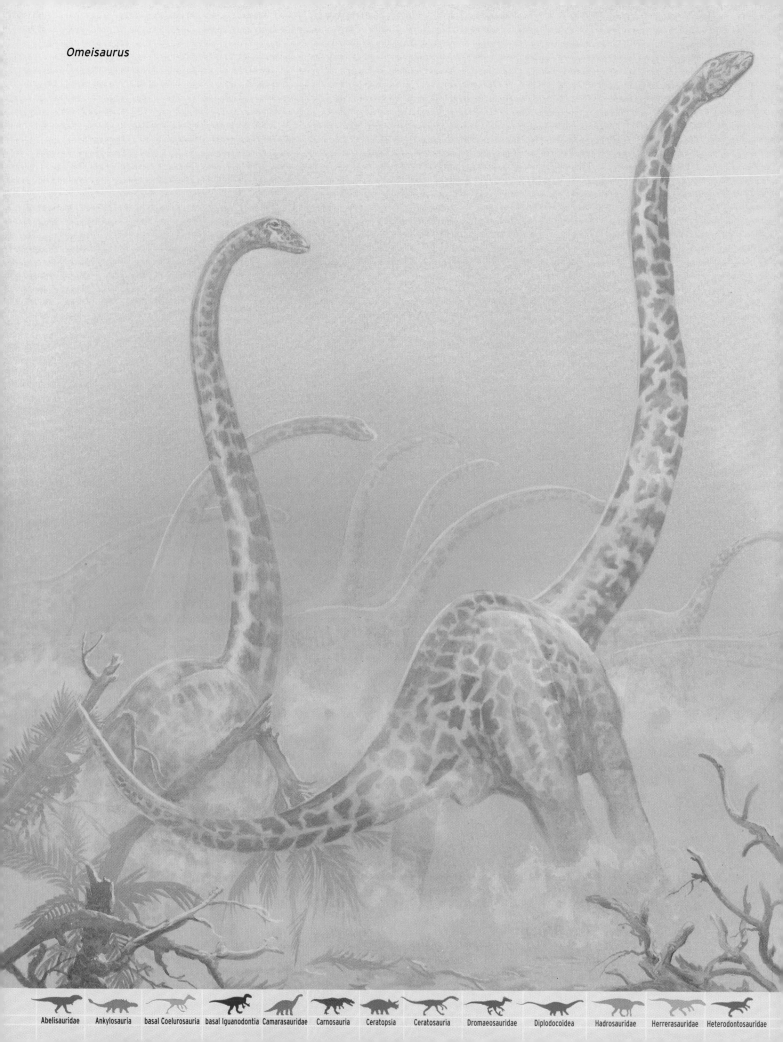

Omeisaurus

Abelisauridae Ankylosauria basal Coelurosauria basal Iguanodontia Camarasauridae Carnosauria Ceratopsia Ceratosauria Dromaeosauridae Diplodocoidea Hadrosauridae Herrerasauridae Heterodontosauridae

Ohmdenosaurus

ohm-den-oh-**sor**-uhss
NAMED AFTER: Ohmden, Germany
CLASSIFICATION: Saurischia, Sauropoda, Primitive sauropods
LENGTH: 30 ft (9.1 m)
TIME: Early Jurassic, 191 million years ago
PLACE: Germany
DIET: plants
DETAILS: *Ohmdenosaurus* was once mistaken for a plesiosaur when its lower leg bone was incorrectly identified as the arm of that aquatic reptile. This dinosaur may be a vulcanodontid, a primitive, plant-eating sauropod with some features, such as the shape of its ankle, that are more like the bones of earlier prosauropods.

"Oligosaurus" (oh-**lig**-uh-**sor**-uhss) Not a valid scientific name. See *Rhabdodon.*

Omeisaurus

uh-**may**-**sor**-uhss or oh-**may**-**sor**-uhss
NAMED AFTER: Mount Omei quarry area, China
CLASSIFICATION: Saurischia, Sauropoda, Camarasauridae
LENGTH: 50 ft (15.2 m)
TIME: Late Jurassic, 156 million years ago
PLACE: China
DIET: plants
DETAILS: This medium-size sauropod had an unusually high, long neck. Several *Omeisaurus* with skulls still intact were found among other dinosaurs at a quarry in southern China. Since the animals died together, it is supposed that they lived in herds. *Omeisaurus* had a short body and limbs like the enormously long-necked *Mamenchisaurus,* also from Jurassic China.

"Omosaurus" (**oh**-mo-**sor**-uhss). Not a valid scientific name. See *Dacentrurus.*

"Onychosaurus" (**on**-ick-oh-**sor**-uhss) Not a valid scientific name. See *Rhabdodon.*

Opisthocoelicaudia

oh-pis-thoh-**see**-lih-**kaw**-dee-uh
NAME MEANS: "hollow-backed tail vertebrae"
CLASSIFICATION: Saurischia, Sauropoda, Macronaria
LENGTH: 40 ft (12.2 m)
TIME: Late Cretaceous, 75 million years ago
PLACE: Mongolia
DIET: plants

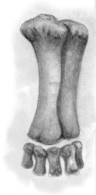

Opisthocoelicaudia
feet and
shin bones

DETAILS: First thought to be a camarasaur, and more recently a titanosaur, *Opisthocoelicaudia* was one of the last sauropods to have lived in Asia. The remains of this dinosaur might belong to another incompletely known large plant-eater, *Nemegtosaurus*, which was approximately 50 feet (15.2 m) long.

"Oplosaurus" (**op**-loh-**sor**-uhss) Not a valid scientific name. See *Pelorosaurus.*

"Orinosaurus" (oh-**rye**-no-**sor**-uhss) Not a valid scientific name. See *Euskelosaurus.*

"Ornatotholus" (or-**nat**-uh-**thoh**-lus). Not a valid scientific name. See *Stegoceras.*

"Ornithodesmus" (or-**nith**-oh-**dess**-muss) Not a valid scientific name. Once considered a primitive bird, then a pterosaur, then a troodontid or a possible *Deinonychus* relative, this small and little-known meat-eating dinosaur continues to puzzle scientists.

"Ornithoides" (or-nih-**thoy**-deez) Not a valid scientific name. See *Saurornithoides.*

Ornitholestes

or-**nith**-oh-**less**-teez
NAME MEANS: "bird robber"
CLASSIFICATION: Saurischia, Theropoda, basal Coelurosauria

139

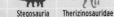

Hypsilophodontidae · Lesothosauria · Macronaria · Ornithomimosauria · Oviraptorosauria · Pachycephalosauria · Primitive sauropods · Prosauropoda · Spinosauria · Stegosauria · Therizinosauridae · Troodontidae · Tyrannosauridae

Ornitholestes

LENGTH: 7 ft (2.1 m)
TIME: Late Jurassic, 145 million years ago
PLACE: Wyoming, Utah, U.S.
DIET: meat
DETAILS: This was a small, agile predator with a crest above its nose. A wolf-size meat-eater, *Ornitholestes* may have been closely related to two groups of far larger meat-eaters; ornithomimids and tyrannosaurs. It was named after a nearly complete skeleton was discovered in 1900.

"Ornithomerus"
(or-**nith**-oh-**mere**-us) Not a valid scientific name. See *Rhabdodon.*

Ornithomimus
or-**nith**-oh-**my**-muss
NAME MEANS: "bird mimic"
CLASSIFICATION: Saurischia, Theropoda, Ornithomimosauria
LENGTH: 12 ft (3.7 m)
TIME: Late Cretaceous, 65 million years ago
PLACE: Colorado, Utah, Montana, Wyoming, U.S.; Alberta, Canada
DIET: meat
DETAILS: Like *Struthiomimus*, this dinosaur had a small head, a toothless mouth, a long neck, and long arms with nimble fingers. Its hind legs and rodlike tail were adapted for speed and agility. *Ornithomimus* was once considered to have been an omnivore, a dinosaur that ate all foods. Recent discoveries indicate ornithomimids had a comb-like filter on their beaks that may have strained small creatures and plants from ponds and lakes, the way modern ducks do. The discovery of this dinosaur in the late 1800s helped to establish the long-legged "ostrich mimic" group.

"Ornithopsis" (or-nith-**op**-siss) Not a valid scientific name. See *Pelorosaurus.*

"Ornithotarsus" (or-**nith**-oh-**tar**-suss) Not a valid scientific name. First thought to be a meat-eater, then a duckbill. Possibly the same dinosaur as *Hadrosaurus.*

140

Ornithomimus

Hypsilophodontidae   Lesothosauria   Macronaria   Ornithomimosauria   Oviraptorosauria   Pachycephalosauria   Primitive sauropods   Prosauropoda   Spinosauria   Stegosauria   Therizinosauridae   Troodontidae   Tyrannosauridae

Ouranosaurus

Orodromeus

or-oh-**droh**-me-us

NAME MEANS: "mountain runner"

CLASSIFICATION: Ornithischia, Hypsilophodontia

LENGTH: 5.6 ft (1.7 m)

TIME: Late Cretaceous, 77 million years ago

PLACE: Montana, U.S.; Alberta, Canada

DIET: plants

DETAILS: This hypsilophodontid had strong, lean hind legs and so was probably a quick two-legged runner. For many years the nests and eggs of *Troodon* were mistaken for those of *Orodromeus*.

"Orosaurus" (**or**-oh-**sor**-uhss) Not a valid scientific name. See *Orinosaurus* and *Euskelosaurus*.

"Orthogoniosaurus" (**or**-thoh-**go**-nee-oh-**sor**-uhss) Not a valid scientific name. Named from a single, badly preserved tooth of a possible large meat-eater.

"Orthomerus" (**or**-thoh-**mere**-uhss) Not a valid scientific name. See *Telmatosaurus*.

"Oshanosaurus" (oh-**shan**-uh-**sor**-uhss) Not a valid scientific name. An unidentifiable small plant-eater.

DETAILS: This large plant-eater had a long, slender snout with a short, horny beak. Unlike other close relatives of *Iguanodon, Ouranosaurus* had a distinctive long spine on each of its backbones, creating a high hump or sail-fin profile. This tall spinal ridge may have been brightly colored to attract mates or to compete with other members of the same species over territory. It may also have served to cool the dinosaur by releasing heat from the many blood vessels in the fin.

Fame!

Remember Dr. Alan Grant, the floppy-hatted hero of the *Jurassic Park* movies? Dr. John R. "Jack" Horner is the real-life model for that character. Horner was born in 1946 in Shelby, Montana, and grew up with a reading problem that his teachers didn't recognize. As a result, he flunked out of college seven times before his disability was recognized.

Today Jack Horner is one of the most famous dinosaur explorers. He has discovered many dinosaurs, including one he named *Orodromeus makelii*, after his best friend, Bob Makela. Dr. Horner has also discovered several *T. rex* skeletons. His specialty is the behavior and evolution of duck-billed dinosaurs. Horner's discoveries of duckbill nests and fossils and his conclusions about how these animals cared for their young have revolutionized our view of dinosaurs.

John R. Horner and Rebecca Lessem, age 7

Othnielia

oth-nee-**ee**-lee-uh

NAMED AFTER: paleontologist Othniel C. Marsh

CLASSIFICATION: Ornithischia, Hypsilophodontia

LENGTH: 4.6 ft (1.4 m)

TIME: Late Jurassic, 156 million years ago

PLACE: Colorado, Utah, Wyoming, U.S.

DIET: plants

Othnielia

DETAILS: *Othnielia* closely resembled *Hypsilophodon*, but differed in the shape of its vertebrae, its more slender hind feet, and its delicate toes.

Ouranosaurus

oo-**ron**-oh-**sor**-uhss

NAME MEANS: "brave lizard"

CLASSIFICATION: Ornithischia, basal Iguanodontia

LENGTH: 24 ft (7.3 m)

TIME: Early Cretaceous, 115 million years ago

PLACE: Niger

DIET: plants

Abelisauridae Ankylosauria basal Coelurosauria basal Iguanodontia Camarasauridae Carnosauria Ceratopsia Ceratosauria Dromaeosauridae Diplodocoidea Hadrosauridae Herrerasauridae Heterodontosauridae

Orodromeus

Hypsilophodontidae   Lesothosauria   Macronaria   Ornithomimosauria   Oviraptorosauria   Pachycephalosauria   Primitive sauropods   Prosauropoda   Spinosauria   Stegosauria   Therizinosauridae   Troodontidae   Tyrannosauridae

Oviraptor

Oviraptor

oh-vih-**rap**-tore

NAME MEANS: "egg robber"

CLASSIFICATION: Saurischia, Theropoda, Oviraptorosauria

LENGTH: 8 ft (2.4 m)

TIME: Late Cretaceous, 70 million years ago

PLACE: Mongolia

DIET: insects?

DETAILS: *Oviraptor* was a long-armed and toothless dinosaur. This dinosaur's odd, toothless skull bore a high crest, a short beak, and a pair of cone-shape prongs on the roof of the mouth. Although the diet of *Oviraptor* is unknown, the strong beak and prongs were ideal for eating eggs as modern egg-eating snakes do. *Oviraptor* was discovered in 1923, near the first nest of dinosaur eggs ever found in Asia. At this site, the plant-eating *Protoceratops* was the most common dinosaur, so *Oviraptor* was thought to have been an "egg thief" who became buried in sand while waiting to steal *Protoceratops* eggs. Seventy years later, more nests were found in China and Mongolia, including a fossilized *Oviraptor* sitting atop the eggs. Other eggs of the same kind included embryonic remains of *Oviraptor,* so this dinosaur was an egg protector, not an egg thief! Additional *Oviraptor* finds have revealed that this dinosaur perched over its clutch of eggs for protection and warmth, a brooding behavior very much like that seen in birds today.

"Ovoraptor" (**oh**-voh-**rap**-tor) Not a valid scientific name. See *Velociraptor.*

Ozraptor

oz-**rap**-tore

NAME MEANS: "Australian plunderer"

CLASSIFICATION: Saurischia, Theropoda, Oviraptorosauria

LENGTH: 10 ft (3 m)

TIME: Middle Jurassic, 169 million years ago

PLACE: Australia

DIET: meat

DETAILS: Named in 1998, this small meat-eater was described based on a single leg bone. The fossil was at first thought to have belonged to an ancient turtle. *Ozraptor* is the first named dinosaur from Western Australia. Oz is a nickname for Australia.

Ozraptor bottom of left shin bone

145

Panoplosaurus (f.)
with dromaeosaurids (b.)

Abelisauridae Ankylosauria basal Coelurosauria basal Iguanodontia Camarasauridae Carnosauria Ceratopsia Ceratosauria Dromaeosauridae Diplodocoidea Hadrosauridae Herrerasauridae Heterodontosauridae

Pachycephalosaurus

pack-ee-**seff**-a-loh-**sor**-uhss

NAME MEANS: "thick-headed lizard"

CLASSIFICATION: Ornithsichia, Pachycephalosauria

LENGTH: 15 ft (4.6 m)

TIME: Late Cretaceous, 65 million years ago

PLACE: Montana, Wyoming, South Dakota, Alaska, U.S.; Alberta, Canada

DIET: plants

DETAILS: Far larger than nearly all other thick-headed dinosaurs, this two-legged plant-eater carried a 10-inch-thick (25.4 cm) layer of bone atop its skull, which was studded with bumps and spikes. It has been suggested that this structure may have been used as a ram for bone-jarring head-on impacts. But recent studies indicate these dinosaurs were not equipped for skull-to-skull collisions. A scattering of bony spikes on the tip of the snout has led some scientists to suggest that *Pachycephalosaurus* might have used its nose for digging up vegetation. This animal's skull was so peculiar that it was mistaken for a giant armadillo-like reptile when it was first discovered.

Pachyrhinosaurus

pack-ee-**rye**-no-**sor**-uhss

NAME MEANS: "thick-nosed lizard"

CLASSIFICATION: Ornithischia, Ceratopsia

LENGTH: 23 ft (7 m)

TIME: Late Cretaceous, 68 million years ago

PLACE: Alaska, U.S.; Alberta, Canada

DIET: plants

DETAILS: *Pachyrhinosaurus* was an especially bulky horned dinosaur. Its skull was powerfully built, from the short knoblike bump on its otherwise hornless snout to its rectangular skull and short, thick teeth. The purpose of a boney bump on its snout is puzzling. According to scientists, one to three straight horns of varying size projected from the middle of the dinosaur's bony frill. The difference in number of horns may have been related to age and sex. *Pachyrhinosaurus* finds in Alaska suggest that this dinosaur may have migrated in herds, heading into northern Alaska in summer during the long

Arctic daylight, when plants grew especially nutritious. A bone bed in Alberta recently produced more than a dozen skulls and hundreds of other *Pachyrhinosaurus* fossils.

Pachyrhinosaurus

"Pachysauriscus" (**pack**-ee-sore-**iss**-cuss) Not a valid scientific name. Now called *Plateosaurus*.

"Pachysaurus" (**pack**-ee-**sor**-uhss) Not a valid dinosaur. See *Plateosaurus*.

"Pachyspondylus" (**pack**-ee-**spon**-dill-uhss) Not a valid scientific name. See *Massospondylus*.

"Palaeopteryx" (**pay**-lee-**op**-tayr-iks) Not a valid scientific name. A puzzling birdlike meat-eater based on just a single limb bone, first thought to belong to a bird.

"Palaeoscincus" (**pay**-lee-oh-**skink**-uhss) Not a valid scientific name. An early dinosaur name (1856) based on a single tooth of an armored dinosaur first thought to belong to a giant lizard.

Panoplosaurus

pan-op-loh-**sor**-uhss

NAME MEANS: "completely armored lizard"

CLASSIFICATION: Ornithischia, Ankylosauria

LENGTH: 18 ft (5.5 m)

TIME: Late Cretaceous, 73 million years ago

PLACE: Montana, U.S.; Alberta, Canada

DIET: plants

DETAILS: This well-known armored dinosaur belonged to the nodosaur armored dinosaurs. *Panoplosaurus*

147

was well protected by a layer of bony plates all the way from its pear-shaped head to its tail. Spikes stuck out from its sides and shoulders. These weapons were probably useful for defense against predators such as *Albertosaurus*. Like other nodosaurs, it did not have a tail club.

"Paraiguanodon" (**par**-uh-ig-**wan**-oh-don) Not a valid scientific name. See *Bactrosaurus*.

Paralititan

pair-a-lih-**tie**-ton
NAME MEANS: "tidal giant"
CLASSIFICATION: Saurischia, Sauropoda, Macronaria
LENGTH: 70 ft (21.3 m)
TIME: Late Cretaceous, 95 million years ago
PLACE: Egypt
DIET: plants

Paralititan upper arm bone

DETAILS: This huge four-legged plant-eater may have been second only to *Argentinosaurus* in size among all known dinosaurs. So far, researchers have uncovered shoulder, arm, and tail bones. The upper arm bone is nearly six feet (1.8 meters) long, almost a foot longer than the upper arm bone on any other Cretaceous dinosaur. *Paralititan* was named in 2001. It was found by University of Pennsylvania graduate students on a recent search for the site of dinosaurs first uncovered by German researchers in 1935. The 1935 dinosaur fossil finds were brought to Germany but destroyed during World War II. Many other large and soon-to-be named animals have been found at this same Egyptian site. It appears to have been the habitat of many huge creatures along an ancient water's edge. Fossils found there include those of crocodiles 35 feet long (10.7 m).

"Paranthodon" (pair-**an**-thoh-don) Not a valid scientific name. This name was taken from stegosaur teeth and the bones of various animals.

"Pararhabdodon" (pair-a-**rab**-doh-don) Not a valid scientific name. It is based upon fragmentary Spanish fossils thought to belong to an iguanodontid, when named in 1993, but now considered a crested duckbill.

Parasaurolophus

pair-a-sore-**oll**-oh-fuss or
pair-a-**sore**-oh-**loaf**-us
NAME MEANS: "near Saurolophus"
CLASSIFICATION: Ornithischia, Hadrosauridae
LENGTH: 30 ft (9.1 m)
TIME: Late Cretaceous, 76 million years ago
PLACE: Utah, New Mexico, U.S.; Alberta, Canada
DIET: plants

Parasaurolophus

DETAILS: This very distinctive duck-billed dinosaur is known for the long, curving, hollow crest along the top of its skull that projected back over its neck. This trumpet-shape crest may have been used to produce low-frequency sounds like those used by elephants or whales to communicate over long distances. It may have contributed to a keen sense of smell, or simply allowed a *Parasaurolophus* to attract a potential mate or to recognize another member of its species. The true function of the crest may be any or all of these — or even something as yet unknown. Two crest shapes, one longer and more gracefully curving, the other shorter and curved sharply downward, may have helped identify males from females, juveniles from adults, or two different closely related species.

Parksosaurus

park-so-**sor**-uhss
NAMED AFTER: Canadian paleontologist William A. Parks
CLASSIFICATION: Ornithischia, Hypsilophodontia
LENGTH: 7 ft (2.1 m)
TIME: Late Cretaceous, 68 million years ago
PLACE: Montana, U.S.; Alberta, Canada
DIET: plants
DETAILS: This small, short-faced, large-eyed dinosaur ran on two legs. The fingers of its forelimbs may have been used for grasping the plants on which it

Parksosaurus

Patagonykus

fed. *Parksosaurus* may have been one of the last North American hypsilophodonts. It is also the first hypsilophodontid known from that continent. A complete skeleton, including a skull, was found in 1922 in Alberta, Canada.

"Paronychodon" (pair-oh-**nick**-oh-don) Not a valid scientific name. A dinosaur named from several teeth of an unidentifiable meat-eater.

"Parrosaurus" (**par**-oh-**sor**-uhss) Not a valid scientific name. Not known from enough bones.

Parvicursor
par-vih-**curse**-or
NAME MEANS: "small runner"
CLASSIFICATION: Saurischia, Theropoda, basal Coelurosauria
LENGTH: 3.3 ft (1 m)

TIME: Late Cretaceous, 84 million years ago
PLACE: Mongolia
DIET: meat
DETAILS: Similar to the birdlike dinosaur *Mononykus,* this small meat-eater had many birdlike characteristics in its skeleton. *Parvicursor* was named in 1996, but few details have yet been published about this swift little dinosaur.

Patagonykus
pat-ah-**gone**-ick-us
NAME MEANS: "Patagonian claw"
CLASSIFICATION: Saurischia, Theropoda, basal Coelurosauria
LENGTH: 6.5 ft (2 m)
TIME: Late Cretaceous, 90 million years ago
PLACE: Argentina
DIET: meat
DETAILS Like the Mongolian *Mononykus,*

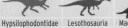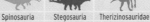

Hypsilophodontidae Lesothosauria Macronaria Ornithomimosauria Oviraptorosauria Pachycephalosauria Primitive sauropods Prosauropoda Spinosauria Stegosauria Therizinosauridae Troodontidae Tyrannosauridae

Patagonykus was a small birdlike dinosaur that ran swiftly on two long legs. How a South American dinosaur could be so similar to a Mongolian one is a great puzzle, especially when *Patagonykus* lived so late in dinosaur time that those continents were no longer linked in any way.

Patagosaurus

pat-ah-**go**-**sor**-uhss
NAME MEANS: "Patagonian lizard"
CLASSIFICATION: Saurischia, Sauropoda, Primitive sauropods
LENGTH: 65 ft (19.8 m)
TIME: Middle Jurassic, 163 million years ago
PLACE: Argentina
DIET: plants
DETAILS: This long-necked, browsing sauropod was named for the region of

Patagosaurus

southwestern Argentina where it was discovered. It was about the size of the large European sauropod *Cetiosaurus*. *Patagosaurus* provided the first proof that large dinosaurs from the Jurassic roamed South America. They may have crossed over from Europe via an ancient connection that linked the continents as the world's single landmass was breaking apart.

"Patricosaurus" (**pat**-rick-oh-**sor**-uhss) Not a valid scientific name. Thought at one time to be a meat-eating dinosaur, the fragmentary fossils may belong in part to a large lizard.

Pawpawsaurus

paw-paw-**sor**-uhss
NAMED AFTER: Paw Paw Formation, Texas
CLASSIFICATION: Ornithischia, Ankylosauria
LENGTH: 15 ft (4.6 m)
TIME: Early Cretaceous, 112 million years ago
PLACE: Texas, possibly Utah, U.S.
DIET: plants

Pawpawsaurus

DETAILS: This stocky armored plant-eater's skull was so well preserved that it revealed a feature unknown in the nodosaurids — small, bony plates on the eyelids of these dinosaurs. The anatomy of the roof of the mouth of *Pawpawsaurus* was primitive compared with the skulls of other nodosaurs like *Sauropelta,* which was discovered in the same region of Texas.

"Pectinodon" (peck-**tin**-oh-don) Not a valid scientific name. See *Troodon.*

"Peishansaurus" (**bay**-shawn-**sor**-uhss) Not a valid scientific name. Named from a fragment of a jawbone that apparently belongs to a small armored dinosaur from China.

"Pekinosaurus" (**pea**-kin-o-**sor**-uhss) Not a valid scientific name. Known only from isolated teeth.

Pelecanimimus

pell-ih-**can**-ih-**my**-muss
NAME MEANS: "pelican mimic," because of the pelicanlike shape of the dinosaur's lower jaw
CLASSIFICATION: Saurischia, Theropoda, Ornithomimosauria
LENGTH: 6.5 ft (2 m)
TIME: Early Cretaceous, 121 million years ago
PLACE: Spain
DIET: meat
DETAILS: Fossil impressions just below the long skull of this strange dinosaur resemble the deep throat pouch of a modern pelican. This dinosaur is one of the few ornithomimids with teeth. More than 200 teeth lined the front of its upper and lower jaws. These are the most teeth known in any theropod dinosaur. Traces of skin impressions were found with *Pelecanimimus*. Scientists are uncertain whether this two-legged meat-eater was covered in a downy coat.

Pelecanimimus

Pellegrinisaurus

pell-ay-**green**-ee-**sor**-uhss

NAMED AFTER: Lake Pellegrini region in northern Patagonia

CLASSIFICATION: Saurischia, Sauropoda, Macronaria

LENGTH: 82 ft (25 m)

TIME: Late Cretaceous, 71 million years ago

PLACE: Argentina

DIET: plants

Pellegrinisaurus back vertebra fragment

DETAILS: This large plant-eating dinosaur was first thought to belong to the same species as another long-necked sauropod from Argentina named *Epachthosaurus*. Based on careful study of the back vertebrae, which were twice as wide and tall as those of *Epachthosaurus* and differently shaped, experts have determined that *Pellegrinisaurus* represents a new kind of large sauropod.

Pelorosaurus

pell-**oh**-roh-**sor**-uhss

NAME MEANS: "colossal lizard"

CLASSIFICATION: Saurischia, Sauropoda, Macronaria

LENGTH: 80 ft (24.4 m)

TIME: Early Cretaceous, 130 million years ago

PLACE: England, Portugal, France

DIET: plants

DETAILS: This gigantic sauropod was one of the first and largest four-legged browsing dinosaurs ever found in Great Britain. *Pelorosaurus* is so similar to the more famous *Brachiosaurus* that some experts have suggested that it may represent a more recent version of the same kind of dinosaur. Rare skin impressions were found alongside one *Pelorosaurus* specimen, revealing a series of six-sided plates. It was named in 1850 by physician Gideon Mantell, who had named the second dinosaur discovered, *Iguanodon*, 25 years earlier.

Pelorosaurus armor plate

Pentaceratops

pen-ta-**sayr**-a-tops

NAME MEANS: "five-horned face"

CLASSIFICATION: Ornithischia, Ceratopsia

LENGTH: 28 feet (8.5 m)

Heads, You're It!

Dinosaurs were fancy animals. From bones, we know their heads were full of horns and frills, bumps and knobs. They may have had many colorful skin patterns, too.

The horned dinosaurs and the duck-billed dinosaurs show a wide variety of head decorations that show differences in the sexes and ages of the animal. Dinosaurs had good eyesight. For them, horns and frills could be signs of warning, displays for attracting mates, or scary weapons for defense against predators or rivals.

Duck-billed dinosaurs had some of the most elaborate headgear. Their crests varied by sex, age, and size as well as species. Some duckbills had foot-long trumpets. Others had helmet crests, and still others were crestless with wrinkly snouts.

TIME: Late Cretaceous, 75 million years ago

PLACE: New Mexico, U.S.

DIET: plants

DETAILS: A horn sat atop *Pentaceratops's* nose, and two more projected above its eyes. Five spikes protruded from its head, and a pair of spiked cheekbones stuck out from its cheeks. The elaborate neck frill of this dinosaur may have

Pentaceratops

been used as a display in attracting a mate or in competition with other members of the species. It might also have served as an attachment point for powerful jaw muscles. Like all of the larger ceratopsians, *Pentaceratops* was a four-legged plant-eater with a beak and scissorlike jaws for shearing through tough vegetation like cottonwoods, palms, and pines.

Phaedrolosaurus

fee-droll-oh-**sor**-uhss

NAME MEANS: "nimble dragon," because of its light build

CLASSIFICATION: Saurischia, Theropoda, Deinonychosauria, Dromaeosauridae

LENGTH: 8 ft (2.4 m)

Hypsilophodontidae Lesothosauria Macronaria Ornithomimosauria Oviraptorosauria Pachycephalosauria Primitive sauropods Prosauropoda Spinosauria Stegosauria Therizinosauridae Troodontidae Tyrannosauridae

TIME: Early Cretaceous, 130 million years ago
PLACE: China
DIET: meat
DETAILS: This small theropod is known only from short, thick teeth with dense serrations for slicing flesh. These were similar to but smaller than the teeth of the larger "raptor" *Deinonychus*. *Phaedrolosaurus* was probably a swift predator.

Phuwiangosaurus

poo-**wyong**-oh-**sor**-uhss
NAMED AFTER: Phu Wiang region of Thailand
CLASSIFICATION: Saurischia, Sauropoda, Macronaria
LENGTH: 64 ft (19.5 m)
TIME: Early Cretaceous, 127 million years ago
PLACE: Thailand
DIET: plants

Phuwiangosaurus
upper leg bone

DETAILS: Like the other giant sauropods, *Phuwiangosaurus* had a long neck and tail, walked on four sturdy legs, and browsed on plants. This massive dinosaur was one of the largest land animals ever to live in Asia.

"Phyllodon" (**fill**-oh-don) Not a valid scientific name. A single tooth found in Portugal indicates that this was some form of hypsilophodontid.

Piatnitzkysaurus

pea-yot-**nit**-skee-**sor**-uhss
NAMED AFTER: Argentine geologist Alejandro Piatnitzky
CLASSIFICATION: Saurischia, Theropoda, Carnosauria
LENGTH: 20 ft (6.1 m)
TIME: Middle Jurassic, 169 million years ago
PLACE: Argentina
DIET: meat
DETAILS: *Piatnitzkysaurus* was a quick, midsize predator with teeth and claws adapted for slashing and slicing. It was probably distantly related to the later, larger, and less primitive North American predator *Allosaurus*.

Pinacosaurus

pin-a-koh-**sor**-uhss or pin-**ack**-oh-**sor**-uhss
NAME MEANS: "plank lizard"

Pinacosaurus

CLASSIFICATION: Ornithischia, Ankylosauria
LENGTH: 18 ft (5.5 m)
TIME: Late Cretaceous, 81 million years ago
PLACE: Mongolia, China
DIET: plants
DETAILS: This club-tailed armored dinosaur was the first of its kind to be discovered in the Gobi Desert. One astounding dig site revealed the skeletons of more than a dozen sheep-size young pinacosaurs huddled together. Experts speculate that the *Pinacosaurus* group may have been smothered by a sudden sandstorm or collapsing sand dune. This dinosaur's club-tipped tail could move side to side, perhaps providing a defense against hungry predators.

Pisanosaurus

pea-**san**-o-**sor**-uhss
NAMED AFTER: Argentine paleontologist Juan A. Pisano
CLASSIFICATION: Ornithischia, Heterodontosauridae
LENGTH: 3.3 ft (1 m)
TIME: Late Triassic, 225 million years ago
PLACE: Argentina
DIET: plants
DETAILS: This fast-moving two-legged plant-eater is the oldest known ornithischian. In this region of South America, the first ornithischians are known from about the same time as the first saurischians.

Piveteausaurus

peeve-toe-**sor**-uhss
NAMED AFTER: French paleontologist Jean Piveteau
CLASSIFICATION: Saurischia, Theropoda, Carnosauria
LENGTH: 36 ft (11 m)
TIME: Middle Jurassic, 163 million years ago
PLACE: France
DIET: meat
DETAILS: Based on just a fossilized braincase, *Piveteausaurus* may have been related to *Eustreptospondylus*. If they were related, this dinosaur would have had a large head, a short neck and forelimbs, and sharply clawed hind limbs.

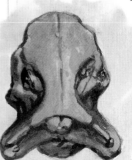
Piveteausaurus
brain case

Piatnitzkysaurus (l.)
and *Hypsilophodon* (r.)

Hypsilophodontidae   Lesothosauria   Macronaria   Ornithomimosauria   Oviraptorosauria   Pachycephalosauria   Primitive sauropods   Prosauropoda   Spinosauria   Stegosauria   Therizinosauridae   Troodontidae   Tyrannosauridae

Planicoxa

plan-i-**coke**-suh

NAME MEANS: "flat hipbone"

CLASSIFICATION: Saurischia, Ornithopoda, basal Iguanodontia

TIME: Early Cretaceous, 130 million years ago

PLACE: Utah, U.S.

DIET: plants

DETAILS: Similar to *Iguanodon,* but smaller, this newly named dinosaur had an unusual hipbone shaped differently than that on any other ornithopod dinosaur.

"Plateosauravus" (**plat**-ee-oh-**sor**-uh-vuss) Not a valid scientific name. See *Euskelosaurus.*

Plateosaurus

plat-ee-oh-**sor**-uhss

NAME MEANS: "broad lizard" or "flat lizard"

CLASSIFICATION: Saurischia, Prosauropoda

LENGTH: 27.5 ft (8.4 m)

TIME: Late Triassic, 219 million years ago

PLACE: Germany, France, Switzerland, Greenland

DIET: plants

DETAILS: One of the earliest large dinosaurs, this heavily built plant-eater had a long neck and a small head. It probably walked slowly on four legs but might have reared up onto two legs to feed. One of the largest and best known of the prosauropod dinosaurs, *Plateosaurus* was named in 1837.

Plateosaurus

Pleurocoelus

ploo-roh-**see**-luss

NAME MEANS: "hollow side"

CLASSIFICATION: Saurischia, Sauropoda, Macronaria

LENGTH: 30 feet (9.1 m)

TIME: Early Cretaceous, 119 million years ago

PLACE: Maryland, Texas, U.S.; England, Portugal

DIET: plants

DETAILS: The long-necked, plant-eating *Pleurocoelus* had a narrow skull. Its teeth were similar to those of *Camarasaurus,* but thinner. Its toes were unusually slender for a sauropod. The fourth toes of its back feet may have had small claws along with three larger claws that other sauropods had. *Pleurocoelus* may have been responsible for the spectacular series of "Brontopodus" ("thunder-foot") footprints preserved in the rock of the Paluxy River of Glen Rose, Texas. Famed dinosaur scientist Othniel C. Marsh of Yale University named this small sauropod in 1888 for the remarkably deep cavities on either side of its backbones.

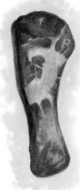

Pleurocoelus
upper leg bone

"Pleuropeltus" (**ploo**-roh-**pel**-tuss) Not a valid scientific name. May be the same as *Danubiosaurus.*

Podokesaurus

poe-**doh**-kee-**sor**-uhss

NAME MEANS: "swift-foot lizard"

CLASSIFICATION: Saurischia, Theropoda, Ceratosauria

LENGTH: 3.5 ft (1.1 m)

TIME: Early Jurassic, 188 million years ago

PLACE: Massachusetts, U.S.

DIET: meat

DETAILS: This little-known meat-eater had a lightly built body with slender, hollow bones. It also featured a long neck, short forelimbs, four-fingered hands, and birdlike feet with three walking toes. Because its proportions and anatomy were similar to *Coelophysis,* some scientists think that *Podokesaurus* may have been a juvenile of that meat-eater. Unfortunately, the single, incomplete specimen of this

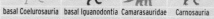

Abelisauridae Ankylosauria basal Coelurosauria basal Iguanodontia Camarasauridae Carnosauria Ceratopsia Ceratosauria Dromaeosauridae Diplodocoidea Hadrosauridae Herrerasauridae Heterodontosauridae

little dinosaur was destroyed in a fire at Mount Holyoke College in Massachusetts nearly a century ago.

Poekilopleuron

peek-ih-loh-**ploo**-ron

NAME MEANS: "varied ribs"

CLASSIFICATION: Saurischia, Theropoda, Carnosauria

LENGTH: 30 ft (9.1 m)

TIME: Middle Jurassic, 175 million years ago

PLACE: France

DIET: meat

Poekilopleuron
upper arm bone

DETAILS: *Poekilopleuron* seems to have been similar to *Torvosaurus* and probably had long and powerful jaws lined with sharp teeth, short forelimbs with three-fingered hands, and strong hind limbs capable of quick bursts of speed. The 1838 description of this large meat-eating dinosaur was based on the discovery of three distinct types of fossilized ribs along with most of a skeleton. Unfortunately, the bones were destroyed during World War II.

"**Polacanthoides**" (**poll**-uh-can-**thoy**-deez) Not a valid scientific name. This dinosaur is incompletely known and could be the same as *Polacanthus*.

Polacanthus

poll-uh-**can**-thuss

NAME MEANS: "many spine"

CLASSIFICATION: Ornithischia, Ankylosauria

LENGTH: 13 ft (4 m)

TIME: Early Cretaceous, 132 million years ago

PLACE: England

DIET: plants

DETAILS: This armored dinosaur had large spines jutting from its back, a bony shield over its hips, and pointed plates along its tail. *Polacanthus* was one of the first armored dinosaurs found. It was first mentioned in 1865 and is now thought to be distinct from *Hylaeosaurus* and *Hoplitosaurus*. Fossils have been found on the Isle of Wight and in Sussex. They may also have been uncovered in Spain.

"**Polyodontosaurus**" (**poll**-ee-oh-**don**-toe-**sor**-uhss) Not a valid scientific name. The same as *Troodon*.

"**Polyonax**" (poll-ee-**oh**-naks) Not a valid scientific name. May be the same as *Triceratops*.

"**Ponerosteus**" (**Pon**-err-**oh**-stee-us) Not a scientifically valid name. Formerly known as "Procerosaurus," and thought to represent a species of *Iguanodon* or even *Tanystropheus* (a reptile, not a dinosaur), it is named "worthless bone" because it may be the poorest fossil specimen ever used to name a dinosaur — a single fragment of bone found in Bohemia, Czech Republic, in the 1870s.

Prenocephale

preen-oh-**seff**-a-lee

NAME MEANS: "sloping head"

CLASSIFICATION: Ornithischia, Pachycephalosauria

LENGTH: 7 ft (2.1 m)

TIME: Late Cretaceous, 77 million years ago

PLACE: Mongolia

DIET: plants

Prenocephale

DETAILS: This thick-headed dinosaur had a high domed skull about eight inches (20.3 cm) deep. Like other pachycephalosaurs, it may have used this solid mass of bone to butt the flanks of predators or rivals. Large eye sockets suggest that this dinosaur may have had exceptional vision.

"**Priconodon**" (pry-**cone**-oh-don) Not a valid scientific name. Identified from a single Maryland tooth of a possible armored dinosaur.

"**Priodontognathus**" (**pry**-o-don-tog-**nay**-thuss) Not a valid scientific name. An armored dinosaur first mistaken for a stegosaur, originally named in 1875 from an upper jawbone.

Probactrosaurus

pro-**back**-troh-**sor**-uhss

NAME MEANS: "before Bactrosaurus"

CLASSIFICATION: Ornithischia, Hadrosauridae

LENGTH: 20 ft (6.1 m)

TIME: Late Cretaceous, 91 million years ago

PLACE: China

DIET: plants

DETAILS: Perhaps this plant-eating dinosaur was a link between the iguanodontids and the duckbills.

Hypsilophodontidae Lesothosauria Macronaria Ornithomimosauria Oviraptorosauria Pachycephalosauria Primitive sauropods Prosauropoda Spinosauria Stegosauria Therizinosauridae Troodontidae Tyrannosauridae

Like the more primitive iguanodontids, its narrow snout contained double-layered banks of tooth rows. The skull and skeleton were similar to the more advanced hadrosaurids, such as one less toe than iguanodontids, only one replacement tooth under each tooth, and a straight ischium, a hipbone. *Probactrosaurus* was named in 1966.

"Proceratops" (pro-**sayr**-a-tops) Not a valid scientific name. See *Ceratops.*

? Proceratosaurus

pro-seh-**rat**-oh-**sor**-uhss
NAME MEANS: "before Ceratosaurus"
CLASSIFICATION: Saurischia, Theropoda, basal Coelurosauria
LENGTH: 10 ft (3 m)
TIME: Middle Jurassic, 175 million years ago
PLACE: England
DIET: meat
DETAILS:

Proceratosaurus

Proceratosaurus was a small meat-eater known only from a partial skull. It had a snout horn that was only about 10 inches long (25.4 cm). Its teeth were cone-shaped and had large roots. These peculiar teeth also had smaller serrations than most other meat-eaters' teeth. Considered by some paleontologists to be the earliest known coelurosaur, *Proceratosaurus* may have been related to *Ornitholestes.*

"Procheneosaurus" (pro-kee-**nee**-oh-**sor**-uhss) Not a valid scientific name. A juvenile lambeosaur that may be *Corythosaurus* or *Lambeosaurus.*

"Procompsognathus" (pro-kom-**sog**-na-thuss or pro-kom-sog-**nay**-thuss) Not a valid scientific name. Long thought to be from a birdlike dinosaur, this animal was named from a skull which belonged to a crocodile-like reptile.

Prosaurolophus

pro-sore-**oll**-oh-fuss or pro-**sor**-oh-**loaf**-uhss
NAME MEANS: "before Saurolophus"
CLASSIFICATION: Ornithischia, Hadrosauridae
LENGTH: 26 ft (7.9 m)
TIME: Late Cretaceous, 73 million years ago
PLACE: Alberta, Canada
DIET: plants
DETAILS: This duck-billed dinosaur has been proposed as an ancestor to *Saurolophus,* a large hadrosaur. *Prosaurolophus* had a flattened head, a short snout, and a very small crest. Like other hadrosaurids, this dinosaur walked on all four legs but could probably rear up onto two legs to run or to grasp plants with its hooflike forefeet.

It was named in 1916 by famed dinosaur collector Barnum Brown.

Protarchaeopteryx

pro-tar-kee-**op**-tayr-iks
NAME MEANS: "first *Archaeopteryx*" or "first ancient wing"
CLASSIFICATION: Saurischia, Theropoda, basal Coelurosauria
LENGTH: 5 ft (1.5 m)
TIME: Early Cretaceous, 127 million years ago
PLACE: China
DIET: insects, reptiles?

Protarchaeopteryx

DETAILS: With its long, hind legs, this dinosaur was probably a swift hunter of small insects, mammals, or reptiles. Turkey-size and feathered, it was anatomically similar to *Archaeopteryx.* Even though it lived later than *Archaeopteryx,* it was more primitive and unable to fly. Chinese and North American scientists who have studied the fossils think that *Protarchaeopteryx* was not a flightless bird but a theropod dinosaur with a feathery covering not used for flight. Perhaps its feathers were for insulation or display. A large feather or featherlike plume

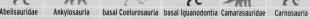

Prosaurolophus

Hypsilophodontidae Lesothosauria Macronaria Ornithomimosauria Oviraptorosauria Pachycephalosauria Primitive sauropods Prosauropoda Spinosauria Stegosauria Therizinosauridae Troodontidae Tyrannosauridae

stood at the end of this dinosaur's tail. *Protarchaeopteryx* was named in 1997.

"Protiguanodon" (pro-tigg-**wah**-no-don) Not a valid scientific name. Now called *Psittacosaurus*.

? Protoavis

pro-toe-ay-viss
NAME MEANS: "first bird"
CLASSIFICATION: Saurischia, Theropoda?
LENGTH: 3 ft (1 m)
TIME: Late Triassic, 220 million years ago
PLACE: Texas, U.S.
DIET: insects

Protoavis

DETAILS: This hotly disputed fossil has been called a Triassic bird by Texas Tech University paleontologist Sankar Chatterjee, who named it. Many other paleontologists disagree, saying that the fragmentary, unarticulated fossils make it impossible to accurately identify. The bones may even have come from several different small animals. For now, the debate over *Protoavis* continues: Is it a bird, a dinosaur, or a mix of dinosaur and other animal remains?

Protoceratops

pro-toe-sayr-a-tops
NAME MEANS: "first horned face"
CLASSIFICATION: Ornithischia, Ceratopsia
LENGTH: 8 ft (2.4 m)
TIME: Late Cretaceous, 85 million years ago
PLACE: Mongolia, China
DIET: plants
DETAILS: Despite its name, this dinosaur was not the direct ancestor of horned dinosaurs. The small plant-eater was a primitive ceratopsian dinosaur with a short, bony neck frill and a parrot-beak snout. Fossil remains from throughout *Protoceratops*'s life cycle have been found, giving paleontologists a good idea of how the dinosaur's proportions changed as it grew from a tiny hatchling to an adult. Two distinct types of adult skulls are known, one with a higher frill and one with a small hornlike bump on the nose. These may demonstrate physical differences between

males and females of the same species. The unique "fighting dinosaurs" fossil assemblage from Mongolia shows, as few fossils do, an exact moment of death: A *Velociraptor* and a *Protoceratops* appear to have died in a sandstorm

Protoceratops

while struggling with each other. The small ceratopsian had clamped its beak around the meat-eater's arm, preventing it from escaping the sandstorm. *Protoceratops* was discovered in 1922 in the Gobi Desert by a team of scientists working under the New York American Museum of Natural History adventurer Roy Chapman Andrews.

Protognathosaurus

pro-tog-nay-thoh-**sor**-uhss
NAME MEANS: "first jaw lizard"
CLASSIFICATION: Saurischia, Sauropoda, Primitive sauropods
LENGTH: 50 ft (15.2 m)

The Real Indiana Jones

Roy Chapman Andrews (1884–1960), the real-life Indiana Jones, carried a pearl-handled revolver, wore a big hat, and traveled the world, hunting for rare objects. And, yes, he *was* afraid of snakes, just like the movie hero!

Andrews was a famous adventurer of the 1920s. His greatest expedition was

Roy Chapman Andrews

conducted over ten years in the Gobi Desert of China and Mongolia. There he found the first nests of dinosaur eggs and the first dinosaur remains from Central Asia. Andrews's team from the American Museum of Natural History in New York named *Oviraptor, Protoceratops,* and *Velociraptor. Protoceratops*'s species name is *andrewsii,* in honor of the great explorer.

TIME: Early Jurassic, 188 million years ago

PLACE: China

DIET: plants

Protognathosaurus lower jaw with teeth

DETAILS: This large browser was possibly a member of the cetiosaur family of sauropods. After studying a thick, heavy jaw fragment containing about 20 teeth, scientists decided that *Protognathosaurus* was more primitive and smaller than most other sauropods.

"Protognathus" (**pro**-tog-**nay**-thuss) Not a valid scientific name; already used for another animal. See *Protognathosaurus.*

Protohadros

pro-toe-**had**-ross

NAME MEANS: "first hadrosaur"

CLASSIFICATION: Ornithischia, Hadrosauridae

LENGTH: 35 ft (10.7 m)

TIME: Late Cretaceous, 99 million years ago

PLACE: Texas, U.S.

DIET: plants

DETAILS: The earliest and most primitive hadrosaur discovered to date, *Protohadros* had a skull that featured a long muzzle with a massive lower jaw. Rows of many-edged teeth indicate that *Protohadros* was less of a plant-grinding specialist than most hadrosaurs, which had flattened batteries of hundreds of teeth. This dinosaur also had less sideways flexibility in its jaws for grinding than did other hadrosaurs. *Protohadros* was found in a river-delta setting, leading some experts to think that its bill

Protohadros

may have acted as a scoop for gathering food out of the water. *Protohadros* was named in 1998.

Psittacosaurus

sit-**tack**-oh-**sor**-uhss

NAME MEANS: "parrot lizard" or "parrot-beak lizard"

CLASSIFICATION: Ornithischia, Ceratopsia

LENGTH: 6.6 ft (2 m)

TIME: Early Cretaceous, 119 million years ago

PLACE: Mongolia, China, Thailand

DIET: plants

DETAILS: This small plant-eater had a parrotlike beak at the tip of its short snout. *Psittacosaurus* appears to represent an evolutionary link between small two-legged plant-eaters and large horned dinosaurs such as *Triceratops*. Since its teeth are worn down, *Psittacosaurus* appears to have fed on particularly tough vegetation. It may have used its nimble hands and strong beak to grasp and tear plants it crushed in its teeth. A *Psittacosaurus* fossil recently found in China had tall bristles sticking up along the top of its tail. Perhaps the bristles were designed to attract mates.

Psittacosaurus

"Pteropelyx" (tayr-**op**-eh-licks) Not a valid scientific name.

"Pterospondylus" (**tayr**-o-**spon**-dill-us) Not a valid scientific name.

Pyroraptor

pie-roh-**rap**-tore

NAME MEANS: "fire raider," because of its discovery following a forest fire

CLASSIFICATION: Saurischia, Theropoda, Deinonychosauria, Dromaeosauridae

LENGTH: 5.5 ft (1.7 m)

TIME: Late Cretaceous, 69 million years ago

PLACE: France

DIET: meat

DETAILS: The fossilized remains of this small, quick predator include the large, curved "raptor" claw on the inner walking toe of each foot. This talon could be raised up off the ground while running or extended for a deadly slashing kick. But *Pyroraptor*'s small and distinctive skeleton suggests that European "raptors" may have entered the region from Asia or North America during the Early Cretaceous Period. Then they may have become smaller in isolation at the end of dinosaur time. It has been suggested that *Pyroraptor,* named in 2000, should belong to the same genus as the very similar *Variraptor,* the first European "raptor."

Qantassaurus

Abelisauridae Ankylosauria basal Coelurosauria basal Iguanodontia Camarasauridae Carnosauria Ceratopsia Ceratosauria Dromaeosauridae Diplodocoidea Hadrosauridae Herrerasauridae Heterodontosauridae

Q

Qantassaurus

kwon-tuh-**sor**-uhss

NAMED AFTER: QANTAS Airlines

CLASSIFICATION: Ornithischia, Hypsilophodontia

LENGTH: 6.5 ft (2 m)

TIME: Early Cretaceous, 110 million years ago

PLACE: Australia

DIET: plants

DETAILS: Known only from a skull bone with at least one tooth intact, this little biped roamed Australia at a time when that continent was within the Antarctic Circle. It may have had large eyes and a large brain to help it adapt to winter darkness. *Qantassaurus* had a shortened jaw, unlike the longer snouts of other known Australian hypsilophodonts such as *Atlascopcosaurus*. Because QANTAS Airlines helped fund dinosaur research and exhibitions in Australia, this small hypsilophodont was named in that company's honor in 1999.

Qinlingosaurus

chin-ling-oh-**sor**-uhss

NAME MEANS: "Qin Ling lizard," after the mountains of Shaanxi Province, China

CLASSIFICATION: Saurischia, Sauropoda, Macronaria

LENGTH: 70 ft (21.3 m)

TIME: Late Cretaceous, 99 million years ago

PLACE: China

DIET: plants

DETAILS: An enormous pelvis and a handful of other fossil remains are all that are known of this huge plant-eater. Like other long-necked sauropods, *Qinlingosaurus* probably had a small head and a long tail and walked on four powerful, pillarlike legs.

Quaesitosaurus

kwee-**sigh**-toe-**sor**-uhss

NAME MEANS: "extraordinary lizard"

CLASSIFICATION: Saurischia, Sauropoda, Diplodocidimorpha

LENGTH: 50 ft (15.2 m)

TIME: Late Cretaceous, 85 million years ago

Quaesitosaurus

PLACE: Mongolia

DIET: plants

DETAILS: The skull of *Quaesitosaurus* strongly resembles that of another gigantic sauropod of the southern Gobi, *Nemegtosaurus*. But *Quaesitosaurus* features a much narrower snout and an unusually slanted canal at the back of the skull. This large opening for a possible sound-communicating nerve suggests that *Quaesitosaurus* may have had an excellent sense of hearing. Only the skull of this huge plant-eater has been found. This is quite unusual, as the fragile skulls of long-necked dinosaurs are rarely preserved. Their much more massive limb and backbones are far more commonly found.

Quilmesaurus

keel-may-**sor**-uss

NAMED FOR: The Quilme Indians of Argentina

CLASSIFICATION: Saurischia, Abelisauridae

LENGTH: 20 ft (6.1 m)

TIME: Late Cretaceous, 75 million years ago

DIET: meat

DETAILS: Known from just two hind-leg bones with an unusual knee shape, this newly named and mysterious meat-eater looks very primitive for its time, late in dinosaur life. Perhaps this animal was capable of hopping!

Quilmesaurus lower leg bone

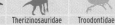

Rebbachisaurus

Abelisauridae   Ankylosauria   basal Coelurosauria   basal Iguanodontia   Camarasauridae   Carnosauria   Ceratopsia   Ceratosauria   Dromaeosauridae   Diplodocoidea   Hadrosauridae   Herrerasauridae   Heterodontosauridae

"Rahona" (**rah**-hoo-nah) Not a valid scientific name; already used for another animal. This dinosaur is called *Rahonavis*.

? Rahonavis

rah-hoo-**nay**-viss

NAME MEANS: "menace from the clouds bird"

CLASSIFICATION: Saurischia, Theropoda, Dromaeosauridae?

LENGTH: 2 ft (61 cm)

TIME: Late Cretaceous, 83.5 million years ago

PLACE: Madagascar

DIET: meat, possibly insects

DETAILS: This mysterious creature is similar to both prehistoric birds and to the swift, deadly "raptor." Some experts suggest that it was a "raptor" dromaeosaur, equipped with a slashing claw on the second toe of its foot. Others point out its very birdlike qualities, including a hipbone very similar to that of modern birds. What appear to be quill or feather attachment marks in the fossilized forearms suggest *Rahonavis* had feathers. About the size of a crow, *Rahonavis*

Rahonavis

was slightly larger than *Archaeopteryx;* its remains were very well preserved. This dinosaur was named in 1998.

"Rapator" (rap-**ay**-tore) Not a valid scientific name. An Australian meat-eater known from only a strange toe bone. May be "Walgettosuchus."

Rapetosaurus

rah-**pay**-too-**sor**-uhss

NAMED AFTER: Rapeto, mythical giant in Malagasy folklore

CLASSIFICATION: Saurischia, Sauropoda, Macronaria

LENGTH: 50 ft (15.2 m)

TIME: Late Cretaceous, 65 million years ago

PLACE: Madagascar

DIET: plants

DETAILS: Named in 2001, this is the most complete titanosaur skeleton ever found. Titanosaurs were the largest and most numerous in kinds of all the giant plant-eaters. The skeleton was uncovered in 1995 by researchers from Madagascar and the United States.

"Rayososaurus" (rye-**oh**-so-**sor**-uhss) Not a valid scientific name. See *Rebbachisaurus*.

Rebbachisaurus

reb-**bash**-ih-**sor**-uhss

NAMED AFTER: Ait Rebbach Berber tribe in Morocco

CLASSIFICATION: Saurischia, Sauropoda, Macronaria

LENGTH: 68 ft (20.7 m)

TIME: Late Cretaceous, 99 million years ago

PLACE: Morocco, Niger

DIET: plants

DETAILS: This massive four-legged plant-eating browser had a small head, a long, graceful neck and a whiplike tail. *Rebbachisaurus* is distinguished from other sauropods by its unusually tall, rigid back. Some scientists think it may even have carried a sail or fin on its spine. The discovery of *Rayososaurus*, a South American sauropod nearly identical to *Rebbachisaurus*, supports the theory that there was still a land connection between Africa and South America during the Early Cretaceous, long after it was commonly thought the two continents had separated.

"Regnosaurus" (**reg**-no-**sor**-uhss) Not a valid scientific name. Named by the physician Gideon Mantell, who labeled the second dinosaur, *Iguanodon,* this poorly preserved dinosaur might belong to a sauropod but is now thought to be part of a stegosaur.

"Revueltosaurus" (rev-**wail**-toe-**sor**-uhss) Not a valid scientific name. Named from isolated teeth.

163

Rhabdodon

Rhabdodon

rab-doh-don

NAME MEANS: "fluted tooth"

CLASSIFICATION: Ornithischia, basal Iguanodontia

LENGTH: 14.5 ft (4.4 m)

TIME: Late Cretaceous, 65 million years ago

PLACE: France, Romania, Austria, Hungary

DIET: plants

DETAILS: One of the last surviving members of the iguanodontid family, *Rhabdodon* seems to have been similar to *Camptosaurus*. It was smaller than other iguanodontids and lived long after them. Why? Perhaps *Rhabdodon* and other European dinosaurs of the Late Cretaceous were primitive and small because they lived in what was then an isolated group of islands.

"Rhadinosaurus" (**rad**-in-oh-**sor**-uhss) Not a valid scientific name.

"Rhodanosaurus" (**rod**-an-oh-**sor**-uhss) Not a valid scientific name.

Rhoetosaurus

ree-toe-**sor**-uhss

NAMED AFTER: Rhoetus, a Greco-Roman mythological giant

CLASSIFICATION: Saurischia, Sauropoda, Primitive sauropods

LENGTH: 50 ft (15.2 m)

TIME: Early Jurassic, 181 million years ago

PLACE: Australia

DIET: plants

DETAILS: *Rhoetosaurus* was a heavy long-necked plant-eater and one of the most primitive sauropods. It had a boxy head, spoon-shape teeth, and front and back legs of nearly the same length. Its tail was more rigid than those of most sauropods, especially at the base. Its thighbone alone was about five feet (1.5 m) long.

Rhoetosaurus

Richardoestesia

(rick-**are**-doh-ess-**tee**-zee-uh)

NAMED AFTER: paleontologist Richard Estes

CLASSIFICATION: Saurischia, Theropoda, Deinonychosauria, Dromaeosauridae

LENGTH: 5 ft (1.5 m)

TIME: Late Cretaceous, 80 million years ago

PLACE: Alberta, Canada

DIET: meat

DETAILS: This small "raptor"-like dinosaur is known only from a pair of lower jaws with sharp teeth. Originally this dinosaur was thought to be *Chirostenotes* but the teeth and small jaw of *Richardoestesia* cannot be linked to *Chirostenotes* or any other known dinosaur.

"Rioarribasaurus" (**ree**-oh-uh-**ree**-buh-**sor**-uhss) Not a valid scientific name. See *Coelophysis*.

Riojasaurus

ree-**oh**-hah-**sor**-uhss

NAMED AFTER: La Rioja, an Argentine province

CLASSIFICATION: Saurischia, Prosauropoda

LENGTH: 36 ft (11 m)

TIME: Late Triassic, 225 million years ago

PLACE: Argentina

DIET: plants

DETAILS: One of the earliest large plant-eating dinosaurs, this prosauropod walked on all fours, though it could probably stand on its hind feet. It had a long, slender neck and a small skull. Its limbs and tail were particularly large for a prosauropod.

Riojasaurus

Rocasaurus

roh-kuh-**sahr**-uss

NAMED AFTER: city of General Roca in southern Argentina

CLASSIFICATION: Saurischia, Sauropoda, Macronaria

LENGTH: 27 ft (8.2 m) (juvenile)

PLACE: Argentina

TIME: Late Cretaceous, 70 million years ago

DIET: plants

DETAILS: *Rocasaurus* is a titanosaur, one of the giant four-legged dinosaurs common throughout the world (except for North America) in the Cretaceous Period. It is known only from a partial skeleton of a juvenile, so its adult length has yet to be determined. It was recently named and may be a close relative of *Saltasaurus*.

Ruehleia

roo-**lee**-yuh

NAMED FOR: Hugo Ruehle von Lilienstern, a famous German paleontologist

CLASSIFICATION: Saurischia, Prosauropoda

LENGTH: 16 ft (4.9 m)

PLACE: Germany

TIME: Late Triassic, 210 million years ago

DIET: plants

DETAILS: *Ruehleia* was similar to *Plateosaurus*, a better known and larger European prosauropod of the Late Triassic. Until recently it was confused with *Plateosaurus*, though it is smaller.

Saltasaurus

Abelisauridae | Ankylosauria | basal Coelurosauria | basal Iguanodontia | Camarasauridae | Carnosauria | Ceratopsia | Ceratosauria | Dromaeosauridae | Diplodocoidea | Hadrosauridae | Herrerasauridae | Heterodontosauridae

Saichania

sigh-**kah**-nee-uh

NAME MEANS: "beautiful one," because of its remarkable preservation as a fossil

CLASSIFICATION: Ornithischia, Ankylosauria

LENGTH: 24 ft (7.3 m)

TIME: Late Cretaceous, 79 million years ago

PLACE: Mongolia

DIET: plants

DETAILS: Like all ankylosaurs, *Saichania* was a tanklike plant-eater. Fossil remains of this heavily armored, club-tailed animal were so well preserved that they revealed new features that may apply to other species in the ankylosaurid family. For example, along with the usual armored back plates, *Saichania* showed bony armor on its belly. Now paleontologists wonder whether stomach armor may have been more common than previously thought among armored dinosaurs. The size of this dinosaur's nostrils and nasal cavities indicate that it may have had a keen sense of smell.

Saichania

Saltasaurus

salt-uh-**sor**-uhss

NAMED AFTER: Salta Province, Argentina

CLASSIFICATION: Saurischia, Sauropoda, Macronaria

LENGTH: 40 ft (12.2 m)

TIME: Late Cretaceous, 83 million years ago

PLACE: Argentina

DIET: plants

DETAILS: When *Saltasaurus* was excavated in Argentina, paleontologists were astounded to find that this long-necked sauropod carried armor plates on its body. The first of the armored titanosaurids known, *Saltasaurus* was discovered with only eight pieces of armor, suggesting that the entire body was not plated. The 4.5-inch-long (11.4 cm) plates may have been scattered across the dinosaur's back as defense against large predators. About 550 quarter-inch wide (6.4 mm) bony bumps were also discovered with the skeleton. These bumps appear to have acted as a light protective covering over the dinosaur's back and sides. *Saltasaurus* appears to have been related to *Neuquensaurus*.

"Saltopus" (**salt**-oh-pus) Not a valid scientific name. This poorly preserved fossil may not be a dinosaur.

"Sanpasaurus" (**sahn**-pah-**sor**-uhss) Not a valid scientific name. Based on fragments of both an iguanodontid and a sauropod found in China.

Santanaraptor

san-**tan**-oh-**rap**-tor

NAME MEANS: "Santana robber," after the Santana Formation of northeastern Brazil

CLASSIFICATION: Saurischia, Theropoda, basal Coelurosauria

LENGTH: 6 ft (1.8 m)

TIME: Late Cretaceous, 112 million years ago

PLACE: Brazil

DIET: meat

DETAILS: *Santanaraptor* was probably a swift hunter of small prey. Its few fossil remains were discovered with a fossilized imprint of a patch of skin. This impression shows that this small meat-eating dinosaur had skin deeply creased in cross-hatched patterns, with no indication of scales, feathers, or bumps like the skin patterns known for some other dinosaurs.

Santanaraptor foot

"Sarcolestes" (**sar**-koh-**less**-teez) Not a valid scientific name. This is one of the most ancient of all nodosaurs. Originally described as a meat-eater, the poorly preserved fossils of "Sarcolestes" actually belonged to an enormous armored plant-eater nodosaur. Its thick skull was similar to those of the bone-headed pachycephalosaurs.

"Sarcosaurus" (**sar**-koh-**sor**-uhss) Not a valid scientific name. This meat-eater was named from bits of fossil found in Great Britain.

167

Saturnalia

sat-turn-**ay**-lee-uh

NAME MEANS: "carnival dinosaur," after the Roman holiday of Saturnalia

CLASSIFICATION: Saurischia, Sauropoda, Prosauropoda

LENGTH: 5 ft (1.5 m)

TIME: Late Triassic, 227 million years ago

PLACE: Brazil

DIET: plants

DETAILS: This small and primitive ancestor of the giant plant-eating dinosaurs was described based on parts from three individuals, including a right hind limb, a foot, a pelvic bone, a small skull, and serrated and leaf-shape teeth.

Saurolophus

sore-**oll**-oh-fuss or sore-oh-**loaf**-us

NAME MEANS: "lizard crest" or "crested lizard"

CLASSIFICATION: Ornithischia, Hadrosauridae

LENGTH: 32 ft (9.8 m)

TIME: Late Cretaceous, 72 million years ago

PLACE: Alberta, Canada; Mongolia

DIET: plants

DETAILS: *Saurolophus* lacked the hollow head-crest of the lambeosaur duckbills but bore a bony, spikelike crest above and between its eyes. The excavation of strikingly similar hadrosaurid fossils in Mongolia supports the theory that connections between the now-separate continents of Asia and North America allowed dinosaurs to cross over during the Late Cretaceous. *Saurolophus* was named in 1912 by Barnum Brown, the fossil hunter who found *Tyrannosaurus rex* and many other dinosaurs in the North American West. A nearly complete *Saurolophus* skeleton was unearthed, including fossilized skin impressions.

Saurolophus

Sauropelta

sore-oh-**pell**-tuh

NAME MEANS: "lizard shield"

CLASSIFICATION: Ornithischia, Ankylosauria

LENGTH: 19 ft (5.8 m)

TIME: Early Cretaceous, 116 million years ago

PLACE: Montana, Wyoming, Utah, U.S.

DIET: plants

DETAILS: *Sauropelta* was a medium-size armored dinosaur that lacked the bony, clubbed tail of the related ankylosaurs. The dinosaur's long hind legs gave it an arched spine. Sharp triangular spikes were strategically placed just in front of the shoulders, probably as a defense against the teeth and claws of predators.

Saurophaganax

sore-oh-**fay**-ga-naks

NAME MEANS: "reptile-eater master" or "king of the reptile-eaters"

CLASSIFICATION: Saurischia, Theropoda, Carnosauria

LENGTH: 40 ft (12.2 m)

TIME: Late Jurassic, 154 million years ago

PLACE: Oklahoma, U.S.

DIET: meat

DETAILS: The massive *Saurophaganax* was perhaps the largest hunter of the Jurassic Period. A huge relative of *Allosaurus*, *Saurophaganax* probably used its bladelike teeth and big claws to bring down prey, including even the giant plant-eaters of its time. Utah paleontologist Dan Chure suggested this name in 1995 for fossil material attributed to an extremely large meat-eating allosaurid that was discovered in Oklahoma during the Great Depression of the 1930s but was never extensively studied. A similar dinosaur had once been called "Saurophagus," but that name is no longer considered scientifically valid.

"Saurophagus" (sore-**off**-a-guss) Not a valid scientific name. Already used for another animal; this may be the same dinosaur as *Saurophaganax*.

"Sauroplites" (**saw**-ruh-**ply**-teeze) Not a valid scientific name. An armored Chinese dinosaur named from just a few fragmentary fossils and armor plates.

Sauroposeidon

sore-oh-po-**sye**-don

NAME MEANS: "earthquake-god lizard," after Poseidon, Greek god of oceans and earthquakes

CLASSIFICATION: Saurischia, Sauropoda, Macronaria

LENGTH: 98 ft (29.9 m)

TIME: Early Cretaceous, 112 million years ago

Sauroposeidon

Hypsilophodontidae Lesothosauria Macronaria Ornithomimosauria Oviraptorosauria Pachycephalosauria Primitive sauropods Prosauropoda Spinosauria Stegosauria Therizinosauridae Troodontidae Tyrannosauridae

PLACE: Oklahoma, U.S.

DIET: plants

DETAILS: Perhaps the tallest and longest-necked of all dinosaurs, the titanic *Sauroposeidon* stretched an estimated 60 feet (18.3 m) from its toes to the top of its raised head. It probably fed off high evergreen branches just like *Brachiosaurus* did. *Sauroposeidon* carried a remarkably elongated neck, which may have been 40 feet (12.2 m) long or more. This dinosaur is known so far from several neck vertebrae that measure 10 feet long. They are the longest of any such bones known in dinosaurs. *Sauroposeidon* was named in 2000.

Saurornithoides

sore-**or**-nith-**oy**-deez

NAME MEANS: "lizard-bird form," because of the similarities of its skull to that of birds

CLASSIFICATION: Saurischia, Theropoda, Deinonychosauria, Troodontidae

LENGTH: 7 ft (2 m)

TIME: Late Cretaceous, 85 million years ago

PLACE: Mongolia

DIET: meat

DETAILS: A swift and smart little hunter, much like its close North American cousin *Troodon*, *Saurornithoides* probably scoured the Gobi Desert for small mammals or reptiles. This large-brained, small meat-eater was a very birdlike dinosaur. *Saurornithoides* and *Troodon* each had a skull like that of a bird's head. The great similarity between the two troodontids is evidence that Asia and North America were connected shortly before these dinosaurs' time.

Saurornitholestes

sore-oh-**nith**-oh-**less**-teez

NAME MEANS: "lizard-bird robber"

CLASSIFICATION: Saurischia, Theropoda, Deinonychosauria, Dromaeosauridae

LENGTH: 6 ft (1.8 m)

TIME: Late Cretaceous, 76 million years ago

PLACE: Alberta, Canada

DIET: meat

DETAILS: This small, lightly built meat-eater had a large head with a narrow snout. Highly flexible wrists and long forelimbs gave *Saurornitholestes* nimble fingers and grip. A long, curved claw that snapped out from the second toe of each foot made this "raptor" relative a lethal predator. A long, stiff tail provided balance for running and leaping. Very similar to *Velociraptor* and *Deinonychus*, its relatives from Asia and North America, *Saurornitholestes* provides yet more evidence for the presence of Late Cretaceous land connections between the two continents.

Scelidosaurus

skell-i-doh-**sor**-uhss

NAME MEANS: "hind-limb lizard"

CLASSIFICATION: Ornithischia, Ankylosauria

LENGTH: 13.5 ft (4.1 m)

TIME: Early Jurassic, 200 million years ago

PLACE: England

DIET: plants

DETAILS: Despite its powerful rear legs, this primitive armored dinosaur walked on all fours. *Scelidosaurus* carried both bony armor and small, rounded scales. Skin impressions were found with the dinosaur's fossilized bones, offering scientists a rare view of the arrangement of those plates and scales. Sir Richard Owen named this dinosaur in 1859. He had coined the word *dinosaur* 18 years earlier.

Scipionyx

sip-ee-**on**-iks or **skip**-ee-**on**-iks

NAME MEANS: "Scipio's claw," after the famed Roman general Scipio

CLASSIFICATION: Saurischia, Theropoda, basal Coelurosauria

LENGTH: 10 ft (3 m)

TIME: Early Cretaceous, 121 million years ago

PLACE: Italy

DIET: meat

DETAILS: This small meat-eater is closely related to *Compsoganthus*.

Scipionyx

Abelisauridae　Ankylosauria　basal Coelurosauria　basal Iguanodontia　Camarasauridae　Carnosauria　Ceratopsia　Ceratosauria　Dromaeosauridae　Diplodocoidea　Hadrosauridae　Herrerasauridae　Heterodontosauridae

Saurornithoides

Hypsilophodontidae　Lesothosauria　Macronaria　Ornithomimosauria　Oviraptorosauria　Pachycephalosauria　Primitive sauropods　Prosauropoda　Spinosauria　Stegosauria　Therizinosauridae　Troodontidae　Tyrannosauridae

Its fossils belonged to a youngster just nine inches (22.9 cm) long, which must have died very soon after hatching. The preservation of this fossil is among the most remarkable of any dinosaur ever found. It is complete except for a small portion of its tail and feet. The skeleton appears to include fossil evidence of soft tissue; impressions in rock show several internal organs, including the thorax, a part of the throat. *Scipionyx*'s remains indicate that its gut was small. This means the dinosaur had a fast, efficient metabolism and processed food quickly. The first dinosaur material ever described from Italy, the *Scipionyx* was named in 1998. Fossilized internal parts of a dinosaur are almost completely unknown beyond this specimen.

"Scolosaurus" (**skoh**-luh-**sor**-uhss) Not a valid scientific name. See *Euoplocephalus*.

Scutellosaurus

skoo-**tell**-oh-**sor**-uhss
NAME MEANS: "little-shield lizard"
CLASSIFICATION: Ornithischia, Ankylosauria
LENGTH: 4 ft (1.2 m)
TIME: Early Jurassic, 200 million years ago
PLACE: Arizona, U.S.
DIET: plants
DETAILS: This small plant-eater had a long tail and carried more fully developed armor than any other known primitive dinosaur. More than 300 plates with six different shapes were found with the fossilized skeleton of *Scutellosaurus*. Long hind limbs suggest that this dinosaur may have walked on its hind legs. Its wide pelvis and long torso, however, indicate that it may have moved on all fours. *Scutellosaurus* was a distant ancestor of the armored dinosaurs of the Jurassic and Cretaceous Periods.

Scutellosaurus

Secernosaurus

see-**sayr**-no-**sor**-uhss
NAME MEANS: "separated lizard"
CLASSIFICATION: Ornithischia, Hadrosauridae
LENGTH: 20 ft (6.1 m)

TIME: Late Cretaceous, 73 million years ago
PLACE: Argentina
DIET: plants
DETAILS: This small duck-billed dinosaur was one of the first hadrosaurids to be discovered in the Southern Hemisphere. It migrated from North America when the continents were linked near the end of dinosaur time, just as some dinosaurs from South America moved northward. *Secernosaurus* may have had a crest on its head, but its remains are too incomplete to be certain of this.

Segisaurus

Segisaurus

seg-ih-**sor**-uhss
NAMED AFTER: Segi Canyon in Arizona
CLASSIFICATION: Saurischia, Theropoda, Ceratosauria
LENGTH: 3.3 ft (1 m)
TIME: Early Jurassic, 200 million years ago
PLACE: Arizona, U.S.
DIET: meat
DETAILS: A young specimen of this small meat-eater was found with its hind limbs and feet flexed beneath its body. This unusual posture has led some scientists to think that *Segisaurus* could have squatted down like a modern-day chicken. This dinosaur's feet were especially well adapted for clawing, leading to more speculation about its behavior. The fingers of its short forelimbs seem well designed for raking a meal of insects or small animals out of the ground. *Segisaurus* had a clavicle, which was unusual in dinosaurs, but is common as the "wishbone" in birds.

Segnosaurus

seg-nuh-**sor**-uhss
NAME MEANS: "slow lizard"
CLASSIFICATION: Saurischia, Theropoda, Therizinosauridae

Segnosaurus lower jaw

LENGTH: 29.5 ft (9 m)

TIME: Late Cretaceous, 97.5 million years ago

PLACE: Mongolia

DIET: plants?

DETAILS: *Segnosaurus* appears to have been a strong but slow-moving dinosaur with a long neck, bulky body and limbs, and a heavy tail. It was the first member of the mysterious segnosaurid family discovered. These medium-size dinosaurs had characteristics of both two-legged and four-legged animals, and of plant-eaters, and of meat-eaters. *Segnosaurus*'s large claws, however, were better adapted for killing than the claws of *Allosaurus*.

Seismosaurus

size-moe-**sor**-uhss

NAME MEANS: "earthquake lizard"

CLASSIFICATION: Saurischia, Sauropoda, Diplodocoidea

LENGTH: 135 ft (41.1 m)

TIME: Late Jurassic, 156 million years ago

PLACE: New Mexico, U.S.

DIET: plants

Seismosaurus

DETAILS: Half a football field in length, this "earth shaker" is the longest dinosaur unearthed to date. Known from much of the rear end of an enormous individual, *Seismosaurus* appears to have been a relatively slim, low-slung dinosaur much like the whip-tailed *Barosaurus* and *Diplodocus*. A group of smooth, rounded stones discovered where the *Seismosaurus*'s stomach once was indicates that *Seismosaurus* swallowed small rocks. Inside the dinosaur's gizzard, these rocks helped crush the plants the dinosaur had nipped with its teeth and swallowed into an easily digested pulp. Giant sauropods may have needed this aid to digestion because they had such small heads, simple teeth, and weak jaws.

Sellosaurus

sell-oh-**sor**-uhss

NAME MEANS: "saddle lizard," because of its wide, flat tail vertebrae

CLASSIFICATION: Saurischia, Prosauropoda

LENGTH: 20 ft (6.1 m)

TIME: Late Triassic, 219 million years ago

PLACE: Germany

DIET: plants

Shamosaurus skull

DETAILS: This early prosauropod was of medium size. Small stomach stones, or gastroliths, were found along with a skeleton of this animal.

Shamosaurus

shah-moe-**sor**-uhss

NAME MEANS: "desert lizard"

CLASSIFICATION: Ornithischia, Ankylosauria

LENGTH: 23 ft (7 m)

TIME: Early Cretaceous, 119 million years ago

PLACE: Mongolia

DIET: plants

DETAILS: *Shamosaurus* is the earliest known club-tailed armored dinosaur from China. Its small skull was ornamented with small bumps of bone. *Shamosaurus* resembled the Mongolian club-tailed ankylosaur.

Shanshanosaurus

shawn-**shawn**-oh-**sor**-uhss

NAMED AFTER: Shanshan Zhan Turpan Basin, China

CLASSIFICATION: Saurischia, Theropoda, Tyrannosauridae

LENGTH: 8.5 ft (2.6 m) or more (based on a juvenile)

TIME: Late Cretaceous, 83 million years ago

PLACE: China

DIET: meat

DETAILS: This small meat-eater was a scientific mystery for almost 40 years. *Shanshanosaurus* is now known to be a baby tyrannosaurid, the smallest one yet discovered.

How big it might have grown as an adult is not known.

Shantungosaurus

shawn-**doong**-oh-**sor**-uhss

NAMED AFTER: Shandong Province, China

CLASSIFICATION: Ornithischia, Hadrosauridae

LENGTH: 50 ft (15.2 m)

TIME: Late Cretaceous, 83 million years ago

PLACE: China

Shantungosaurus

DIET: plants

DETAILS: *Shantungosaurus* is the largest of all known duck-billed dinosaurs. Apart from its enormous size, this four-legged plant-eater was very much like North America's *Edmontosaurus*. Like all flat-headed hadrosaurs, *Shantungosaurus* had a long, broad skull with a short beak and densely packed teeth for efficiently crushing plants. Many of this dinosaur's skeletons are now known, but few have been scientifically described.

Shanxia

shawn-**she**-uh

NAMED AFTER: Shanxi Province in China
CLASSIFICATION: Ornithischia, Ankylosauria
LENGTH: 12 ft (3.7 m)
TIME: Late Cretaceous, 99 million years ago
PLACE: China
DIET: plants

DETAILS: This sturdy four-legged armored plant-eater had distinctive elongated and slender triangular spikes protruding from the back of its head. Excavated in northeastern China, this incomplete skeleton included a piece of armor and fragments of a wide skull.

"**Shanyangosaurus**" (shawn-**yong**-oh-**sor**-uhss) Not a valid scientific name. This small Chinese meat-eater is based on isolated limb bones.

Shunosaurus

shoe-no-**sor**-uhss

NAMED AFTER: old name for Sichuan Province, China
CLASSIFICATION: Saurischia, Sauropoda, Primitive sauropods

Shunosaurus

LENGTH: 46 ft (14 m)
TIME: Middle Jurassic, 175 million years ago
PLACE: China
DIET: plants

DETAILS: *Shunosaurus* was a long-necked browser with an unusual feature – a tail club. The spectacularly well-preserved remains of this unusual sauropod, found in 1983, revealed a knobby, bony club at the end of its short tail. This small but solid weapon might have been swung to cause serious damage to predatory dinosaurs.

Shuvosarus

? Shuvosarus

Shoe-vo-**sor**-uhss

NAMED AFTER: Shuvo, son of paleontologist Sankar Chatterjee
CLASSIFICATION: Saurischia, Theropoda?
LENGTH: 5 ft (1.5 m)
TIME: Late Triasssic, 210 million years ago
PLACE: Texas, U.S.
DIET: meat

DETAILS: This little known and mysterious animal has just become a dinosaur, again! In 1993, it was first described from a few bones and a toothless skull

The Tale of the Tail

Dinosaur tails came in many shapes and sizes. Some dinosaurs had club tails that they used for defense or show. Most club tails are known only from one group of armored tanklike dinosaurs, the ankylosaurs. *Shunosaurus* was among the few sauropods with a club tail that we know of.

Other dinosaurs, such as the duckbills, had frilly edges on the skin of their long tails. Duckbill tails were probably used for balance and perhaps for swiping at rivals or predators. Other dinosaurs may have had brightly colored tails to show off for mates or signal to their herds. Giant plant-eaters of the *Diplodocus* family had whiplike tails more than 20 feet (6.1 m) long! By snapping their tails these animals could produce a thundering sound to frighten off predators.

Abelisauridae Ankylosauria basal Coelurosauria basal Iguanodontia Camarasauridae Carnosauria Ceratopsia Ceratosauria Dromaeosauridae Diplodocoidea Hadrosauridae Herrerasauridae Heterodontosauridae

fragment as a very early member of the ornithomimids. Ornithomimids are toothless, meat-eating "ostrich" dinosaurs. In 1995, other scientists argued that *Shuvosaurus* was a more primitive reptile, not a dinosaur at all. But new studies indicate that it was a primitive meat-eater after all, though probably not an ornithomimid.

Shuvuuia

shoe-**voo**-ee-uh
NAME MEANS: "bird"
CLASSIFICATION: Theropoda, basal Coelurosauria
LENGTH: 3.3 ft (1 m)
TIME: Late Cretaceous, 83.5 million years ago
PLACE: Mongolia
DIET: meat
DETAILS: This unusual *Mononykus*-like meat-eater had a birdlike skull with a snout that could bend upward. *Shuvuuia* was once thought to be a flightless bird. Scientists now think it is a dinosaur. Its fossils include two very well-preserved skulls. The dinosaur was named in 1998.

Siamosaurus

sigh-**am**-o-**sor**-uhss
NAME MEANS: "Siamese lizard," after the ancient word for Thailand
CLASSIFICATION: Saurischia, Theropoda, Spinosauria
LENGTH: 30 ft (9.1 m)
TIME: Late Jurassic, 163 million years ago
PLACE: Thailand
DIET: meat, possibly fish

DETAILS: Known only from teeth that closely resemble those of the North African meat-eater *Spinosaurus,* this large carnivore may have lived primarily on fish. *Siamosaurus* had smooth, compressed teeth, similar to those of fish-eating marine reptiles like plesiosaurs and amphibious crocodiles. These teeth were better suited for piercing than for slicing or tearing flesh. A quick-snapping jaw gave this dinosaur a firm grip on a mouthful of wriggling fish. Like other spinosaurids, *Siamosaurus* may have had three-fingered hands and tall back spines that supported a sail.

Siamosaurus teeth

Siamotyrannus

sigh-**am**-o-tie-**ran**-us
NAME MEANS: "Siamese tyrant"
CLASSIFICATION: Saurischia, Theropoda, Tyrannosauridae
LENGTH: 25 ft (7.6 m)
TIME: Early Cretaceous, 110 million years ago
PLACE: Thailand
DIET: meat
DETAILS: Recently discovered, this partial skeleton may represent the oldest known tyrannosaur. Several researchers doubt, however, that this large meat-eater belongs to the tyrannosaur family and cannot identify it further from the fossils known so far.

Sigilmassasaurus

see-jill-**mah**-saw-**sor**-uhss
NAMED AFTER: Sigilmassa, ancient capital of Taflalt, Morocco
CLASSIFICATION: Saurischia, Theropoda, Spinosauria
LENGTH: 20 ft (6.1 m)
TIME: Late Cretaceous, 95 million years ago
PLACE: Morocco, Egypt
DIET: meat
DETAILS: The few known fossils of this large meat-eating dinosaur suggest it may have been a relative of *Carcharodontosaurus*. But *Sigilmassasaurus* had an unusually flexible neck and a small head. Bones from other parts of its body were found in Egypt by German scientists in the 1930s but were destroyed in Germany during World War II bombing.

"Siluosaurus" (suh-**loo**-oh-**sor**-uhss) Not a valid scientific name. A mysterious plant-eater based on two teeth found on the Silk Road in Central Asia.

Silvisaurus

sill-vih-**sor**-uhss
NAME MEANS: "forest lizard"
CLASSIFICATION: Ornithischia, Ankylosauria
LENGTH: 13 ft (4 m)
TIME: Late Cretaceous, 116 million years ago
PLACE: Kansas, U.S.
DIET: plants
DETAILS: This primitive armored dinosaur had

Silvisaurus skull

Sinornithosaurus

large protective spikes on its sides. Like other armored dinosaurs, *Silvisaurus* had large sinus chambers in its skull. These may have amplified the dinosaur's sounds in much the same way as a voice box makes our speech louder. Not much is preserved of this animal, so it is unknown whether it carried a club on its tail.

"Sinocoelurus" (**sine**-oh-see-**loor**-us) Not a valid scientific name. Based on the four teeth uncovered, this animal may not be a dinosaur at all.

Sinornithoides

sine-**or**-nith-**oy**-deez

NAME MEANS: "Chinese bird form"

CLASSIFICATION: Saurischia, Theropoda, Troodontidae

LENGTH: 3.6 ft (1.1 m) or larger (based on juvenile)

TIME: Early Cretaceous, 121 million years ago

PLACE: China

DIET: meat

DETAILS: This small meat-eater had a shorter skull but still looked much like troodontids, which lived more than 40 million years later in North America. These similarities suggest this form of dinosaur was highly successful, and so changed little over long periods of time. *Sinornithoides* may have grown nearly twice as large as the one specimen known, which was a youngster found curled up like a cat. At first, researchers mistook it for a small psittacosaur, a plant-eater. It may, in fact, be one of the most birdlike of all small meat-eating dinosaurs.

Sinornithosaurus

sine-or-nith-oh-**sor**-uhss

NAME MEANS: "Chinese bird lizard"

CLASSIFICATION: Saurischia, Theropoda, Deinonychosauria, Dromaeosauridae

LENGTH: 5 ft (1.5 m)

TIME: Early Cretaceous, 125 million years ago

PLACE: China

DIET: meat

DETAILS: *Sinornithosaurus* had slender arms, possibly with the same large range of motion of a bird's wings. Its arms had a featherlike covering as well. The feathers are preserved in the form of fossil impressions that show patches of strands about 1.4 inches (3.6 cm) long around different parts of this dinosaur's body. The downy coat was not completely preserved; perhaps it covered the head and most of the body. *Sinornithosaurus* was described based on a fairly complete but scattered skeleton, including a skull just over five inches (12.7 cm) long. Its birdlike shoulders and forelimbs seem to be very much like those of the smaller, flying *Archaeopteryx*. *Sinornithosaurus* was not equipped for flight, so the feathery layer must have served some other function, possibly to keep the dinosaur warm or to provide a display for attracting a mate. This dinosaur's forelimbs are about 80% as long as the hind limbs, making them proportionally among the longest arms on any meat-eating dinosaur. Portions of the right foot at the end of one strong, sleek leg show that *Sinornithosaurus* had the slashing sickle-claw characteristic of dromaeosaurid dinosaurs. *Sinornithosaurus* was named in 1999.

Sinosauropteryx

Sinosauropteryx

sine-oh-sore-**op**-tayr-iks

NAME MEANS: "Chinese dragon feather"

CLASSIFICATION: Saurischia, Theropoda, basal Coelurosauria

LENGTH: 4 ft (1.2 m)

TIME: Early Cretaceous, 140 million years ago

PLACE: China

DIET: meat, including lizards and mammals

DETAILS: A two-foot-long (61 cm) youngster of this little predatory dinosaur was found in the sediments of an ancient lake in the Liaoning Province of northeastern China. The remains were so well preserved that even tiny, featherlike structures lining the back and tail are clearly visible. Initially misidentified as a primitive bird, *Sinosauropteryx* is in fact a small theropod, closely related to *Compsognathus*. Three individuals have been unearthed to date. These finds are of special significance because traces of soft tissue were preserved along with the bone. Eyes, internal organs, stomach contents, and even unlaid eggs still in the oviducts make this one of the most detailed dinosaur fossils ever found.

Sinosauropteryx has the longest tail for its size of any known meat-eating dinosaur. The first of

Hypsilophodontidae   Lesothosauria   Macronaria   Ornithomimosauria   Oviraptorosauria   Pachycephalosauria   Primitive sauropods   Prosauropoda   Spinosauria   Stegosauria   Therizinosauridae   Troodontidae   Tyrannosauridae

Spinosaurus (t.)
and Hypsilophodon (b.)

Abelisauridae   Ankylosauria   basal Coelurosauria   basal Iguanodontia   Camarasauridae   Carnosauria   Ceratopsia   Ceratopsia   Dromaeosauridae   Diplodocoidea   Hadrosauridae   Herrerasauridae   Heterodontosauridae

its three fingers ended in an enlarged slashing claw. Featherlike filaments appear to have covered most of the dinosaur's body, perhaps serving to keep the small animal warm. Examination of the preserved stomach contents shows that *Sinosauropteryx* ate small prey, including lizards and mammals. A pair of eggs discovered within a female's body indicate that *Sinosauropteryx* laid two eggs at a time, as *Troodon* is thought to have done.

"Sinosaurus" (**sine**-oh-**sor**-uhss) Not a valid scientific name. This animal is based upon a partial jaw that may have belonged to a primitive reptile.

Sinraptor

sine-**rap**-tor

Sinraptor

NAME MEANS:
"Chinese plunderer"

CLASSIFICATION:
Saurischia, Theropoda, Carnosauria

LENGTH: 23 ft (7 m)

TIME: Late Jurassic, 154 million years ago

PLACE: China

DIET: meat

DETAILS: This large meat-eating dinosaur shows interesting similarities not only to *Allosaurus,* a similar-sized meat-eater from the same time in North America, but to later and even larger carnivores such as *Giganotosaurus* from the Southern Hemisphere. *Sinraptor*'s closest relative was the Chinese meat-eater of a similar time, *Yangchuanosaurus.* The first *Sinraptor* skull showed bite marks that scientists think came from other *Sinraptor* individuals battling for mates, territory, dominance, defense, or food.

Sonorasaurus

so-**nor**-uh-**sor**-uhss

NAMED AFTER: the Sonoran Desert in Mexico and U.S.

CLASSIFICATION: Saurischia, Sauropoda, Macronaria

LENGTH: 51 ft (15.5 m)

TIME: Early Cretaceous, 112 million years ago

PLACE: Arizona, U.S.

DIET: plants

DETAILS: This medium-size sauropod was about 30% smaller than its more famous relative, *Brachiosaurus.* Like other brachiosaurids, *Sonorasaurus* had high front legs, a sloping back, and a long neck that it held high in the air. *Sonorasaurus* had only two small claws on its hind feet; some brachiosaurids, including *Pleurocoelus,* had four. A tooth of the giant theropod *Acrocanthosaurus* was found embedded in the bones of *Sonorasaurus,* suggesting that it feasted on the dead or dying plant-eater. Found in 1995 near Tucson, Arizona, *Sonorasaurus* was named in 1998. Before being scientifically described, it was first mistakenly identified as a hadrosaurid, then a prosauropod, and then a therizinosaur. *Sonorosaurus* was found with a collection of stomach stones called gastroliths, used to help grind food.

"Sphenospondylus" (**sfee**-noh-**spon**-dih-lus). Not a valid scientific name. See *Iguanodon.*

Spinosaurus

spy-no-**sor**-uhss

NAME MEANS: "spine lizard"

CLASSIFICATION: Saurischia, Theropoda, Spinosauria

LENGTH: 45 ft (13.7 m)

TIME: Late Cretaceous, 97.5 million years ago

PLACE: Egypt, Morocco

DIET: meat

DETAILS: This giant sail-backed meat-eater may have been among the largest carnivores ever to walk the earth. The bones of its back featured unusual, tall spines. These spines may have been connected by a membrane of skin, giving this dinosaur a distinctive sail-like fin similar to that of the far more ancient mammal-like reptile *Dimetrodon.* The function of this fin remains unknown. It may have served as a display to attract mates, or acted as a heat regulator to cool the dinosaur down on hot days. Like other spinosaurids, *Spinosaurus* had narrow jaws full of sharp, conical teeth. This dinosaur was named in 1915, but its remains, which had been brought to Germany, were destroyed in Allied bombing raids during World War II. Recently more *Spinosaurus* fossils have been found in Egypt. In the movie *Jurassic Park III* its size was greatly exaggerated to make it a *T. rex*–chasing villain. However, a fragmentary find suggests this animal may have grown up to 60 feet (18 m) long!

"**Spondylosoma**" (**spon**-dill-oh-**so**-muh) Not a valid scientific name. Fragmentary fossils, including two teeth, suggest it was a primitive plant-eater from Brazil.

Staurikosaurus

store-ick-oh-**sor**-uhss

NAME MEANS: "Southern Cross lizard," after the constellation visible in the Southern Hemisphere
CLASSIFICATION: Saurischia, Theropoda, Herrerasauridae
LENGTH: 7 ft (2.1 m)
TIME: Late Triassic, 231 million years ago
PLACE: Brazil
DIET: meat
DETAILS: This small South American meat-eaters appears to have been among the earliest and most primitive of all dinosaurs. Like the larger *Herrerasaurus*, a possible relative, *Staurikosaurus* had a slender neck and long, muscular legs with five-toed feet. Its forearms were small, with four-fingered hands. Later, more advanced theropod dinosaurs would lose digits, walking on three toes and grasping or slashing with three-clawed hands or, in the case of the advanced tyrannosaurids, only two fingers.

Staurikosaurus

Stegoceras

steg-**oss**-e-russ

NAME MEANS: "roof horn"
CLASSIFICATION: Ornithischia, Pachycephalosauria
LENGTH: 7 ft (2.1 m)
TIME: Late Cretaceous, 67 million years ago
PLACE: Montana, U.S.; Alberta, Canada
DIET: plants

Stegoceras

DETAILS: Like all of the pachycephalosaurs, *Stegoceras* had a dense layer of protective bone atop its skull. This thickened skull bone was originally mistaken for the bony core of a ceratopsian dinosaur's horn. *Stegoceras* became the dinosaur's somewhat misleading name in 1902.

"**Stegopelta**" (steg-oh-**pell**-tuh) Not a valid scientific name. See *Nodosaurus*.

"**Stegosaurides**" (**steg**-oh-sor-**eye**-deez) Not a valid scientific name.

Stegosaurus

steg-o-**sor**-uhss

NAME MEANS: "plated lizard"
CLASSIFICATION: Ornithischia, Stegosauria
LENGTH: 29.5 ft (9 m)
TIME: Late Jurassic, 156 million years ago
PLACE: Colorado, Utah, Wyoming, U.S.
DIET: plants
DETAILS: *Stegosaurus* was the first of the plate-backed dinosaurs to be discovered, and it remains one of the largest of that group known so far. A small-headed plant-eater, *Stegosaurus* carried two rows of alternating bony plates, the largest more than two feet (61 cm) tall, arranged along its back from neck to tail. A pair of long spikes projected from each side of the tail near the tip; these could perhaps be swiped back and forth to ward off predators. Small bony disks embedded in the dinosaur's skin provided some protection for its vulnerable throat and hips and may have covered other parts of the body as well. The function of the flattened, diamond-shape back plates remains

180

Abelisauridae   Ankylosauria   basal Coelurosauria   basal Iguanodontia   Camarasauridae   Carnosauria   Ceratopsia   Ceratosauria   Dromaeosauridae   Diplodocoidea   Hadrosauridae   Herrerasauridae   Heterodontosauridae

Stegosaurus

Hypsilophodontidae Lesothosauria Macronaria Ornithomimosauria Oviraptorosauria Pachycephalosauria Primitive sauropods Prosauropoda Spinosauria Stegosauria Therizinosauridae Troodontidae Tyrannosauridae

uncertain. They may have been used as display to attract a mate or to compete with rivals. Or perhaps these plates helped regulate temperature, cooling the dinosaur down when it became too warm. There was once a popular misconception that this dinosaur had two brains. In fact, the second "brain" was a nerve center in the hips, a feature *Stegosaurus* shared with several other dinosaurs.

"Stenonychosaurus" (sten-**on**-ick-oh-**sor**-uhss) Not a valid scientific name. See *Troodon*.

Stenopelix skeleton, seen from above

Stenopelix

sten-**op**-eh-licks
NAME MEANS: "narrow pelvis"
CLASSIFICATION: Ornithischia, Hypsilophodontidae
LENGTH: 5 ft (1.5 m)
TIME: Early Cretaceous, 144 million years ago
PLACE: Germany
DIET: plants
DETAILS: This little plant-eater has had a long and complicated scientific history since its discovery in 1857. Once thought to be related to the two-legged *Hypsilophodon, Stenopelix* was later grouped with the primitive horned dinosaurs, the parrot-beaked psittacosaurs. Subsequently, this dinosaur was reclassified as a thick-skulled dinosaur, a pachycephalosaur. *Stenopelix* may have been related to the common ancestor of both the horned and the dome-skulled dinosaurs.

"Stenotholus" (sten-oh-**thoh**-luss) Not a valid scientific name. See *Stygimoloch*.

"Stephanosaurus" (**steff**-a-no-**sor**-uhss) Not a valid scientific name. This name was based on fossils from several different dinosaurs, including *Lambeosaurus*.

"Stereocephalus" (**stare**-ee-oh-**seff**-a-luss) Not a valid scientific name. See *Euoplocephalus*.

"Sterrholophus" (stir-**oll**-oh-fuss) Not a valid scientific name. See *Triceratops*.

? Stokesosaurus

stoke-so-**sor**-uhss
NAMED AFTER: Utah paleontologist William Lee Stokes
CLASSIFICATION: Saurischia, Theropoda, Tyrannosauridae
LENGTH: 13.5 ft (4.1 m)
TIME: Late Jurassic, 156 million years ago
PLACE: Utah, U.S.
DIET: meat
DETAILS: This small to midsize meat-eater had a strange ridge running down the middle of its pelvic bone. It may also have had a short, stubby snout, but the few fossils known make *Stokesosaurus* difficult to identify. It may have been a very early tyrannosaurid.

Stokesosaurus pelvic bone

"Strenusaurus" (**stren**-uh-**sor**-uhss) Not a valid scientific name. See *Riojasaurus*.

"Streptospondylus" (**strep**-toe-**spon**-dill-us) Not a valid scientific name. A theropod known only from a few bones, this animal may be related to *Spinosaurus*.

Struthiomimus

strew-thee-oh-**my**-muss
NAME MEANS: "ostrich mimic"
CLASSIFICATION: Saurischia, Theropoda, Ornithomimosauria
LENGTH: 13 ft (4 m)
TIME: Late Cretaceous, 76 million years ago
PLACE: Wyoming, Utah, U.S.; Alberta, Canada
DIET: small reptiles and insects
DETAILS: Because this birdlike bipedal dinosaur's skull, neck, leg, and feet so closely resembled those of the modern-day ostrich, it was named for that large flightless bird. As large as an ostrich but only midsize for its ornithomimid family, this toothless dinosaur no doubt relied on its speed and eyesight to hunt for food and evade predators. Judging from its long legs and light body, it was one of the fastest of all dinosaurs. Its hands were

Struthiomimus

large and powerful, equal in length to its upper arm. Each hand had three long, clawed fingers.

Struthiosaurus

strew-thee-oh-**sor**-uhss

NAME MEANS: "ostrich lizard"

CLASSIFICATION: Ornithischia, Ankylosauria

LENGTH: 7 ft (2.1 m)

TIME: Late Cretaceous, 83 million years ago

PLACE: Austria, France, Hungary

DIET: plants

DETAILS: First assigned to an order of "bird-headed" reptiles, then described as a meat-eating dinosaur, *Struthiosaurus* was finally classified as a member of the ankylosaurs. Known originally from only a single piece of a skull, *Struthiosaurus* appears to have been a primitive, clubless dinosaur and is among the smallest ankylosaur dinosaurs known. Only one-fourth the length of the North American nodosaurids, *Struthiosaurus* may have been the last of its kind to survive in Europe. This little tanklike dinosaur was named in 1870.

Stygimoloch

stid-jih-**moll**-ock

NAMED AFTER: after the mythical river Styx of the Greek underworld and the demon sun god Moloch

CLASSIFICATION: Ornithischia, Pachycephalosauria

LENGTH: 7 ft (2.1 m)

TIME: Late Cretaceous, 68 million years ago

Stygimoloch

183

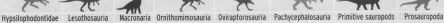

Hypsilophodontidae   Lesothosauria   Macronaria   Ornithomimosauria   Oviraptorosauria   Pachycephalosauria   Primitive sauropods   Prosauropoda   Spinosauria   Stegosauria   Therizinosauridae   Troodontidae   Tyrannosauridae

PLACE: Montana, U.S.

DIET: plants

DETAILS: This ferocious-looking dinosaur with a crown of long spikes was a plant-eater and not a large one. *Stygimoloch* was a dome-headed pachycephalosaur with a distinctive array of long spikes rising from its skull. The largest of these horns was nearly four inches (10.2 cm) long. As with other pachychephalosaurs, it is no longer thought that this dinosaur used its skull for head-butting – which would have been very painful for pointy-headed *Stygimoloch*.

"Stygivenator" (**stid**-jih-vee-**nay**-tore) Not a valid scientific name.

Styracosaurus

sty-**rack**-oh-**sor**-uhss

NAME MEANS: "spike lizard"

CLASSIFICATION: Ornithischia, Ceratopsia

LENGTH: 18 ft (5.5 m)

TIME: Late Cretaceous, 77 million years ago

PLACE: Alberta, Canada

DIET: plants

DETAILS: This impressive horned dinosaur was named for its ornate frills and horns. The bony neck frill features many long, tapering spikes. Perhaps the fearsome frill array evolved in order to make this plant-eater seem larger and more intimidating to predators like *Albertosaurus,* which roamed Late Cretaceous North America at the same time. The large collar of frill spikes may have been used in displays for competition over territory or mating.

Suchomimus

sue-koh-**my**-muss

NAME MEANS: "crocodile mimic"

CLASSIFICATION: Saurischia, Theropoda, Spinosauria

LENGTH: 36 ft (11 m)

TIME: Early Cretaceous, 121 million years ago

PLACE: Niger

DIET: meat (possibly fish)

DETAILS: The long, narrow snout of this large theropod inspired its name in 1998. *Suchomimus* was a spinosaur, very much like England's *Baryonyx*. The teeth in its four-foot-long skull (1.2 m) are stout cones with grooves, unlike the smooth, needle-like spearing teeth of another relative, *Spinosaurus*. Like *Baryonyx,* *Suchomimus* had powerful forearms with large, curving talons and a massive thumb claw, ideal for spearing fish or tearing into other prey. Tall spines along the dinosaur's back may have been connected in a sail over its hips. If, as its skull shape suggests, *Suchomimus* was a fish-eater, it may have waded into rivers as bears do. Then it would have used its

Suchomimus

Abelisauridae   Ankylosauria   basal Coelurosauria   basal Iguanodontia   Camarasauridae   Carnosauria   Ceratopsia   Ceratosauria   Dromaeosauridae   Diplodocoidea   Hadrosauridae   Herrerasauridae   Heterodontosauridae

Styracosaurus

Hypsilophodontidae   Lesothosauria   Macronaria   Ornithomimosauria   Oviraptorosauria   Pachycephalosauria   Primitive sauropods   Prosauropoda   Spinosauria   Stegosauria   Therizinosauridae   Troodontidae   Tyrannosauridae

Syntarsus

hooked thumb claws and crocodile-like snout to catch a meal. *Suchomimus* might also have been able to swim, using its powerful hind legs and tail to propel it through the water.

Supersaurus

sue-per-**sor**-uhss

NAME MEANS: "super lizard"

CLASSIFICATION: Saurischia, Sauropoda, Diplodocoidea

LENGTH: 110 ft (33.5 m)

Supersaurus shoulder bones

TIME: Late Jurassic, 154 million years ago

PLACE: Colorado, U.S.

DIET: plants

DETAILS: This astoundingly long sauropod was found in Colorado's Dry Mesa Dinosaur Quarry and named based on incomplete fossil material. Even incomplete, however, the sheer size of *Supersaurus* is impressive. The shoulder bone alone is more than eight feet (2.4 m) long. Weighing an estimated 50 tons (75.4 t), this enormous plant-eater probably had a narrow head atop its remarkably long neck. *Supersaurus* was named by Utah dinosaur-hunter "Dinosaur Jim" Jensen in 1973.

"Syngonosaurus" (sing-**go**-no-**sor**-uhss) Not a valid scientific name. See *Anoplosaurus.*

Syntarsus

sin-**tar**-suss

NAME MEANS: "fused tarsus," because of its fused anklebones

CLASSIFICATION: Saurischia, Theropoda, Ceratosauria

LENGTH: 10 ft (3 m)

TIME: Early Jurassic, 195 million years ago

PLACE: Arizona, U.S.; Zimbabwe

DIET: meat

DETAILS: The latest word is that this dinosaur may be the same as *Coelophysis,* found in New Mexico.

Heads Up!

Big. Thick. Bumpy. Fossils show that there were all kinds of dinosaur heads. The largest of all belong to the horned dinosaurs. New finds of *Torosaurus* and *Pentaceratops* show skulls more than 9 feet (2.7 m) long. With their heads covered with many bumps and points, *Stygimoloch* and the other thick-headed dinosaurs had some of the most highly decorated skulls. Perhaps these bumps and points were supposed to make the dinosaur appear more frightening. Many scientists had thought that thick-headed dinosaurs butted heads as rams do today. But recent studies indicate that these animals could not have successfully bonked heads. They would only have slid off the sides of each others' heads or hurt themselves. Instead, *Stygimoloch* may have banged each other in the sides with their hard skulls.

Syntarsus had a small head, a long neck, and large, well-developed hands with three-clawed fingers. The remains of 30 *Syntarsus* individuals were excavated from a single locality in Zimbabwe. They may have been victims of a sudden flood. Two skeletal types, one 15% larger than the other, may represent males and females. Most paleontologists think that the larger skeletons belonged to females, as is true among most birds. In 2001, a scientist discovered that an insect had been named *Syntarsus* before the dinosaur. So, he renamed the dinosaur *Megapnosaurus,* which means "big dead lizard." The scientist was poking fun at dinosaurs.

"Syrmosaurus" (sir-moe-**sor**-uhss) Not a valid scientific name. See *Pinacosaurus.*

"Szechuanosaurus" (such-**wah**-no-**sor**-uhss) Not a valid scientific name. A midsize Chinese meat-eater known from just a few bones and teeth; possibly related to *Sinraptor.*

Hypsilophodontidae Lesothosauria Macronaria Ornithomimosauria Oviraptorosauria Pachycephalosauria Primitive sauropods Prosauropoda Spinosauria Stegosauria Therizinosauridae Troodontidae Tyrannosauridae

Talarurus

Abelisauridae Ankylosauria basal Coelurosauria basal Iguanodontia Camarasauridae Carnosauria Ceratopsia Ceratosauria Dromaeosauridae Diplodocoidea Hadrosauridae Herrerasauridae Heterodontosauridae

Talarurus

tal-a-**roo**-russ

NAME MEANS: "wicker tail," from Greek for its interlocking tailbones and tendons

CLASSIFICATION: Ornithischia, Ankylosauria

LENGTH: 16.5 ft (5 m)

TIME: Late Cretaceous, 97.5 million years ago

PLACE: Mongolia

DIET: plants

DETAILS: This midsize armored dinosaur had spikes on its sides and an unusual, well-preserved tail. Its tail vertebrae wove together with hardened tendons to make a powerful structure. The stocky, four-legged *Talarurus* had a long, narrow skull.

Tangvayosaurus

tong-**vie**-oh-**sor**-uhss

NAMED AFTER: the village of Tang Vay, Laos

CLASSIFICATION: Saurischia, Sauropoda, Macronaria

LENGTH: 50 ft (15.2 m)

TIME: Early Cretaceous, 121 million years ago

PLACE: Laos

DIET: plants

DETAILS: This truck-size dinosaur was not large for a titanosaur. Based on two skeletons, both missing their skulls, *Tangvayosaurus* was similar to *Phuwiangosaurus,* a Late Jurassic sauropod from Thailand. Finding dinosaurs in the dense jungles of Southeast Asia is unusual, as opposed to the usual desert outcroppings, which make fossils easily visible. *Tangvayosaurus* was named in 1999.

Tanius

tah-nee-us

NAMED AFTER: Chinese geologist H. C. Tan

CLASSIFICATION: Ornithischia, Hadrosauridae

LENGTH: 30 ft (9.1 m) or more

TIME: Late Cretaceous, 88.5 million years ago

PLACE: China

DIET: plants

DETAILS: This large plant-eater had a low, flat skull. Since there is no evidence of a crest on its head, it may have belonged to a crestless branch of the duckbill family. Some scientists speculate that

Tanius, which was named in 1929, was the female form of the spike-crested *Tsintaosaurus.* This is definitely not the case.

"Tanystrosuchus" (tan-**iss**-troh-**sue**-cuss) Not a valid scientific name. See *Halticosaurus.*

Tarascosaurus

tar-**ask**-oh-**sor**-uhss

NAMED AFTER: a legendary monster in town of Tarascon, France

CLASSIFICATION: Saurischia, Theropoda, Ceratosauria, Abelisauridae

LENGTH: 20 ft (6.1 m)

TIME: Late Cretaceous, 75 million years ago

PLACE: France

DIET: meat

DETAILS: A member of the abelisaurs, *Tarascosaurus* had a large skull, double-edged teeth, strong hind limbs, and large, talon-bearing toes. Similar meat-eaters roamed South America, India, and Africa during the Late Cretaceous Period. This suggests that a common ancestor of these meat-eaters made use of land connections to spread across what later became separate continents.

Tarbosaurus

tar-**boh**-**sor**-uhss

NAME MEANS: "alarming lizard"

CLASSIFICATION: Saurischia, Theropoda, Tyrannosauridae

LENGTH: 40 ft (13 m)

TIME: Late Cretaceous, 74 million years ago

PLACE: Mongolia

DIET: meat

Tarbosaurus skull

DETAILS: This large tyrannosaurid is a close Asian cousin to *T. rex* and nearly as large. *Tarbosaurus* had a four-foot skull and teeth nearly six inches (15.2 cm) long. *Tarbosaurus* was a hunter of *Saurolophus* and sauropods in Asia. A bone bed of *Tarbosaurus* was recently found, indicating this dinosaur may have hunted in packs.

189

Tarchia

tar-kee-uh

NAME MEANS: "brainy one," because of its unusually large braincase

CLASSIFICATION: Ornithischia, Ankylosauria

LENGTH: 18 ft (5.5 m)

TIME: Late Cretaceous, 78 million years ago

PLACE: Mongolia

DIET: plants

DETAILS: *Tarchia* is among the largest of the Asian club-tailed armored plant-eaters. It wielded an especially hefty tail club.

Tarchia

Tatisaurus

dah-dee-**sor**-uhss

NAMED AFTER: Dadi area of southern China

CLASSIFICATION: Ornithischia, Ankylosauria

LENGTH: 6.5 ft (2 m)

TIME: Early Jurassic, 200 million years ago

PLACE: China

DIET: plants

DETAILS: This little animal was one of the earliest of all armored dinosaurs, along with *Bienosaurus,* also from China. A fragment from a left jawbone, including teeth, helped paleontologists identify this small plant-eater. Slender, with simple teeth, *Tatisaurus* may have had mammal-like cheek pouches to keep plant material in its mouth while it chewed. When first discovered, *Tatisaurus* was thought to be a hypsilophodontid plant-eater.

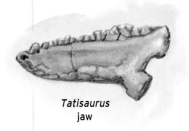

Tatisaurus jaw

"**Taveirosaurus**" (tah-**vay**-roo-**sor**-uhss). Not a valid scientific name. Possibly tiny, thick-headed plant-eater named from only teeth, found in Portugal.

"**Tawasaurus**" (dah-wah-**sor**-uhss) Not a valid scientific name. See *Lufengosaurus.*

"**Technosaurus**" (**teck**-no-**sor**-uhss). Not a valid scientific name. Perhaps the oldest and most primitive ornithischian dinosaur, this dinosaur now appears to be a hodgepodge of fossil bones mixed in with prosauropod hatchling bones.

Tecovasaurus

teck-**oh**-vah-**sor**-uhss

NAME MEANS: "Tecovas lizard"

CLASSIFICATION: Ornithischia, Lesothosauria

LENGTH: 6 ft (1.8 m)

TIME: Late Triassic, 225 million years ago

PLACE: Arizona, Texas, U.S.

DIET: plants

DETAILS: This primitive, small plant-eater was named from just five teeth, the smallest one only a fraction of an inch (2 mm) high.

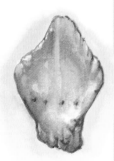

Tecovasaurus tooth

Tehuelchesaurus

tay-**wail**-chay-**sor**-uhss

NAMED AFTER: Tehuelche people of Argentina

CLASSIFICATION: Saurischia, Sauropoda, Camarasauridae?

LENGTH: about 50 ft (15.2 m)

TIME: Middle Jurassic, 164 million years ago

PLACE: Argentina

DIET: plants

DETAILS: This long-necked dinosaur is similar to a smaller Chinese sauropod, *Omeisaurus,* of the same time. It is set apart by the shape and heaviness of its limbs. Both skin impressions and half a skeleton were discovered. *Tehuelchesaurus* was named in 1999.

"**Teinurosaurus**" (tie-**new**-roh-**sor**-uhss) Not a valid scientific name. This dinosaur was named from a single backbone thought first to belong to a plant-eater, then a meat-eater.

Telmatosaurus

tell-mat-oh-**sor**-uhss

NAME MEANS: "marsh lizard"

CLASSIFICATION: Ornithischia, Hadrosauridae

LENGTH: 16 ft (4.9 m)

TIME: Late Cretaceous, 83 million years ago

PLACE: Romania, France

DIET: plants

DETAILS: When plant-eating *Telmatosaurus* lived in Europe near the close of the dinosaur era, the continent was a string of islands. The isolated

Telmatosaurus

dinosaurs were primitive and dwarfed in size, including this half-size duckbill. Fossilized eggs and embryonic duckbill remains found in Transylvania may have belonged to this primitive, flat-headed hadrosaur.

Tendaguria

ten-duh-**goo**-ree-uh

NAMED AFTER: the Tendaguru fossil site in Tanzania

CLASSIFICATION: Saurischia, Sauropoda, Macronaria

LENGTH: 60 ft (18.3 m)

TIME: Late Jurassic, 154 million years ago

PLACE: Tanzania

DIET: plants

DETAILS: *Tendaguria,* a long-necked sauropod, was named in 2000. Though recently discovered, it comes from a region where many large plant-eaters, including a species of *Brachiosaurus,* were found early in the 20th century. This giant four-legged plant-eater looked somewhat like the well-known sauropod *Camarasaurus,* but little else is known about this dinosaur.

Tenontosaurus

ten-**on**-to-**sor**-uhss

NAME MEANS: "tendon lizard," because of the hardened tendons found in its tail fossils

CLASSIFICATION: Ornithischia, basal Iguanodontia

LENGTH: 23 ft (7 m)

TIME: Early Cretaceous, 116 million years ago

PLACE: Montana, Wyoming, Utah, Texas, Oklahoma, U.S.

DIET: plants

DETAILS: This plant-eater could walk on two legs or on all fours, depending upon need or terrain. It had a skull similar to that of *Iguanodon.* Its long arms appear to have been muscular. Hardened tendons in *Tenontosaurus's* long tail helped balance its bulky body. Unfortunately for *Tenontosaurus,* it was likely one of the favorite meals of the sickle-clawed predator *Deinonychus.* Teeth from that meat-eater have been found near *Tenontosaurus* remains. One possible Montana kill site of a *Tenontosaurus*

shows that it may have taken down several members of a pack of *Deinonychus* before it was killed, perhaps holding off the hunters with swipes of its powerful tail. *Tenontosaurus* has been excavated in swampy Cretaceous settings along with the remains of turtles and crocodiles. This suggests that *Tenontosaurus* may have preferred to live in wetlands.

"**Tetragonosaurus**" (tet-rag-**oh**-no-**sor**-uhss) Not a valid dinosaur. See *Lambeosaurus.*

Texasetes

teks-uh-**see**-teez

NAME MEANS: "Texas resident"

CLASSIFICATION: Ornithischia, Ankylosauria

LENGTH: 10 ft (3 m)

TIME: Early Cretaceous, 112 million years ago

PLACE: Texas, U.S.

DIET: plants

DETAILS: Fossils found in Texas indicate that *Texasetes* was a small nodosaur, an armored dinosaur with no defensive club at the end of its tail. It is the most complete ankylosaur of its time known from the Gulf Coast region of North America. The unearthed skeleton lacked ribs, backbones, and much of its armor and long bones. The rest of the animal probably washed away when a stream carried it into the ancient sea.

"**Thecocoelurus**" (**theek**-o-see-**lure**-us) Not a valid scientific name. Known only from fragmentary bones. A recent study suggests this animal may be an oviraptorid.

Tenontosaurus

Thecodontosaurus

theek-o-**don**-to-**sor**-uhss

NAME MEANS: "socket-tooth lizard"

CLASSIFICATION: Saurischia, Prosauropoda

LENGTH: 10 ft (3 m)

TIME: Late Triassic, 225 million years ago

PLACE: England

DIET: plants, possibly meat

DETAILS: *Thecodontosaurus* is a relatively small and primitive two-legged plant-eater. Its distinctive teeth resemble those of the modern monitor lizard, suggesting that it may have been an omnivore, eating both plants and meat. Identified in 1836, *Thecodontosaurus* was among the earliest dinosaurs named.

"Thecospondylus" (**theek**-oh-**spon**-dill-us) Not a valid scientific name. See *Calamospondylus*.

Therizinosaurus

thair-ih-zie-no-**sor**-uhss

NAME MEANS: "reaping lizard"

CLASSIFICATION: Saurischia, Theropoda, Therizinosauridea

LENGTH: 36 ft (11 m)

TIME: Late Cretaceous, 77 million years ago

PLACE: Mongolia

DIET: plants, possibly insects or fish

DETAILS: Once thought to have been a sprawling, turtle-like aquatic reptile, *Therizinosaurus* remains a mysterious dinosaur. Therizinosaurs show similarities to both meat-eating and plant-eating animals. This "reaping lizard" was named for its enormous two-foot (61 cm) hand claws, whose purpose is unclear. They may have been wielded as attack weapons or as a defense against predators. These record-size claws might have been used to rake branches, or to dig for insects in anthills or rotting tree trunks. This dinosaur's large

body and arms are similar to an unrelated and much more recent animal, the extinct mammal known as the giant ground sloth.

"Therosaurus" (**thair**-oh-**sor**-uhss) Not a valid scientific name. See *Iguanodon*.

Thescelosaurus

thesk-el-oh-**sor**-uhss

NAME MEANS: "surprising lizard"

CLASSIFICATION: Ornithischia, Hypsilophodontidae

LENGTH: 12 ft (3.7 m)

TIME: Late Cretaceous, 77 million years ago

PLACE: Colorado, Montana, South Dakota, Wyoming, U.S.; Alberta, Saskatchewan, Canada

DIET: plants

DETAILS: This stocky plant-eater had a small head and a long tail. Its unusually

Thescelosaurus

Eggs-actly How Big?

Even huge dinosaurs started out small. Many of them hatched from eggs that were often no bigger than grapefruits. The biggest dinosaur egg may have belonged to a therizinosaur. It was almost two feet (61 cm) long, or as long as two footballs. Of course a hatched therizinosaur would grow to be about 30 feet (9.1 m) long!

Meat-eating dinosaurs such as *Troodon* had long, narrow eggs shaped like little loaves of French bread. A *Troodon*'s egg was about five inches (12.6 cm) long. Plant-eaters' eggs were more rounded, like the grapefruit-size eggs of *Hypselosaurus*, a large plant-eater. Some dinosaur eggs were pebbly on the outside; other dinosaur species had smooth-shelled eggs. One Chinese duck-billed dinosaur nest had 24 eggs in it!

meat-eating dinosaur nest and egg in close-up

Abelisauridae   Ankylosauria   basal Coelurosauria   basal Iguanodontia   Camarasauridae   Carnosauria   Ceratopsia   Ceratosauria   Dromaeosauridae   Diplodocoidea   Hadrosauridae   Herrerasauridae   Heterodontosauridae

short legs suggest that this particular hypsilophodontid may have walked on all fours more often than its relatives did. The first nearly complete dinosaur skeleton to be discovered, *Thescelosaurus* remained sealed in a crate and untouched from its excavation in 1891 until 1913. When paleontologists were finally able to study the neglected bones, they discovered that they belonged to a previously undescribed species of small dinosaur.

"Thespesius" (thess-**pea**-see-us) Not a valid scientific name. A duck-billed dinosaur known from isolated bones.

Tianchisaurus

tyen-chur-**sor**-uhss

NAMED AFTER: for Lake Tianchi (Heavenly Pool) in China

CLASSIFICATION: Ornithischia, Ankylosauria

LENGTH: 10 ft (3 m)

TIME: Middle to Late Jurassic, 169 million years ago

PLACE: China

DIET: plants

DETAILS: *Tianchisaurus* lived early in time for an armored dinosaur. Anklyosaurs survived 100 million years later into the Late Cretaceous Period. *Tianchisaurus* was referred to informally as "Jurassosaurus," in honor of the film *Jurassic Park*. The film's director, Steven Spielberg, donated money to Chinese dinosaur research (arranged by the author of this book). The dinosaur has already been formally named *Tianchisaurus* to honor the lake in northern China near where it was discovered. The club-tailed dinosaur's tongue-twisting species name, *nedegoapeferima,* is formed from the first two letters of the last names of most of the *Jurassic Park* cast, such as *ne* for Sam Neill, *de* for Laura Dern, *go* for Jeff Goldblum, and *a* for Richard Attenborough.

Tianchisaurus armor plates

Tianzhenosaurus

tyen-juh-no-**sor**-uhss

NAMED AFTER: Tianzhen region of China

CLASSIFICATION: Ornithischia, Ankylosauria

LENGTH: 10 ft (3 m)

TIME: Late Cretaceous, 90 million years ago

PLACE: China

DIET: plants

DETAILS: Known from a nearly complete fossilized skull and named in 1998, this small armored dinosaur had two horns that protruded backward at the top and rear of its skull. The length of *Tianzhenosaurus*'s snout and the shape of its nostrils differ from *Saichania* and *Pinacosaurus,* two other club-tailed ankylosaurids found in the region. Protective bony knobs of irregular sizes covered the top of this dinosaur's head.

"Tichosteus" (tie-**koh**-stee-us) Not a valid scientific name. This dinosaur is based on a single vertebra of an ornithopod.

Tienshanosaurus

tyen-**shawn**-oh-**sor**-uhss

NAMED AFTER: Tienshan Mountains (Heavenly Mountains) in China

CLASSIFICATION: Saurischia, Sauropoda, Macronaria

LENGTH: 39 ft (11.9 m)

TIME: Late Jurassic, 163 million years ago

PLACE: China

DIET: plants

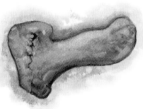

Tienshanosaurus shoulder blade with healed injury

DETAILS: Unusually short limbs set this dinosaur apart from otherwise similar and even larger sauropods. This plant-eater had a sloping head and peglike teeth. The first of these dinosaurs found (1920s) had a strangely roughened shoulder blade, the result of an injury or disease.

Timimus

tim-**eye**-muss

NAMED AFTER: Thomas Rich, son of paleontologists Patricia and Thomas Rich, and Australian dinosaur digger Timothy Flannery

CLASSIFICATION: Saurischia, Theropoda, Ornithomimosauria

LENGTH: 10 ft (3 m)

TIME: Early Cretaceous, 112 million years ago

PLACE: Australia

DIET: meat

DETAILS: *Timimus* is known only from a single slender leg bone. Although this dinosaur is generally classified as a member of the ostrichlike ornithomimosaur sprinters, some scientists think it may have been some other form of meat-eater.

Timimus

Titanosaurus

tie-**tan**-oh-**sor**-uhss

NAMED AFTER: the Titans of Greek mythology

CLASSIFICATION: Saurischia, Sauropoda, Macronaria

LENGTH: 66 ft (20.1 m)

TIME: Late Cretaceous, 83 million years ago

PLACE: India, Argentina, England

DIET: plants

DETAILS: Many species have been grouped within the titanosaurs, the most common of all sauropods. This particular member of the titanosaur family, named in 1877, was described based on just two vertebrae discovered in India. *Titanosaurus* had forward sloping skulls and limbs that were roughly equal in length. Cannonball-shape dinosaur eggs, which were also found in India, may have belonged to *Titanosaurus* or a related member of the sauropod giants.

Tochisaurus

toe-kee-**sor**-uhss

NAME MEANS: "ostrich-foot lizard"

CLASSIFICATION: Saurischia, Theropoda, Deinonychosauria, Troodontidae

LENGTH: 8 ft (2.4 m)

TIME: Late Cretaceous, 77 million years ago

PLACE: Mongolia

DIET: meat

DETAILS: This troodontid was slender with a narrow foot, suggesting that the dinosaur's legs were well suited to quick bursts of speed. Like all troodontids, *Tochisaurus* would have had a large brain and may have been a particularly cunning hunter of small prey.

"Tomodon" (**toe**-moe-don). Not a valid scientific name. Already used for another animal; see *Diplotomodon*.

"Tornieria" (tore-**near**-ee-uh) Not a valid scientific name. See *Barosaurus*.

Torosaurus

tore-oh-**sor**-uhss

NAME MEANS: "perforated lizard"

CLASSIFICATION: Ornithischia, Ceratopsia

LENGTH: 26 ft (7.9 m)

TIME: Late Cretaceous, 70 million years ago

PLACE: Wyoming, Utah, South Dakota, Montana, New Mexico, Texas, U.S.; Saskatchewan, Canada

DIET: plants

DETAILS: This horned dinosaur, first identified in 1891, had the longest skull known of any animal ever to walk the earth. From the tip of its parrotlike beak to the end of its bony neck frill, the head of *Torosaurus* stretched a full 8.5 feet (2.6 meters). A large pair of openings on the huge frill of the dinosaur helped lighten the massive structure but made it useless as a defensive shield. *Torosaurus* was a relatively rare horned dinosaur according to fossil finds.

Torosaurus skull

Torvosaurus

tore-voh-**sor**-uhss

NAME MEANS: "savage lizard"

CLASSIFICATION: Saurischia, Theropoda, Carnosauria

LENGTH: 31 ft (9.4 m)

TIME: Late Jurassic, 156 million years ago

PLACE: Colorado, Wyoming, U.S.

DIET: meat

DETAILS: This bulky dinosaur was a powerful predator. Unlike *Allosaurus* and many

Torvosaurus

Abelisauridae | Ankylosauria | basal Coelurosauria | basal Iguanodontia | Camarasauridae | Carnosauria | Ceratopsia | Ceratosauria | Dromaeosauridae | Diplodocoidea | Hadrosauridae | Herrerasauridae | Heterodontosauridae

other meat-eaters of its time, *Torvosaurus's* upper arms were long and its forearms and pelvis were short. These primitive features indicate that *Torvosaurus* may have been more closely related to early large theropods like *Megalosaurus* and *Erectopus* than *Allosaurus,* though *Allosaurus* lived in the same time and territory.

"Trachodon" (**track**-uh-**don**) Not a valid scientific name. First named from only a few teeth, then used as a grab-bag name for many duck-billed dinosaurs until they were more clearly identified. See *Hadrosaurus, Edmontosaurus,* and *Anatotitan.*

Triceratops

try-**sayr**-a-tops
NAME MEANS: "three-horned face"
CLASSIFICATION: Ornithischia, Ceratopsia
LENGTH: 29.5 ft (9 m)
TIME: Late Cretaceous, 68 million years ago

PLACE: Wyoming, Montana, South Dakota, Colorado, U.S.; Alberta, Saskatchewan, Canada
DIET: plants
DETAILS: *Triceratops* was one of the largest of all the horned dinosaurs. It is unusual because it lacked windowlike openings in the short, solid frill of bone on its neck. Its scissoring teeth were probably adapted for slicing through tough, fibrous plants. A stocky four-legged dinosaur, *Triceratops* may have weighed as much as five tons. It appears to have lived in small groups as opposed to the enormous herds of other horned dinosaurs.

Triceratops horns were long, thin, pointed and probably covered with a sheath of dense keratin, a substance like human fingernails. The horns were even longer and sharper than they appear from fossil remains. They may have been an effective defense against a larger predator such as *Tyrannosaurus rex.* The horns were probably used in display and mating contests with other *Triceratops.* The sturdy frill that fanned out from

Triceratops

the back of the dinosaur's skull may have been more useful as a protective shield for its neck than were the more delicate, thin-boned frills of most ceratopsians. Perhaps these broad displays were brightly colored to attract a mate, to warn off predators, or to identify the species to other horned dinosaurs. Othniel C. Marsh, the 19th-century Yale University scientist who named *Triceratops* and many other dinosaurs, originally thought that the horns of *Triceratops* belonged to a prehistoric bison.

"Trimucrodon" (try-**mook**-roh-don) Not a valid scientific name. Known only from a tooth.

Troodon

troh-uh-don

NAME MEANS: "wounding tooth"
CLASSIFICATION: Saurischia, Theropoda, Deinonychosauria, Troodontidae
LENGTH: 11.5 ft (3.5 m)
TIME: Late Cretaceous, 76 million years ago
PLACE: Montana, Wyoming, Alaska, U.S.; Alberta, Canada
DIET: meat
DETAILS: *Troodon* was one of the smartest of all dinosaurs. This lightly built, speedy theropod had a long neck, nimble fingers, a variety of serrated teeth, and birdlike legs. All of these features and

Troodon

My, What Big Teeth You Have!

Dinosaur teeth were as varied as the great beasts themselves. Most meat-eaters, like *Troodon*, for example, had notches on the edges of their teeth. *Troodon*'s teeth were less than an inch (2.5 cm) long, with wide grooves. Other meat-eaters had teeth with many small grooves, like the edge of a steak knife. These edges helped saw through meat. *T. rex* had huge, thick teeth the size of bananas.

Some plant-eaters had 1,000 teeth in their jaws. Plant-eaters' teeth were designed for slicing, grinding, or raking plants. *Triceratops*'s teeth

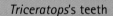
T. rex tooth and root

snipped like scissors. *Stegosaurus* had leaf-shape teeth. And the biggest dinosaurs, giant plant-eaters like *Brachiosaurus*, often had just a few pencil- or spoon-shape teeth for pulling plants into their mouths. These dinosaurs chopped up plants in their huge guts, not in their small jaws.

Dinosaurs replaced their teeth throughout their lives. New teeth were constantly moving into the spaces left by older, worn-out teeth. A full set of choppers meant bad news for their prey or any leafy greens in their way.

excellent senses probably made this small meat-eater an excellent hunter of mammals, birds, and small dinosaurs. The enlarged "killing claw" on the second toe of each hind foot suggests that Troodon may also have fed on larger prey, if it hunted in groups. Although the slender predator weighed only an estimated 50 pounds (22.7 kgs), its brain weighed two ounces (56.7 g) and was the size of an avocado pit. Compared with its size, this is a bigger brain than living reptiles and even some birds have. *Troodon* had unusually large eyes, suggesting keen eyesight even in twilight. It was named in 1856 on the basis of a tooth. Several other dinosaurs, no longer valid, were named from teeth that later proved to be part of the varied collection of tooth shapes within *Troodon*'s jaws.

Tsagantegia

tsah-gone-**tay**-ghee-uh

NAMED AFTER: Tsagan Teg region of the southeastern Gobi Desert

CLASSIFICATION: Ornithischia, Ankylosauria

LENGTH: 15 ft (4.6 m)

TIME: Late Cretaceous, 85 million years ago

PLACE: Mongolia

DIET: plants

DETAILS: This long-snouted member of the club-tailed armored dinosaurs had a particularly flat head and long snout. It was named in 1994.

Tsintaosaurus

ching-dow-**sor**-uhss

NAMED AFTER: Qingdao, China

CLASSIFICATION: Ornithischia, Hadrosauridae

LENGTH: 33 ft (10 m)

TIME: Late Cretaceous, 75 million years ago

PLACE: China

DIET: plants

Tsintaosaurus

DETAILS: This large crested duckbill had a peculiar unicorn-hornlike spike on its head. This long, thin, hollow, hornlike crest grew to more than a foot (30.5 cm) projected forward and upward from its forehead. Some scientists thought that this crest was merely a displaced bone, forced upward during fossilization. But closer study revealed that the spiky bone was truly a feature of this peculiar-looking duckbill.

"Tugulusaurus" (too-**goo**-loo-**sor**-uhss) Not a valid scientific name. Probably mistakenly called an ostrichlike ornithomimid dinosaur. The true identity of this large meat-eater from China is uncertain.

Tuojiangosaurus

twaw-jyong-oh-**sor**-uhss

NAMED AFTER: Tuo River, China

CLASSIFICATION: Ornithischia, Stegosauria

LENGTH: 23.5 ft (7.2 m)

TIME: Late Jurassic, 163 million years ago

PLACE: China

DIET: plants

DETAILS: Known from a nearly complete skeleton, *Tuojiangosaurus* had a typical stegosaur skull with an elongated face and spoon-shape teeth. Two rows of narrow triangular plates stretched across the dinosaur's back, from its neck over its shoulders, down to the middle of its tail. Four defensive spikes adorned the tip of this powerful tail. The spikes might have scared away any predator looking to attack this plant-eater from the rear.

Turanoceratops

too-**ron**-o-**sayr**-a-tops

NAMED AFTER: Turanian Platform, a geological feature of Central Asia

CLASSIFICATION: Ornithischia, Ceratopsia

LENGTH: 5–6 ft? (80–96 cm?)

TIME: Late Cretaceous, 97.5 million years ago

Tuojiangosaurus

Hypsilophodontidae   Lesothosauria   Macronaria   Ornithomimosauria   Oviraptorosauria   Pachycephalosauria   Primitive sauropods   Prosauropoda   Spinosauria   Stegosauria   Therizinosauridae   Troodontidae   Tyrannosauridae

Tyrannosaurus (l.) and *Triceratops* (r.)

Abelisauridae Ankylosauria basal Coelurosauria basal Iguanodontia Camarasauridae Carnosauria Ceratopsia Ceratosauria Dromaeosauridae Diplodocoidea Hadrosauridae Herrerasauridae Heterodontosauridae

PLACE: Uzbekhistan

DIET: plants

DETAILS: This apparently horned dinosaur is known from just a few skull bones, a shoulder blade, and teeth and jaw parts. If it is indeed a horned dinosaur, as is suspected, it may be the first of the horned dinosaurs known from Asia.

Tylocephale

tye-luh-**seff**-uh-lee

NAME MEANS: "swelling head"

CLASSIFICATION: Ornithischia, Pachycephalosauria

LENGTH: 7 ft (2.1 m)

TIME: Late Cretaceous, 80 million years ago

PLACE: Mongolia

DIET: plants

DETAILS: Remains of one damaged skull show this bone-headed dinosaur was unique among the thick-headed dinosaurs in that its dome was highly raised in the front. The small but sturdy *Tylocephale* ate plants and may have engaged in ritual side-butting with other members of its species.

Tylocephale

"Tylosteus" (tie-**loh**-stee-us) Not a valid scientific name. See *Pachycephalosaurus*.

Tyrannosaurus

tie-**ran**-oh-**sor**-uhss

NAME MEANS: "tyrant lizard"

CLASSIFICATION: Saurischia, Theropoda, Tyrannosauria

LENGTH: 41 ft (12.5 m)

TIME: Late Cretaceous, 68 million years ago

PLACE: Montana, Wyoming, Colorado, New Mexico, South Dakota, U.S.; Alberta, Saskatchewan, Canada

DIET: meat

DETAILS: The most famous and most popular of all dinosaurs, *Tyrannosaurus* is still considered the deadliest, though no longer the largest, meat-eater. *Tyrannosaurus* had low, bumpy crests above its eyes. Its massive, dagger-toothed skull was capable of delivering a powerful, bone-shearing bite. It could tear off as much as 200 pounds (90.7 kgs) of meat in one rip. Its teeth, the largest of any carnivore, were as long as bananas. They were thick enough to break through bone and sharp enough to slice meat. The dinosaur's two-clawed arms were strongly muscled and had 10 times the power of the strongest human arms.

Was *Tyrannosaurus* a predator or a scavenger? It is a subject of considerable popular debate though not scientifically answerable. Most likely both behaviors were common, and *T. rex* consumed animals already dead whenever possible. "Sue," the most complete and famous *T. rex* fossil, shows bite marks on its face, perhaps from another *T. rex*. made during fighting or mating. Recent fossil finds have suggested that tyrannosaurs may have gathered or hunted together, perhaps in small family groups. *Tyrannosaurus rex* from North America had a cousin in Mongolia and China, named *Tarbosaurus* (once known as *Tyrannosaurus bataar*).

King of the Fossil Hunters

Barnum Brown (1873–1963) was the *T. rex* of dinosaur hunters, a giant among fossil finders. In the 50 years he worked with the American Museum of Natural History in New York, Brown unearthed hundreds of dinosaur bones. His expeditions took him across the western United States to Alberta, Canada, and far off to India. Brown discovered the world's first and third known skeletons of

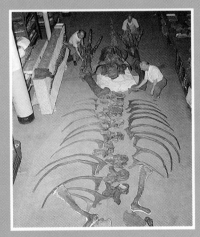

Tyrannosaurus rex, as well as many other new kinds of dinosaurs.

Brown was a man of style. Despite all the dirt and the dust, he liked to wear fancy fur coats and gold glasses and sport a cane on his expeditions. The famous dinosaur hunter was named after the equally famous circus promoter P. T. Barnum.

Barnum Brown

Hypsilophodontidae   Lesothosauria   Macronaria   Ornithomimosauria   Oviraptorosauria   Pachycephalosauria   Primitive sauropods   Prosauropoda   Spinosauria   Stegosauria   Therizinosauridae   Troodontidae   Tyrannosauridae

Udanoceratops

Abelisauridae Ankylosauria basal Coelurosauria basal Iguanodontia Camarasauridae Carnosauria Ceratopsia Ceratosauria Dromaeosauridae Diplodocoidea Hadrosauridae Herrerasauridae Heterodontosauridae

Udanoceratops

oo-**don**-oh-**sayr**-a-tops

NAMED AFTER: Udan Sayr fossil region in Mongolia

CLASSIFICATION: Ornithischia, Ceratopsia

LENGTH: 15 ft (4.6 m)

TIME: Late Cretaceous, 86 million years ago

PLACE: Mongolia

DIET: plants

DETAILS: This dinosaur was the largest member of the protoceratopsian plant-eaters. Before it was found, *Montanoceratops* of the North American West was the largest known protoceratopsian dinosaur. But *Udanoceratops* had a skull 50% larger than *Montanoceratops*.

"Ugrosaurus" (**oog**-roh-**sor**-uhss) Not a valid scientific name. This dinosaur's bone came from a diseased *Triceratops*.

"Uintasaurus" (you-**in**-tuh-**sor**-uhss) Not a valid scientific name. Now known as *Camarasaurus*.

"Ultrasauros" (**ull**-tra-**sor**-uhss) Not a valid scientific name. This name was originally "Ultrasaurus," before scientists realized that that name had already been given to a South Korean sauropod dinosaur, itself named from too few bones to be valid. "Ultrasauros" was then determined to be composed of parts of *Supersaurus* and a large *Brachiosaurus*. For several years, this Colorado find was considered the largest dinosaur, an honor now held by *Argentinosaurus*.

? Unenlagia

oon-en-**log**-ee-uh

NAME MEANS: "half bird," in the language of the Mapuche Indian's of Patagonia

CLASSIFICATION: Saurischia, Theropoda, Dromaeosauridae?

LENGTH: 8.25 ft (2.5 m)

TIME: Late Cretaceous, 93.5 million years ago

PLACE: Argentina

DIET: meat

DETAILS: A very birdlike dinosaur, *Unenlagia* might have had feathers. *Unenlagia* may have shared a common ancestor with *Archaeopteryx*. Some researchers suggest that this dinosaur, which was named in 1997, is more closely related to raptor dromaeosaurids than it is to *Archaeopteryx*.

Unenlagia femur

Unquillosaurus

oong-**kee**-yoh-**sor**-uhss

NAMED AFTER: Unquillo River, Argentina

CLASSIFICATION: Saurischia, Theropoda, basal Coelurosauria

LENGTH: 9.75 ft (3 m)

TIME: Late Cretaceous, 83 million years ago

PLACE: Argentina

DIET: meat

DETAILS: *Unquillosaurus* is shrinking, at least in the estimates of scientists.

Unquillosaurus pelvis

"Dinosaur Jim" Digs Bones

"Dinosaur Jim" Jensen (1925–1998) traveled far and wide, looking for adventure — and fossils. He found both, everywhere from Alaska to Argentina. Jensen worked for Harvard University as a handyman and fossil collector, before returning to his native Utah to run Brigham Young University's fossil-collection program. In the 1960s, Jensen identified *Supersaurus* and "Ultrasaurus," parts of giant plant-eaters among the largest animals yet known. He also discovered large meat-eaters from the Late Jurassic Period in Colorado and Utah. With his pith helmet and booming voice, big "Dinosaur Jim" was a popular figure in paleontology.

Utahraptor

Abelisauridae   Ankylosauria   basal Coelurosauria   basal Iguanodontia   Camarasauridae   Carnosauria   Ceratopsia   Ceratosauria   Dromaeosauridae   Diplodocoidea   Hadrosauridae   Herrerasauridae   Heterodontosauridae

Originally thought to have been 36 feet (11 m) in length, *Unquillosaurus* has been considerably downsized with further study of its few remains. Some researchers think that this was the same animal as the birdlike predator *Unenlagia,* also found in Argentina.

Utahraptor

yoo-tah-**rap**-tore

NAME MEANS: "Utah plunderer"

CLASSIFICATION: Saurischia, Theropoda Deinonychosauria, Dromaeosauridae

LENGTH: 19.5 ft (5.9 m)

TIME: Early Cretaceous, 125 million years ago

PLACE: Utah, U.S.

DIET: meat

DETAILS: This giant dromaeosaurid is the largest "raptor" yet known. It's twice the size of *Deinonychus.* Perhaps the deadliest of all dinosaur predators, *Utahraptor* had a huge, sickle-like slashing talon on each foot and flattened, bladelike claws on its hands. Its long, stiffened tail provided balance while running, leaping, or kicking at prey with its lethal slashing claws. Its claw was discovered after paleontologist James Kirkland, awaiting an order of pancakes in a Utah diner, stopped in a nearby rock shop and saw several dinosaur bones. He located the quarry where the armored dinosaur bones were found. There his research team found the enormous front limb claw of *Utahraptor,* a weapon nearly a foot (30.5 cm) long.

On Your Mark, Get Set, Go!

How fast could dinosaurs run? *Ornithomimus* may have run 35 miles (56 km) per hour, *T. rex* 15 miles (24 km) per hour (or far slower, according to a recent study), and huge *Apatosaurus* only 3 miles (5 km) per hour. Footprints are our only evidence of dinosaur speed. And most of these footprints were left by animals walking through mud. Scientists speculate that the fastest dinosaurs may have run more than 35 miles (56 km) per hour on dry land.

That's faster than any of us can run! The ornithomimids were probably the fastest of all dinosaurs. Their long legs and light bodies were built for speed.

However, most dinosaurs were slow compared to animals today. The giant plant-eaters, and even perhaps *T. rex,* may never have run at all. But no matter how slow it was, wouldn't you want to keep your distance from a *T. rex*?

Velociraptor

Abelisauridae   Ankylosauria   basal Coelurosauria   basal Iguanodontia   Camarasauridae   Carnosauria   Ceratopsia   Ceratosauria   Dromaeosauridae   Diplodocoidea   Hadrosauridae   Herrerasauridae   Heterodontosauridae

"Valdoraptor" (**val**-doh-**rap**-tore) Not a valid scientific name. Based on a bone fragment of a left foot from England, this dinosaur was originally thought to be an ankylosaur. The fossil does belong to some sort of meat-eater, but which kind is not known.

Valdosaurus

val-doh-**sor**-uhss

NAMED AFTER: Wealden Formation, England

CLASSIFICATION: Ornithischia, basal Iguanodontia

LENGTH: 10 ft (3 m)

TIME: Early Cretaceous, 144 million years ago

PLACE: England, Romania, possibly Niger

DIET: plants

DETAILS: This little-known, relatively small dinosaur was probably a primitive iguanodontid. *Valdosaurus* was first thought to be a hypsilophodontid, a smaller plant-eater. It is, in fact, very similar to *Dryosaurus*. Its existence in Africa and Europe supports the idea that animals crossed between the two continents, which must have been linked at this time.

Variraptor

var-ih-**rap**-tore

NAMED AFTER: Var River of southern France

CLASSIFICATION: Saurischia, Theropoda, Deinonychosauria, Dromaeosauridae

LENGTH: 8.25 ft (2.5 m)

TIME: Late Cretaceous, 71 million years ago

PLACE: France

DIET: meat

Variraptor backbone

DETAILS: *Variraptor* is the first "raptor" discovered in Europe. This clawed predator is a relative of *Deinonychus* and *Velociraptor* and was a smart and nimble hunter.

"Vectisaurus" (**vek**-tih-**sor**-uhss) Not a valid scientific name. See *Iguanodon*.

"Velocipes" (vee-**loss**-ih-peez) Not a valid scientific name. Known only from a single bone.

Velociraptor

vee-**loss**-ih-**rap**-tore

NAME MEANS: "swift robber"

CLASSIFICATION: Saurischia, Theropoda, Deinonychosauria, Dromaeosauridae

LENGTH: 6.5 ft (2 m)

TIME: Late Cretaceous, 85 million years ago

PLACE: Mongolia, China

DIET: meat

DETAILS: This "raptor" dromaeosaurid was made famous in the movie *Jurassic Park*. Unlike its man-size movie version, the real *Velociraptor* was no bigger than a German Shepherd dog. It was a small, lightly built predator with a long, low snout and large eyes. Like all dromaeosaurids, *Velociraptor* had a relatively large brain, long, flexible arms, and fingers tipped with sharp grasping talons. Its long, straight tail was stiffened by rodlike tendons. The long, straight tails of the "raptors" gave them balance for running, leaping, and delivering deadly slashing kicks to their prey. These kicks were made all the more devastating by the large hook claw that snapped forward from the second toe of each foot. The famed "fighting dinosaurs" fossils found in Mongolia show a *Velociraptor* battling the small ceratopsian *Protoceratops*. *Velociraptor* was smart, fast, and deadly for a dinosaur.

Velocisaurus

vee-**loss**-ih-**sor**-uhss

NAME MEANS: "swift lizard"

CLASSIFICATION: Saurischia, Theropoda, Ceratosauria

LENGTH: 4 ft (1.2 m)

TIME: Late Cretaceous, 73 million years ago

PLACE: Argentina

DIET: meat

DETAILS: The leg and foot bones of this small, lightly built theropod suggest that it was a very fast runner, well equipped for chasing down small prey such as mammals, lizards, and insects. This dinosaur's limb bones most closely resemble those of the ceratosaur meat-eaters, but *Velocisaurus*'s relationship to other dinosaurs is not clear.

205

Vulcanodon

Abelisauridae Ankylosauria basal Coelurosauria basal Iguanodontia Camarasauridae Carnosauria Ceratopsia Ceratosauria Dromaeosauridae Diplodocoidea Hadrosauridae Herrerasauridae Heterodontosauridae

Venenosaurus

veh-**nee**-no-**sahr**-uss

NAMED AFTER: the Poison Strip rock formation of Utah

CLASSIFICATION: Saurischia, Sauropoda, Macronaria

LENGTH: 67 ft (20.4 m)

TIME: Early Cretaceous, 130 million years ago

PLACE: Utah, U.S.

DIET: plants

DETAILS: This large and primitive titanosaur is one of the few of these giant sauropods found in North America. Its presence in the Early Cretaceous of North America, recently discovered, proves that titanosaurs did not simply migrate north to North America in the Late Cretaceous (see *Alamosaurus*) as had been previously thought.

Volkheimeria

volk-high-**mere**-ee-uh

NAMED AFTER: paleontologist Wolfgang Volkheimer

CLASSIFICATION: Saurischia, Sauropoda, Macronaria

LENGTH: 40 ft (12.2 m)

TIME: Middle Jurassic, 169 million years ago

PLACE: Argentina

DIET: plants

DETAILS: This primitive long-necked sauropod resembles dinosaurs known from the same time in Madagascar, such as *Bothriospondylus*. This resemblance supports the view that during the Jurassic Period South America was closely linked to the African landmass, including what would eventually form the island of Madagascar.

Vulcanodon

vull-**kay**-no-don

NAME MEANS: "Vulcan's tooth," after the Roman god of fire, because the fossils were first found near an ancient lava flow

CLASSIFICATION: Saurischia, Sauropoda, Primitive sauropods

LENGTH: 21 ft (6.5 m)

TIME: Early Jurassic, 200 million years ago

PLACE: Zimbabwe

DIET: plants

DETAILS: The long-necked plant-eater *Vulcanodon* was originally classified as an advanced prosauropod. It is now generally considered by paleontologists to have been a sauropod, which were more advanced and often larger four-legged plant-eaters than prosauropods. If so, *Vulcanodon* was one of the earliest, most primitive, and prosauropod-like members of the sauropod dinosaurs. The teeth for which *Vulcanodon* was named in 1972 actually came from a predatory dinosaur that may have been scavenging the plant-eater's remains.

Volkheimeria

Hypsilophodontidae Lesothosauria Macronaria Ornithomimosauria Oviraptorosauria Pachycephalosauria Primitive sauropods Prosauropoda Spinosauria Stegosauria Therizinosauridae Troodontidae Tyrannosauridae

Xenotarsosaurus (b.)
and *Patagonykus* (f.)

Abelisauridae Ankylosauria basal Coelurosauria basal Iguanodontia Camarasauridae Carnosauria Ceratopsia Ceratosauria Dromaeosauridae Diplodocoidea Hadrosauridae Herrerasauridae Heterodontosauridae

"Wakinosaurus" (wah-**keen**-oh-**sor**-uhss) Not a valid scientific name. This dinosaur is known only from a partial tooth.

"Walgettosuchus" (**wall**-get-oh-**sue**-cuss) Not a valid scientific name. Only part of a backbone has ever been found for this Australian dinosaur.

"Walkeria" (wah-**keer**-ee-uh). Not a valid scientific name; already used for another animal. See *Alwalkeria*.

Wannanosaurus

wah-**non**-oh-**sor**-uhss

NAMED AFTER: Wannan, Southern Anhui region of China

CLASSIFICATION: Ornithischia, Pachycephalosauria

LENGTH: 2 ft (61 cm)

TIME: Late Cretaceous, 83 million years ago

PLACE: China

DIET: plants

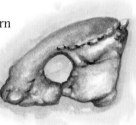

Wannanosaurus skull

DETAILS: This tiny two-legged dinosaur was a very primitive flat-headed member of the thick-skulled pachycephalosaur dinosaurs. Only *Yaverlandia* may have been a more primitive among all the thick-headed plant-eaters.

Wuerhosaurus

woo-**uhr**-huh-**sor**-uhss

NAMED AFTER: Wuerho, a town in China

CLASSIFICATION: Ornithischia, Stegosauria

LENGTH: 25 ft (7.6 m)

TIME: Early Cretaceous, 138 million years ago

PLACE: China

DIET: plants

DETAILS: A large stegosaur, *Wuerhosaurus* had shorter front limbs

Wuerhosaurus

and a larger neck than *Stegosaurus*. *Wuerhosaurus* is the last known member of the plate-backed dinosaurs. Most stegosaurs are known from the earlier Jurassic Period.

Xenotarsosaurus

zen-oh-**tar**-so-**sor**-uhss

NAME MEANS: "strange-ankle lizard"

CLASSIFICATION: Saurischia, Theropoda, Ceratosauria, Abelisauridae

LENGTH: 20 ft (6.1 m)

TIME: Late Cretaceous, 83 million years ago

PLACE: Argentina

DIET: meat

DETAILS: This little-known meat-eater was named for its oddly fused anklebones. These fossilized leg elements suggest that *Xenotarsosaurus* was not a very fast runner. Perhaps it scavenged rather than chased down prey. It may have been related to *Carnotaurus* of South America and the earlier ceratosaurs of North America.

"Xiaosaurus" (shyow-**sor**-uhss) Not a valid scientific name. Known from only partial remains that indicate that it was a primitive ornithischian dinosaur.

Xuanhanosaurus

shwen-hahn-oh-**sor**-uhss

NAMED AFTER: Xuanhan County, China

CLASSIFICATION: Saurischia, Theropoda, Carnosauria

LENGTH: 20 ft (6.1 m)

TIME: Middle to Late Jurassic, 175 million years ago

PLACE: China

DIET: meat

DETAILS: This primitive meat-eater had powerful forelimbs. Dong Zhiming, the Chinese scientist who named it, suggested that *Xuanhanosaurus* might have walked on all four legs because of its unusually long and primitive front limbs. If so, it would be the only known four-legged meat-eater among dinosaurs. Other paleontologists do not agree with Dong. They think this dinosaur walked on its hind legs as other meat-eaters did.

Yangchuanosaurus

Abelisauridae   Ankylosauria   basal Coelurosauria   basal Iguanodontia   Camarasauridae   Carnosauria   Ceratopsia   Ceratosauria   Dromaeosauridae   Diplodocoidea   Hadrosauridae   Herrerasauridae   Heterodontosauridae

"**Yaleosaurus**" (**yale**-oh-**sor**-uhss) Not a valid scientific name. See *Anchisaurus*.

Yandusaurus

yen-doo-**sor**-uhss
NAMED AFTER: Yandu ("salt capital"), the former name of Zijong, a town in Sichuan Province, China
CLASSIFICATION: Ornithischia, Hypsilophodontia
LENGTH: 5 ft (1.5 m)
TIME: Middle Jurassic, 175 million years ago
PLACE: China
DIET: plants
DETAILS: *Yandusaurus* was a light, primitive member of the hypsilophodontids. Its large eyes and nimble hands probably helped this small dinosaur gather plants for its meals. It is known from two nearly complete skeletons, both with skulls.

Yangchuanosaurus

yong-chwah-no-**sor**-uhss
NAMED AFTER: Yangchuan County, Sichuan Province, China
CLASSIFICATION: Saurischia, Theropoda, Carnosauria
LENGTH: 34.5 ft (10.5 m)
TIME: Late Jurassic, 163 million years ago
PLACE: China
DIET: meat

Yangchuanosaurus

DETAILS: A large predator at least the size of *Allosaurus*, *Yangchuanosaurus* had low horns above and in front of its eyes. Unlike *Allosaurus*, which lived later in North America, *Yangchuanosaurus* had a small fourth finger, not just three fingers on its hands. Three of those fingers carried sharp talons. This dinosaur was more closely related to *Sinraptor* than to *Allosaurus*. *Yangchuanosaurus* had a shorter snout and fewer teeth than the smaller, but more famous, *Allosaurus*.

Yaverlandia

yay-vur-**land**-ee-uh
NAMED AFTER: Yaverland Point on the Isle of Wight, England
CLASSIFICATION: Ornithischia, Pachycephalosauria
LENGTH: 3 ft (1 m)
TIME: Early Cretaceous, 125 million years ago
PLACE: England
DIET: plants
DETAILS: *Yaverlandia* was a very early pachycephalosaur, a thick-headed, small plant-eater that walked on its hind legs. Some scientists now think that *Yaverlandia* was more advanced than previously thought, despite its relatively ancient age for a thick-headed dinosaur.

"**Yibinosaurus**" (yi-bin-oh-sor-uhss) Not a valid scientific name. A sauropod dinosaur from the Early Jurassic of China that has yet to be formally described.

Yimenosaurus

yee-**muh**-no-**sor**-uhss
NAMED AFTER: Yimen County, Yunnan Province, southern China
CLASSIFICATION: Saurischia, Prosauropoda
LENGTH: 30 ft (9.1 m)
TIME: Early Jurassic, 200 million years ago
PLACE: China
DIET: plants
DETAILS: *Yimenosaurus* appears to have been a primitive prosauropod with a short skull. This long-necked, small-headed dinosaur may have been a plateosaur, a type of prosauropod best known from Europe, not China.

Yunnanosaurus

you-**non**-oh-**sor**-uhss
NAMED AFTER: Yunnan region of southern China
CLASSIFICATION: Saurischia, Prosauropoda
LENGTH: 23 ft (7 m) or more?
TIME: Early Jurassic, 200 million years ago
PLACE: China
DIET: plants
DETAILS: A 23-foot-long (7 m) skeleton shows that this dinosaur was a large member of the long-necked, small-headed prosauropods. But the individual found may have been a juvenile, suggesting that these prosauropods may have grown to well over 30 feet (9.1 m) long.

Zuniceratops

Abelisauridae | Ankylosauria | basal Coelurosauria | basal Iguanodontia | Camarasauridae | Carnosauria | Ceratopsia | Ceratosauria | Dromaeosauridae | Diplodocoidea | Hadrosauridae | Herrerasauridae | Heterodontosauridae

"Zapsalis" (**zap**-sal-is). Not a valid scientific name. See *Paronychodon*.

Zephyrosaurus

zeff-ear-oh-**sor**-uhss

NAMED AFTER: Zephyrus, mythical Greek god of the west wind

CLASSIFICATION: Ornithischia, Hypsilophodontidae

LENGTH: 6 ft (1.8 m)

TIME: Early Cretaceous, 119 million years ago

PLACE: Montana, U.S.

DIET: plants

DETAILS: *Zephyrosaurus* was probably a member of the hypsilophodontids. Like other members of that dinosaur group, this was a small, lightly built, two-legged animal with a short beak and large eyes.

"Zigongosaurus" (dzuh-**goong**-o-**sor**-uhss) Not a valid scientific name. This dinosaur may yet prove to be a valid form of giant Chinese plant-eater. See *Mamenchisaurus*.

Zizhongosaurus

dzuh-joong-o-**sor**-uhss

NAMED AFTER: Zizhong County, China

CLASSIFICATION: Saurischia, Sauropoda, Primitive sauropods

LENGTH: 30 ft (9.1 m)

TIME: Early Jurassic, 200 million years ago

PLACE: China

DIET: plants

DETAILS: This dinosaur was a small, primitive member of the long-necked plant-eaters known as sauropods.

Zuniceratops

zoo-nee-**sayr**-uh-tops

NAMED AFTER: Zuni people of New Mexico

CLASSIFICATION: Ornithischia, Ceratopsia

LENGTH: 11.5 ft (3.5 m)

TIME: Late Cretaceous, 92 million years ago

PLACE: New Mexico, U.S.

DIET: plants

DETAILS: *Zuniceratops* was a small, primitive horned dinosaur. Its frilled and beaked skull had surprisingly large horns above the eyes. It is the oldest ceratopsian for which brow horns are known. The recent discovery of this and other early horned dinosaurs in North America may indicate that horned dinosaurs are known as far back in North America as they are in Asia. So it is not clear on which continent these dinosaurs evolved.

Hypsilophodontidae   Lesothosauria   Macronaria   Ornithomimosauria   Oviraptorosauria   Pachycephalosauria   Primitive sauropods   Prosauropoda   Spinosauria   Stegosauria   Therizinosauridae   Troodontidae   Tyrannosauridae

New information about dinosaurs and fossils is always being unearthed. Here are some recent updates.

Agnosphitys

agg-no-**sfie**-tiss

NAME MEANS: "unknown begetter"

CLASSIFICATION: Saurischia, Theropoda?

LENGTH: 28 in (70 cm)

TIME: Late Triassic, 230 million years ago

PLACE: England

DIET: meat

DETAILS: Described in 2002, this small, primitive dinosaur is only known from a few bones and teeth found in a quarry in England. Paleontologists are not sure how it should be classified, which explains its unusual name. It could be related to *Herrerasaurus*, but some scientists think it may be too primitive to be a true dinosaur.

Aletopelta

a-**lee**-toe-**pel**-tuh

NAME MEANS: "wandering shield"

CLASSIFICATION: Ornithischia, Ankylosauria

LENGTH: 20 ft (6 m)

TIME: Late Cretaceous, 82 million years ago

PLACE: California, U.S.

DIET: plants

DETAILS: The region where this armored dinosaur was found is part of an ancient geological plate that drifted north from Mexico millions of years ago and ended up as part of southern California. That's why the genus was named "wandering shield;" because its fossils were moved north along with the pieces of the North American continent.

Anabisetia

an-uh-bee-**set**-ee-uh

NAMED AFTER: Ana Biset, Argentine archaeologist

CLASSIFICATION: Ornithischia, Ornithopoda, basal Iguanodontia

LENGTH: 6 ft (1.8 m)

TIME: Late Cretaceous, 95 million years ago

PLACE: Argentina

DIET: plants

DETAILS: *Anabisetia* is a small running ornithopod known from parts of a number of skeletons. Little of its skull has been found, which makes this dinosaur difficult to classify. Its hands probably could grasp. The discovery of this dinosaur shows that iguanodontians already existed in South America before the continent connected with North America later in the Late Cretaceous Period.

Aucasaurus

ow-kah-**sor**-uhss

NAME MEANS: "Auca Mahuevo lizard"

CLASSIFICATION: Saurischia, Theropoda, Ceratosauria

LENGTH: 20 ft (6 m)

TIME: Late Cretaceous, 80 million years ago

PLACE: Argentina

DIET: meat

DETAILS: Remains of this medium-sized theropod were found in the badlands of Auca Mahuevo in Patagonia in southern Argentina. *Aucasaurus* was related to the strange horned meat-eater *Carnotaurus* but had a longer skull with bumps instead of "horns" on its forehead. Its bones were found near the nests of giant titanosaur sauropod dinosaurs, which could mean *Aucasaurus* hunted young sauropods.

Bienosaurus

byen-oh-**sor**-uhss

NAMED FOR: Mei Nien Bien, a famous Chinese paleontologist

CLASSIFICATION: Ornithischia, Ankylosauria?

LENGTH: 40 in (1 m)

TIME: Early Jurassic, 190 million years ago

PLACE: China

DIET: plants

DETAILS: *Bienosaurus* was a small armored dinosaur whose teeth looked like those of both ankylosaurs and stegosaurs. Only part of a skull and jaw are known.

Cedarpelta

see-dar-**pel**-tuh

NAME MEANS: "Cedar Mountain shield"

CLASSIFICATION: Ornithischia, Ankylosauria

LENGTH: 28+ ft (9+ m)

TIME: Early Cretaceous, 110 million years ago

PLACE: Utah, U.S.

DIET: plants

DETAILS: This ankylosaur is one of the biggest known. It was found in the Cedar Mountain Formation in eastern Utah. Some news stories called it "Bilbeyhallorum" when scientists first announced their discovery.

Crichtonsaurus

cry-tin-**sor**-uhss

NAMED AFTER: Michael Crichton, author of *Jurassic Park; The Lost World*

CLASSIFICATION: Ornithischia, Ankylosauria

LENGTH: 15 feet (4.5 m)

TIME: Late Cretaceous, 65 million years ago

PLACE: China

DIET: Plants

DETAILS: An entire skeleton of this mid-sized club-tailed dinosaur was recently uncovered near the city of Beipiao in northeastern China by Dong Zhiming, China's leading dinosaur scientist for many decades. The dinosaur was named by Dong for Michael Crichton at the request of this book's author to honor Crichton for his role in popularizing dinosaurs and dinosaur research.

Epidendrosaurus

ep-i-**den**-droh-**sor**-uhss

NAME MEANS: "tree-climbing lizard"

CLASSIFICATION: Saurischia, Theropoda, Coelurosauria

LENGTH: 5.8 in (14.5 cm) (juvenile)

TIME: Late Jurassic?, 145 million years ago?

PLACE: Inner Mongolia, China

DIET: insects?

DETAILS: This strange, tiny dinosaur had long fingers and long toes that helped it climb trees. The third finger on its hand is extremely long and may have been used to dig for insects under tree bark.

Erliansaurus

uhr-lyen-**sor**-uhss

NAMED AFTER: city of Erlian in Inner Mongolia, China

CLASSIFICATION: Saurischia, Theropoda, Therizinosauridae

LENGTH: 8.5 ft (2.57 m)

TIME: Late Cretaceous, 85 million years ago

PLACE: Inner Mongolia, China

DIET: plants?

DETAILS: A newly described dinosaur from Inner Mongolia, *Erliasaurus* seems to be intermediate between primitive and advanced therizinosauroids. It had a relatively short neck.

Gobisaurus

go-bee-**sor**-uhss

NAME MEANS: "Gobi Desert lizard"

CLASSIFICATION: Ornithischia, Ankylosauria

LENGTH: 24 ft (7 m)

TIME: Early Cretaceous, 112 million years ago

PLACE: Inner Mongolia, China

DIET: plants

DETAILS: This large ankylosaur was very similar to *Shamosaurus*, but the shape of its head was longer. *Gobisaurus's* fossils were found in 1959, though scientists did not study the bones and name this dinosaur until 2001.

Hesperosaurus

hess-puh-ro-**sor**-uhss

NAME MEANS: "western lizard"

CLASSIFICATION: Ornithischia, Stegosauria

LENGTH: 20 ft (6 m)

TIME: Upper Jurassic, 153 million years ago

PLACE: Wyoming, U.S.

DIET: plants

DETAILS: *Hesperosaurus* is the earliest stegosaur found so far in North America. It is more primitive than *Stegosaurus* and had low, oval-shaped plates along its back and four spikes on its tail. The fossil skeleton was found in the western United States but is now in a museum in Japan.

Incisivosaurus

in-**sigh**-sih-vo-**sor**-uhss

NAME MEANS: "incisor lizard" for its large front teeth

CLASSIFICATION: Saurischia, Theropoda, Oviraptorosauria

LENGTH: 4 ft (1.2 m)

TIME: Early Cretaceous, 128 million years ago

PLACE: Liaoning Province, China

DIET: plants

DETAILS: *Incisivosaurus* is the earliest known oviraptorosaur and still has teeth in its jaws. Its top two front teeth are amazingly large and look similar to the big gnawing teeth of rabbits and rodents. Scientists think this "buck-toothed" dinosaur ate plants even though it was a theropod.

Jiangshanosaurus

jeeong-**shah**-no-**sor**-uhss

NAME MEANS: "Jiangshan County lizard"

CLASSIFICATION: Saurischia, Sauropoda, Macronaria

LENGTH: 60 ft (18 m)

TIME: Early Cretaceous, 112 million years ago

PLACE: China

DIET: plants

DETAILS: This sauropod from Jiangshan County in Zhejiang Province, China, is similar in some ways to *Alamosaurus* from North America, but not all of its skeleton is known yet.

Liaoceratops

leeow-**sayr**-uh-tops

NAME MEANS: "Liaoning horned face"

CLASSIFICATION: Ornithischia, Ceratopsia

LENGTH: 3 ft (1 m)

TIME: Early Cretaceous, 125 million years ago

PLACE: Liaoning Province, China

DIET: plants

DETAILS: *Liaoceratops* is one of the most primitive horned dinosaurs ever found. It was only about as big as a terrier dog. *Liaoceratops* had a small horn under each of its eyes, but no horn on its nose. It also had a frill on the back of its head where jaw muscles were probably attached. In some ways it was similar to "parrot dinosaurs" like *Psittacosaurus.*

Neimongosaurus

nay-**mon**-go-**sor**-uhss

NAME MEANS: "Inner Mongolia lizard"

CLASSIFICATION: Saurischia, Theropoda, Therizinosauridae

LENGTH: around 10 ft (3 m)

TIME: Late Cretaceous, 88 million years ago

PLACE: Inner Mongolia, China

DIET: plants?

DETAILS: Nei Mongol is another name for Inner Mongolia, in northern China, where this dinosaur was found. *Neimongosaurus* had a short tail and a longer neck and longer forelimbs than other known therizinosaurs. It also had hollowed-out airspaces in some of its bones.

Pukyongosaurus

pook-**yong**-o-**sor**-uhss

NAMED AFTER: Pukyong National University in South Korea

CLASSIFICATION: Saurischia, Sauropoda, Camarasauridae

LENGTH: 50 ft (15 m)

TIME: Early Cretaceous, 120 million years ago

PLACE: South Korea

DIET: plants

DETAILS: This sauropod from Korea is only known from a few bones, but it may be related to *Euhelopus.*

"Saltriosaurus" (**salt**-ree-oh-**sor**-uhss) Not a valid scientific name. This theropod discovered near Saltrio, Italy, has not been officially described yet and scientists are still preparing its bones. It lived during the Early Jurassic Period and was about 27 ft (8 m) long. It may be related to *Allosaurus.*

Scansoriopteryx

scan-**sor**-ee-**op**-te-ricks

NAME MEANS: "climbing wing"

CLASSIFICATION: Saurischia, Theropoda, Coelurosauria

LENGTH: 5.8 in (14.5 cm) (juvenile)

TIME: Early Cretaceous, 125 million years ago

PLACE: Liaoning Province, China

DIET: insects?

DETAILS: This strange, tiny dinosaur looked very

similar to *Epidendrosaurus* and had an extremely long third finger on its hands. The fossil of *Scansoriopteryx* is of a juvenile, and shows it had hair-like "feathers" on its body. It likely climbed trees and might have used its long third finger to dig for insects.

Sinovenator

sigh-no-vee-**nay**-tor
NAME MEANS: "Chinese hunter"
CLASSIFICATION: Saurischia, Theropoda, Troodontidae
LENGTH: 40 in (1 m)
TIME: Early Cretaceous, 125 million years ago
PLACE: Liaoning Province, China
DIET: meat
DETAILS: This small meat eater is a primitive troodontid. Scientists were excited to find that some of its bones were similar to the bones of dromaeosaurids, showing that both types of small meat-eating dinosaurs are closely related. Its body was about the size of a chicken, and it had a long, thin tail. It probably had a feather-like covering, but the fossils found so far don't preserve any soft tissues.

Teyuwasu

tay-oo-**wah**-soo
NAME MEANS: "big lizard"
CLASSIFICATION: Dinosauria, Herrerasauridae?
LENGTH: 10 feet (3 m)
TIME: Late Triassic, 210 million years ago
PLACE: Brazil
DIET: meat?
DETAILS: This possible early meat-eating dinosaur is only known from two leg bones, a femur and tibia, once mistakenly thought to belong to an armored archosaur.

"Zupaysaurus" (soo-pie-**sor**-uhss) Not a valid scientific name. This early theropod from Argentina has not been officially described yet. It was around 10–14 ft (3–4 m) long and lived during the Late Triassic Period. "Zupay" is a local name for the devil.

A

advanced Used here to describe features that have evolved within a dinosaur group as more specialized than those of other members of its group. For instance, a two-fingered hand is an *advanced* feature in meat-eating dinosaurs. It evolved in tyrannosaurs from the more primitive condition of three or more fingers.

Age of Dinosaurs Dinosaurs lived from the Late Triassic Period (228 million years ago) until the end of the Cretaceous Period (65 million years ago), a long time for one life-form to exist.

atmosphere The layer of gases that surrounds a planet.

B

beak A horny, toothless mouth part that is found on birds and on some dinosaurs. More lightweight than teeth, it is also used to bite and tear food.

Aralosaurus see page 37

bird-hipped *See* Ornithischian

bone beds Dinosaur fossils sometimes are found in big groups called bone beds. Fires, or simply a strong stream flow bringing bones to a bend in an ancient river could have produced such concentrations of bones, often of many kinds of dinosaurs.

bone-headed A descriptive term for the thick, flattened, or rounded skull top of some dinosaurs, particularly the pachycephalosaurids. Also referred to as "thick-headed."

browse To feed on shoots, leaves, and bark of shrubs and trees.

C

camouflage A natural color scheme or pattern that allows an animal to hide by blending in with its surroundings to avoid detection.

carnivore (kar-nih-vor) A meat-eating animal.

climate The average weather conditions in a particular part of the world. (*Weather* is the day-to-day variation in climate.)

Chirostenotes see page 60

continent A large landmass. The seven continents today are North America, Europe, Asia, Africa, South America, Australia, and Antarctica. In the Triassic Period there was only one continent, Pangaea; and in the Jurassic Period, Pangaea split into two continents, forming Gondwana and Laurasia.

crest Used here to describe a ridge or other projection found on the skulls of many dinosaurs, particularly the lambeosaurine hadrosaurs.

Cretaceous (kree-tay-shus) The third and last period of the Mesozoic era and of dinosaur life, the Cretaceous Period lasted from 145 million to 65 million years ago.

Lambeosaurus see page 113

D

dinosaurs A highly successful and varied group of land animals with fully upright postures and *S*-curved necks that lived from the Late Triassic (228 million to 200 million years ago) through the Jurassic (200 million through 145 million years ago) and Cretaceous Periods (145 million to 65 million years ago). Crocodilians are often thought of as the closest living relatives of dinosaurs, but most scientists consider birds the dinosaurs' descendants.

display This word has many meanings. Here it is used to describe the anatomical features and behaviors that dinosaurs, like modern animals, use to frighten rivals or attract mates. These displays can include large crests or spikes, creating color on body parts, making ritual motions, and many more attention-getting actions.

E

environment The living conditions of animals, including landscape, climate, plants, and other animals.

evolve To change over many generations; to produce a new species, body feature, or way of life.

F

Family A grouping of similar genera, closely related groups of animals.

formation A geological term for the strata of rock deposited at a particular time in a region.

fossilized Turned into fossil.

fossils Remains or traces of once-living plants or animals that are preserved, usually in rock.

frill Used here to describe the bony border or fringe of a dinosaur's skull, particularly the sometimes enormous, decorative fringe of bone on the horned, or ceratopsian, dinosaurs.

Deinonychus
left foot
see page 68

G

gastrolith A stomach stone. In this case small rocks swallowed by many plant-eating dinosaurs to aid in digestion. Gastroliths grind food within the animal's gizzard. Some meat-eating dinosaurs had gastroliths, perhaps to aid in balance while swimming.

Gondwana (gawnd-wah-nah) The more southern of the two supercontinents formed by the breakup of Pangaea in the Age of Dinosaurs. Gondwana included land that is now Australia, South America, Africa, Antarctica, Madagascar, and India.

H

habitat The local area in which an animal or plant lives; for example, a desert, forest, or lake.

herbivore (er-bih-vor) A plant-eating animal.

horn A pointed body part that may have a bony core.

Antarctosaurus
see page 36

I

impression A mark or print in the surface of the ground or a rock made by something pressing against or in it.

Brachyceratops
see page 48

J

Jurassic (jur-raa-sick) The second period of the Mesozoic Era and of dinosaur life. The Jurassic Period lasted from 200 million to 145 million years ago.

L

Laurasia (law-ray-zhah) The more northern of the two supercontinents formed by the breakup of Pangaea, around 200 million years ago. Laurasia is made up of what is now North America, Europe, and most of Asia.

lizard-hipped *See* Saurischian.

M

mammals An order of warm-blooded animals with backbones and hair, whose members nurse their babies. Mammals were present throughout the time of the dinosaurs, though they never grew much larger than house cats until after dinosaurs became extinct.

Mesozoic (mezz-uh-zoe-ic) One of the major eras of earth's history, from 245 million to 65 million years ago. It was the time when dinosaurs, flying reptiles, and many other life-forms lived, and when mammals and birds first evolved.

migrate To move from place to place as conditions change, or for mating or reproduction.

O

Ornithischian (**or**-nih-**thih**-skee-un) One of the two lineages of dinosaurs, traditionally defined by hip anatomy. Ornithischians are bird-hipped dinosaurs that, like birds, have a pubic bone that lies parallel to another hipbone, the ischium. Stegosaurs and armored, dome-headed, and duck-billed dinosaurs are ornithischians. All ornithischians are plant-eaters.

P

paleontologist (**pay**-lee-on-**taw**-luh-jist) A scientist who studies fossils of ancient plants or animals.

Pangaea (pan-**jee**-ah) The supercontinent that existed in the Triassic Period, approximately 230 million years ago, when all the landmasses of the earth were joined.

plate A smooth, flat, bony piece that formed part of an armored covering on many dinosaurs, including all ankylosaurs and some titanosaurid sauropods.

Pelorosaurus armor plate see page 151

plesiosaurs (plee-zee-uh-**sores**) Swimming reptiles from the Age of Dinosaurs that were only distantly related to dinosaurs. These animals had squat bodies and limbs shaped like paddles.

predators (**preh**-dah-turs) Meat-eating animals that hunt and kill.

prey An animal that is hunted and eaten by a predator.

primitive Used here to describe dinosaur features that are simple. For instance, among dinosaurs, a five-toed foot is a primitive condition. Individual

kinds of dinosaurs within a group will lose many of their primitive features over millions of years. But sometimes certain primitive features are retained by individual kinds of dinosaurs.

Pterodactyls (**tair**-o-**dack**-tills) Pterosaurs with long necks and short tails that lived in the Jurassic and Cretaceous Periods.

Pterosaurs (**tair**-o-**sores**) Flying reptiles; the first vertebrates to fly.

R

raptor A popular term for dromaeosaurid dinosaurs; small to mid-sized meat-eaters with sickle claws and stiff tails, from the Northern Hemisphere in the Cretaceous Period.

Velociraptor, see page 204

reptiles Cold-blooded animals with backbones and scales. Reptiles crawl or creep on short legs. They reproduce by laying hard-shelled or leathery eggs on land. Snakes, lizards, turtles, and crocodiles are some modern types of reptiles.

S

sailback A descriptive term for the sail-shape arch that may have appeared along the backs of many dinosaurs, as indicated by a prominent series of bony projections along the animals' back vertebrae.

saurischian (saw-**rih**-skee-un) A lineage of dinosaurs based on their long pubic bones. The meat-eating theropods and the giant plant-eating sauropods are saurischians.

sauropod (saw-ro-pod) Large plant-eating saurischian dinosaurs. This group included the largest dinosaurs known, some of which were more than 100 feet (30.5 meters) long.

scavenger (skaa-ven-jur) A meat-eating animal that eats the bodies of animals already dead.

scutes Armor plates found on many plant-eating dinosaurs.

Patagosaurus
see page 150

species A group of organisms that are similar in appearance and might interbreed.

spine A bony, pointed projection, often used here interchangeably with "spike." Spine refers to the large, tapering bone outgrowths on many armored and plate-backed dinosaurs.

T

tail club A large knob of bone at the tip of the tail vertebrae that was present on ankylosaurid armored dinosaurs and some sauropod dinosaurs.

tendons (ten-duns) Pieces of animal tissue that attach muscles to bones.

thecodonts (thee-ko-dahnts) Mostly meat-eaters, these were the earliest of the "ruling reptiles," the archosaur group. This group included the ancestors of dinosaurs, as well as crocodiles and extinct large animals, including pterosaurs, aetosaurs, phytosaurs, and rauisuchians. Thecodonts were common in the Triassic Period.

theropods (thayr-o-podz) Two-legged, meat-eating lizard-hipped dinosaurs ranging in size from tiny hunters smaller than crows to the 42-foot-long (14.3 meters) *Giganotosaurus*.

Giganotosaurus, see page 88

Triassic (try-yaa-sick) The first of the three periods of the Mesozoic Era, and of Age of the Dinosaurs, from 245 million to 200 million years ago.

V

vegetation (veh-jeh-tay-shun) Plant life.

vertebrates (ver-tuh-brayts) Animals with backbones, including fish, mammals, birds, reptiles, amphibians, and dinosaurs.

221

BOOKS

Brett-Surman, Michael, *The Jurassic Park Institute Field Guide,* Random House, 2001.

Dixon, Dougal, *Amazing Dinosaurs,* Boyds Mills Press, Honesdale, Pennsylvania, 2000.

Dixon, Dougal, et al, *The Macmillan Illustrated Encyclopedia of Dinosaurs and Prehistoric Animals,* Collier Books, New York, 1988.

Halls, Kelly Milner, *Dino Trekking,* Wiley & Sons, 1996. The best travel guide and resource for finding museums and digs around the country.

Lambert, David, *The Ultimate Dinosaur Book,* Dorling Kindersley, New York, 1993.

Lessem, Don, *Bigger Than T. Rex,* Crown, New York, 1997. New giant meat-eaters.

Lessem, Don, *Dinosaur Worlds,* Boyds Mills Press, Honesdale, Pennsylvania, 1996. Dinosaurs by habitat and time.

Lessem, Don, *Raptors,* Little Brown, Boston, 1996. The famous dromaeosaurids.

Lessem, Don, *The Special Dinosaurs: (series) Utahraptor, Seismosaurus, Ornithomimids, Troodon,* Lerner Publications, Minneapolis, 1995.

Lessem, Don, *Supergiants,* Little Brown, Boston, 1997. The largest plant-eaters.

Norman, David, *The Illustrated Encyclopedia of Dinosaurs,* Crown, 1991. Dated but still the best-illustrated and written overview of dinosaurs.

Norman, David, *Prehistoric Life,* Macmillan, New York, 1994.

Sloan, Christopher. *Feathered Dinosaurs,* National Geographic Books, 2000.

Svarney, Thomas and Patricia Barnes Svarney, *The Handy Dinosaur Answer Book,* Visible Ink Press, Farmington Hills, Michigan, 1999. Useful information.

VIDEOS

Big Al, BBC/Discovery Channel, 2001

Bigger Than T. Rex, Discovery Channel, 1997

The Case of the Flying Dinosaur, NOVA, 1992

Dinosaurs of the Gobi, NOVA, 1994

The Hunt for China's Dinosaurs, NOVA, 1993

T. Rex *Exposed,* NOVA, 1991

Walking with Dinosaurs, BBC/Discovery Channel, 1999

When Dinosaurs Roamed North America, Discovery Channel, 2001

The Ultimate Guide to T. Rex (1997), Discovery Channel, 1997

FAVORITE WEB SITES

"Dino" Don *http://dinosaurdon.com*

Dinosauricon *http://dinosauricon.com*

The Dinosauria
http://www.ucmp.berkeley.edu/diapsids/dinosaur.html

Dinosaur Interplanetary Gazette
http://www.dinosaur.org/frontpage.html

Society of Vertebrate Paleontology
http://www.museum.state.il.us/svp

University of Arizona's Sci-Info Paleontology & Fossil Resources
http://dizzy.library.arizona.edu/users/mount/paleont.html

Scutellosaurus
see page 172

Lesothosaurus
see page 115

MUSEUMS

American Museum of Natural History
79th Street and Central Park West
New York, NY
(212) 769-5100
http://www.amnh.org

Royal Tyrrell Museum of Palaeontology
Midland Provincial Park
Drumheller, Alberta, Canada
(403) 823-7707
http://www.tyrrellmuseum.com/index.htm

The Museum of Paleontology
University of California at Berkeley
1101 Valley Life Sciences Building
Berkeley, CA 94720-4780
(510) 642-1821
http://www.ucmp.berkeley.edu/index.htm

PALEONTOLOGICAL EXPEDITIONS

Earth Watch
Sponsors a host of dinosaur and other scientific
expeditions that accept volunteers

3 Clocktower Place, Suite 100,
Maynard, MA 01754
1-800-776-0188 or (978) 461-0081

Royal Tyrrell Museum of Palaeontology
Work with museum staff in the world's best
dinosaur dig sites. Weekend day digs May through
August for ages 16 and up or 10 to 15 accompanied
by an adult. Two-hour dig site tours in July and
August. Weeklong field-experience programs in July
and August.

PO Box 7500,
Drumheller, Alberta, Canada
1-888-440-4240

Wyoming Dinosaur Center and Dig Sites
Kid digs for children 8 to 13.
Mid-July to August are the most popular times
but hot!

PO Box 868,
Thermopolis, WY 82443
1-800-455-3466

**Dinosaur Expeditions, Museum of Western
Colorado**
Self-guided tours. Day digs available May through
October on Thursdays and for groups of five or
more.

362 Main Street
Grand Junction, CO 81501
(970) 240-9210

NOTE: Many local science museums participate in
one-day or longer dig programs. Try your
neighborhood science museum's education
department for programs such as
those listed here.

Asiaceratops,
see page 40